International Trade

International Trade

An Introduction to Theory and Policy

Richard Pomfret

Basil Blackwell

Copyright © Richard Pomfret 1991

First published 1991

Basil Blackwell, Inc.
3 Cambridge Center
Cambridge, Massachusetts 02142, USA

Basil Blackwell Ltd
108 Cowley Road, Oxford OX4 1JF, UK

Library of Congress Cataloging in Publication Data
Pomfret, Richard W. T.
  International trade: an introduction to theory and policy/
Richard Pomfret.
    p. cm.
  Includes index.
  Includes bibliographical references.
  ISBN 1–55786–104–8 (hardback) — ISBN 1–55786–105–6
(pbk.)
  1. International trade. 2. Commercial policy. I. Title.
HF1379.P66 1991
382—dc20   90–36316
                                                      CIP

British Library Cataloguing in Publication Data
A CIP catalogue record for this book is available from the British Library.

Typeset in 10½ on 12 pt Plantin
by Colset Private Ltd, Singapore
Printed in Great Britain by
T J Press Ltd, Padstow, Cornwall

Contents

List of Boxes

Preface

This book is a self-contained introduction to international trade theory and policy. It stems from a course which I have taught to MA students at the Johns Hopkins University School of Advanced International Studies in Bologna, Nanjing, and Washington. The SAIS students are not necessarily economics specialists; many come with a limited economics background, and few intend to pursue further studies in economics. The book reflects these origins insofar as it places more emphasis on the application of theory and on current policy issues and less emphasis on formal proofs of theorems than other texts intended for postgraduate economics courses. Most economic concepts are explained from first principles, although the overview of microeconomic theory in chapter 3.1 is terse and readers with only a rudimentary economics background may want to refer to a standard microeconomics text for further explanation.

The book covers the usual international trade topics, with more emphasis than other texts on intraindustry trade and imperfect competition, on discriminatory trade policies, and on why trade barriers exist (the political economy of trade barriers). I have also tried to give many examples of trade policies in action, taking these from a variety of countries; most of the boxes provide such examples. Finally, the last part of the book deals with macro topics that are closely interrelated to trade issues (for example, whether trade policies are appropriate tools for removing balance of payments deficits or aggregate unemployment, and whether exchange rate volatility disrupts trade). This final part is not a full treatment of international finance or open economy macroeconomics, but it is intended to answer questions that typically fall between the cracks in the standard micro/macro division of international economics.

I am grateful to many people who have helped in the preparation of this book. My greatest debt is to the students who have asked questions in class and commented on drafts of the text. My colleagues Max Corden and James Riedel have read parts of the text and discussed the ideas. John Black read the entire text and provided many detailed comments and suggestions which improved the finished product. Any remaining errors are my responsibility, and are left in to keep the reader on his or her intellectual toes. Romesh Vaitilingam, the commissioning editor, has been supportive of the book through all its stages. Janice Delbert, Joy Carper, Pamela Yatsko, Robert Benjamin, and Patricia Calvano prepared the various drafts of the manuscripts.

1

Introduction

International trade requires little definition, nor does its study require much justification for citizens of most of the world's nations. Conceptually the exchange of goods across national boundaries is easy to identify; operationally it is also one of the most easily measurable economic flows. All nations participate in international trade and have long done so, and for most market economies a substantial share of domestic output is exported, and a large part of total expenditure is on imported items. Both consumers and workers are constantly reminded of the importance of international trade in their daily economic lives, and yet for many the visible signs are only the tip of the iceberg, as the larger part of international trade is in intermediate products which are never seen by the ordinary consumer.

International trade is a central concern of governments' economic policies. From the earliest historical times, governments have regulated long-distance trade. They continue to do so, and in democratic societies trade policies frequently emerge as important election issues. This book provides an introduction to the economic analysis of international trade policies, focusing on the effects of various trade policies and using this positive analysis both to determine which trade policies should be adopted and to explain why existing policies have been adopted.

1.1 The Distinctive Features of International Economics

The nation–state is a well-defined unit in the world economy, and trade among nations a measurable phenomenon, but what is the relevance of the nation–state for *analysis* of the world economy? Economists typically analyze exchange by building up from individual decision-making units such as the household or the firm: Why can trade between units from different countries not be treated the same way? In crucial respects it can be (and will be in this book), but there are several ways in which national boundaries modify the analysis by providing discrete breaks without exact parallel within national economies.

Firstly, national boundaries often, but not always, correspond to cultural boundaries. Thus we could view national populations as having distinct tastes or productive abilities. This is not much justification for treating international economics as a separate sub-branch of economics, because in standard microeconomic theory consumers are treated as individuals with different tastes. Moreover, to explain a country's export items by saying they are what that country's residents make particularly well is not a very satisfying explanation of trade patterns.

Secondly, national boundaries represent breaks in the degree of factor mobility. In microeconomic theory labor and capital are assumed to be able to move freely from one economic activity to another. Labor does not, however, move freely from working in one country to working in another; this is partly due to the cultural differences mentioned in the previous paragraph, but mostly in the twentieth century it reflects immigration restrictions. Likewise, international capital movements are often restricted by communications problems or legal obstacles. Thus, it may be more appropriate in analyzing international trade to assume no international factor mobility rather than free mobility. This has been the dominant strand in international trade theory, and almost the entire analysis of parts I–III is based on this assumption. It should, however, be borne in mind that free and no-factor mobility are both extreme assumptions, whether applied to domestic or international factor markets – and that the degree of international factor mobility changes over time.

Thirdly, national boundaries represent breaks in regulatory control. National governments have the power to regulate trade at their national borders, for example by erecting barriers to imports, by subsidizing or restricting exports, by creating a monopoly in issuing the currency which is legal tender, and so forth. Similar barriers to domestic trade may be imposed by state or provincial governments, but these are trivial by comparison with national barriers. Thus, it is particularly in its policy aspects that international economics is a distinctive subject.

To illustrate the above points, let us consider how to analyze trade between Germany and the US. As a first cut, the analysis could be the same as that of trade between Idaho and Montana; it is only when considering the ensuing adjustments in production via factor movements or the possibility of government restrictions that the analysis would require different assumptions. Another potential difference between the analysis of interstate and of international trade is that Idaho and Montana use the same currency whereas Bavaria and Idaho do not. Differing currencies need not matter if trade between the two countries exactly balances (that is, both countries' citizens are content with bartering their export bundle for the others' import bundle);

without the need for IOUs, money facilitates transactions but is only a veil with no effect on resource allocation (as in standard microeconomic theory, if all markets clear then only relative prices matter and the absolute price level is unimportant).

The distinction between balanced and unbalanced trade is at the heart of the division between trade theory and monetary theory in international economics. International trade theory typically assumes balanced trade in order to focus on the fundamental "real" forces behind international exchange. International monetary theory is concerned with alternative methods of dealing with overall imbalance, which leads to analysis of the importance of national monies, the role of exchange rates, and the impact of the international adjustment mechanism on national macroeconomic policies. This division will be maintained in the present book which omits monetary problems until the final part, where they are considered only briefly. Of course, the two subdivisions often overlap in actual policy debates, for example the repeated advocacy of trade measures to reduce the US balance of payments deficit during the 1980s. Nevertheless, the analytic distinction between trade and monetary theory is clear and useful; international trade can be best analyzed without the monetary veil, and a convincing case exists in international monetary theory that microeconomic policies such as trade barriers are inferior instruments for dealing with macroeconomic problems such as an overall imbalance in international payments.

1.2 A Note on Method

In subject matter international trade theory and international monetary theory are extensions of the micro- and macroeconomic theory commonly used to analyze the closed economy. Not surprisingly, their methodology is also similar. Thus international trade theory, like microeconomic theory, starts from assumptions about individual behavior: utility maximization by consumers and profit maximization by producers. The general microeconomic model will be set out in chapter 3, and the remainder of the book consists of relaxing various assumptions (starting with free factor mobility).

The "neoclassical" approach of starting from the smallest units and then analyzing how these units interact in the marketplace is sometimes criticized for being too abstract. Individuals do not always maximize utility or profits without regard to others' welfare. Such a criticism, however, misses the point of theory, which must be to abstract the essential matter from the complex totality of the real world. Even a minor trading nation can be involved in billions of international transactions each year. No trade theory is likely to explain all transactions or even trade in all products, but a good theory should be able to explain a substantial portion of international trade.

Two guiding principles for what follows result from the previous paragraph. Firstly, since simplifying assumptions need to be made, it is always better to make these explicit rather than implicit. The first two parts of the book develop formal models with which to analyze international trade, as the various assumptions are relaxed and changed. The introduction of government intervention is left until last (parts III and IV). Thus, although trade policy is a central concern of the book, it will not be broached until we have put together an analytic tool kit. Moreover, by first applying the explicit models to analyzing international trade with no government intervention we have a yardstick against which to compare the effect of any trade policy; no intervention may not always be the relevant case for comparison, but it will usually be a good starting point.

The second guiding principle is that trade theories should be confronted with empirical tests. For a variety of reasons this is not always possible, and in other cases the tests may not be conclusive. Nevertheless, considerations of empirical relevance have guided the development of international trade theory, and especially in part II it will be desirable to survey some of this empirical literature, both to assess the value of alternative theories and to understand why trade theorists pursued some paths and neglected others. In particular, empirical studies by Leontief in the early 1950s and by Grubel and Lloyd in the 1970s, both of which appeared to invalidate the dominant trade theory, provided fertile stimuli for new developments in international trade theory.

1.3   A Survey of International Trade Flows

Before developing a theory of international trade, let us briefly examine some characteristics of current trade flows. International trade is big business. Every country participates in it. The annual value of international trade in the late 1980s was over $2,000 billion – a large number, and also a large increase over the $150 billion of the early 1950s.[1] Of course, some of this increase reflects inflation, but even after allowing for the increase in prices the volume of world trade grew fourfold in real terms.

---

[1]Since World War II international trade statistics have usually been given in US dollars as this is the major vehicle currency. The currency of account mattered little in the 1950s and 1960s when the major exchange rates were fixed, but in the 1980s valuation in dollars understates the growth of world trade during the first half of the decade and overstates the post-1985 growth.

The variety of goods traded is also great – practically every good produced is traded to some extent. The commodity composition of world trade according to the most common method of classification, the Standard International Trade Classification (SITC), is given in table 1.1. Just over two-thirds of the goods traded are manufactured goods and just under one-third are primary products. The long-term trend has been for the share of manufactures to increase at the expense of primary products, although in the short run the importance of individual raw materials can vary significantly (for example, the share of oil in the value of world trade rose dramatically between 1973 and 1980 after two major price increases, but then fell again in the 1980s). The majority of international trade flows involve intermediate goods rather than goods for final consumption, although trade in automobiles or coffee or clothing is more likely to attract public attention than trade in ball bearings or vehicle parts.

A small number of countries conduct most of world trade. In table 1.2 are listed 24 countries trading more than $40 billion worth of goods in 1986. Together they account for over four-fifths of world trade. In general, smaller countries are more trade-oriented than larger ones (for example, the export/GDP ratios of Botswana and Mauritius – both 63 percent in 1986 – are

Table 1.1 Commodity composition of world trade, 1986

Commodity description	Value of world trade (US$ billion)
Food	227
Raw materials	72
Ores and minerals	73
Fuels	272
Primary products	643
Iron and steel	74
Chemicals	190
Other semi-manufactures	103
Office and telecommunications equipment	121
Road motor vehicles	196
Other machinery and transport equipment	436
Household appliances	68
Textiles	66
Clothing	62
Other consumer goods	116
Manufactures, not classified	45
Total	2,119

Source: GATT *International Trade 1986–87*, p. 175

BOX 1.1 How Accurate are International Trade Statistics?

International trade data are often considered to be among the most reliable economic statistics. International flows of goods pass through a limited number of border crossings, and imports are always and exports often monitored by customs officials, so the flows should be easier to measure than, say, national output or income. There are exceptions: trade in illegal products is by its nature hidden from official inspection, high trade barriers provide an incentive for smuggling, and exports or imports carried by travellers may not be counted. For some economies, especially for countries involved in the drug trade, these discrepancies may be large,[2] but for the major trading nations they are not.

Nevertheless, international agencies assembling nationally collected data on imports and exports consistently find that the world does not balance its trade - which is a logical impossibility because any dollar's worth of imports by one country is a dollar's worth of exports from another country.

The US and Canada have tried to resolve this problem through an agreement made in the early 1970s to reconcile their bilateral trade statistics. Canadian data showed a 1986 merchandise trade surplus with the US of US$11 billion, whereas the US data gave a 1986 trade deficit with Canada of $23 billion. The reconciled estimates showed a Canadian surplus of $13 billion. By far the largest adjustment to the initial data took account of nonreceipt of export documents to the tune of $3 billion in Canada and $10 billion in the US.

The size of these discrepancies is striking (total Canada–US trade was $107–21 billion, depending on whether it is measured by export or by import data), especially as the two North American countries can be included among the nations with the most efficient statistical services. They also show that import statistics are likely to be more reliable than export statistics, because most governments are more careful in monitoring imports than exports.

Source: GATT International Trade 86–87, p. 91

[2]For example, coca is the main export of Bolivia and Peru and refined cocaine is probably Colombia's second largest export, but they are not included in these countries' trade statistics (see The Economist, October 1988).

Table 1.2 Merchandise trade by countries, 1986 (US$ billion)

	Imports (cif)	Exports (fob)	Exports/GDP (percent)
US	387	217	7
West Germany	191	243	30
Japan	128	211	12
France	129	125	22
UK	126	107	26
Italy	99	98	20
USSR	89	97	n.a.
Canada	86	90	27
Netherlands	76	81	54
Belgium–Luxembourg	69	69	69
Switzerland	41	37	37
China	43	31	11
Hong Kong	35	35	112
Sweden	33	37	33
South Korea	32	35	41
Taiwan	24	40	n.a.
Spain	35	27	20
East Germany	25	26	n.a.
Austria	27	23	37
Australia	26	23	16
Singapore	26	23	135
Denmark	23	21	32
Saudi Arabia	20	24	36
Czechoslovakia	21	20	n.a.

n.a. = Not available in the source.
fob (free on board) = Including all costs to get goods on board but still in the harbour of the exporting country.
cif (cost, insurance, freight) = Including fob cost plus freight charges to the point of import, insurance charges, and unloading from ship to pier at the receiving port.
Import data for the USSR, East Germany, and Czechoslovakia are fob, and therefore understated relative to other countries' import data. Trade data for Hong Kong and Singapore include a significant amount of imports for re-export.

Sources: GATT *International Trade 86–87*, p. 156, and World Bank *World Development Report 1988*, table 5

higher than those of most of the countries in table 1.2). Thus, the major trading nations tend to be more important for the international trading system than foreign trade is for them. This is especially true of the largest trading nation, the US, although its ratio of exports and (especially) imports to GDP has increased markedly from the 5 percent of the 1960s. Thus, when discussing trade policy this book will focus on the US, the members of the

European Community, and Japan, which together account for three-fifths of the world's imports; their respective policies affect the rest of the world most, although a country's own trade policy is likely to be most crucial for small open economies.

Part I

Modeling International Trade

2

Why Do Countries Trade With Each Other?

The most straightforward, and longest-held, explanation of international trade is based upon differences in countries' production functions. Because inputs can be combined to produce outputs with differing degrees of efficiency in different parts of the world there are gains from trade between the various regions. This explanation will be referred to as the "classical" model of international trade.

In its simplest form the classical approach emphasizes the unavailability of various goods in different countries. A country may want some good which it does not produce, while a potential supplier in another part of the world wants something which is produced in the first country but not by itself. For example, if Italians wish to wear coats made of arctic fox fur and Canadians want to use olive oil, but arctic fox do not live in Italy and olive trees do not grow in Canada, then trade of furs for oil may be mutually beneficial for Italians and Canadians (although perhaps not for the foxes). Such examples are, however, difficult to find, because few goods cannot be produced in practically every country if sufficient resources are put into the production process. At most, this type of trade is limited to a few natural products; so, as an explanation of international trade, this simplest form of the classical model can be passed by as unimportant as well as uninteresting.

A more plausible situation arises when, although two products can both be produced in two countries, one country has an absolute advantage in the production of one product and the other country has an absolute advantage in producing the other product. Such a situation can be represented by a simple numerical example:

Annual output per worker

	America	Europe
Grain	15 bu.	12 bu.
Cloth	5 yd	6 yd

Assuming simple production functions with the single input labor and constant returns in producing either grain or cloth, America is clearly more efficient at producing grain and Europe at producing cloth. If each country specializes according to its advantage, there are potential gains from trade. Thus, if one American worker switches from cloth to grain production and one European worker from grain to cloth production, then total output in the two countries will be increased by three bushels of grain and one yard of cloth.

What if one country has an absolute advantage in producing no good? The greatest single contribution to international trade theory was the demonstration by David Ricardo in the early nineteenth century that gains from trade still exist, as long as the country specializes in producing the good in which it has a comparative advantage. Consider the following situation in which America is the more efficient producer of both grain and cloth:

Annual output per worker

	America	*Europe*
Grain	15 bu.	8 bu.
Cloth	5 yd	4 yd

Redoing the resource shift of the previous paragraph would increase grain output by seven bushels but reduce cloth output by one yard, which yields no clear verdict on whether there are gains from specialization. However, if two American workers move from cloth to grain production and three European workers move from grain to cloth production, then total grain output increases by six bushels and cloth output by two yards, so that there are indeed potential gains from specialization and trade.

The principle of comparative advantage was clearly stated in Ricardo's 1817 book *On the Principles of Political Economy and Taxation.* His exposition, based on trade in wine and cloth between Portugal and England, became famous, although it was not an ideal example because Portugal had an absolute advantage in wine production and England may have had an absolute advantage in cloth production. Ricardo explicitly pointed out, however, that: "This exchange might even take place, notwithstanding that the commodity imported by Portugal could be produced there with less labour than in England." He also illustrated how the principle of comparative advantage applies to exchange at all levels:

Two men can both make shoes and hats, and one is superior to the other in both employments; but in making hats he can only exceed his competitor by one-fifth or twenty percent, and in making shoes he can excel him by one-third or 33 percent; will it not be for the interest of both, that the superior man should employ himself exclusively in making shoes, and the inferior man in making hats?

All this is within a few pages in the first half of chapter 7 of his book, which also contains a clear statement of how factor mobility reduces variations in opportunity costs within the domestic economy but is less effective across national boundaries.

The examples given in the previous two paragraphs illustrate a very general point: as long as the opportunity cost of producing any good differs between two countries, then there are potential gains from trade. This is an extremely powerful conclusion insofar as it is highly likely for any pair of countries that differences in opportunity costs will be common. Thus the principle of comparative advantage provides a general explanation of why countries trade. Given the existence of potential gains from trade, there is an incentive to trade as long as the gains exceed the costs of transportation.[1]

Numerical examples can be usefully constructed to illustrate the principle of comparative advantage. For other purposes, however, they may not be so useful because it will be less clear whether the results are general or whether they depend on the specific numbers chosen. A more general apparatus is desirable and the choice lies between algebra and geometry, both of which have advantages. This book will rely on diagrammatic analysis because it is intuitively clearer to most people, and requires less mathematical background than the algebra often used in expositions of trade theory. The main drawback of using diagrams is that the printed page has two dimensions, so the formal analysis is restricted to cases with two goods, two countries, two factors of production, and so on, with only occasional informal references to the theoretical implications of moving beyond two-ness.

The gains from trade arising from specialization according to comparative advantage can be illustrated clearly by diagrammatic analysis. Using the data from the previous table and additional information about the labor force in America and Europe, the production possibility frontier for each country can be constructed. Thus, if Europe has six workers and America four workers, the maximum output levels for various allocations of labor between grain and cloth production are:

Europe	Grain	48	40	32	24	16	8	0
	Cloth	0	4	8	12	16	20	24
America	Grain	60	45	30	15	0		
	Cloth	0	5	10	15	20		

---

[1]Transportation costs should be broadly conceived as the costs of doing business internationally as well as of physically moving goods. Little will be said in this book about transportation costs because their role is obvious and for the most part theoretically uninteresting. High transportation costs reduce the volume of trade and shift its composition in favor of goods whose bulk is small relative to their value. In some respects they can be viewed as natural trade barriers with similar effects to the government-imposed trade barriers analyzed in part III.

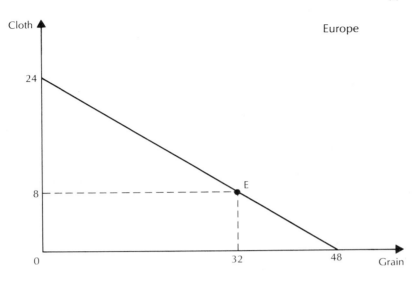

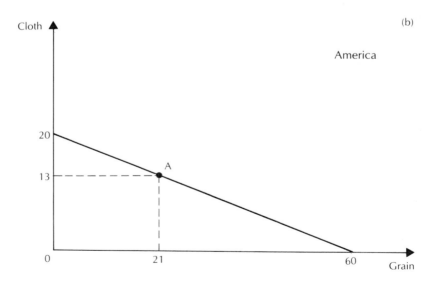

Figure 2.1 Production possibility frontiers: (a) Europe; (b) America.

If labor is perfectly mobile domestically and is divisible one worker can work part-time in grain and part-time in cloth production without affecting productivity), then each country can produce any output mix on or inside their production possibility frontiers (figure 2.1). In the absence of trade each country must consume the same mix of goods as it produces; that is, its production and consumption points must coincide, for example at E for Europe and A for America.

Figure 2.1 indicates that America's comparative advantage lies in grain production. The American production possibility frontier is flatter than the European production possibility frontier because the opportunity cost of producing grain is lower than in Europe. The slope of the PPF is equal to the opportunity cost of producing an additional unit of the good measured on the horizontal axis, in this case the slope is constant and equal to $\frac{1}{3}$ in America and $\frac{1}{2}$ in Europe. Thus, the differences in slopes of the PPFs determine the specialization patterns which will yield gains from trade.

The gains from specialization and trade implicit in figure 2.1 can be made explicit by constructing a box out of the two PPFs. This is done by aligning the output levels which result from specialization according to comparative advantage, in this case with America producing only grain and Europe producing only cloth (figure 2.2). The rectangular box enclosed by the axes of the two PPF diagrams now encompasses all of the possible consumption points in the two countries, given a joint output of 60 bushels of grain and 24 yards of cloth, and assuming no transport costs. Specifically,

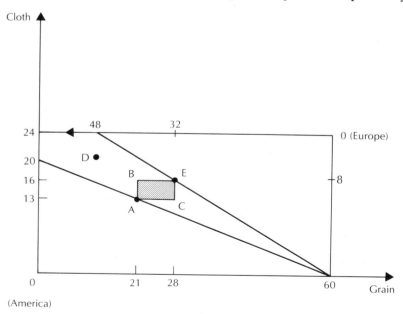

Figure 2.2 Gains from trade in the classical model.

both of the autarchic consumption points, A and E, lie within the box, although if either country were to consume at its autarchic point after trade took place then the other would be able to consume more than it did before trade. If Europe continued to consume 32 bushels of grain and eight yards of cloth, that is post-trade consumption is at point E, then American consumers could enjoy an extra seven bushels of grain and three yards of cloth over their no-trade consumption bundle. Any other consumption point within the rectangle ABEC would involve additional consumption of one or both goods in both countries compared to the no-trade points A and E, with the distribution of the extra seven bushels and three yards depending on exactly where in the rectangle consumption takes place. Since any point inside ABEC leaves both countries better off than they were without trade, the existence of such a rectangle proves the existence of potential gains from trade.

The generality of the classical analysis of gains from trade emerges clearly from figure 2.2. The only requirement for a rectangle such as ABEC to exist is that opportunity costs differ (the PPFs have different slopes). As drawn, figure 2.2 involves total specialization, but the same conclusion would result from partial specialization; for example, if America continued to produce four yards of cloth while Europe specialized totally in cloth production, then the European production block could be aligned with the American block so that the European cloth axis intercepted the American grain axis at 48 bushels and the European grain axis intersected the American cloth axis at 28 yards. Even with incomplete specialization there is a wedge between the two PPFs containing consumption points which are superior to the no-trade situation in the sense that they permit higher consumption of both goods in both countries.

The classical model developed here is a supply-side theory of international trade. Without introducing demand-side considerations the consumption points have to be taken as exogenously determined, and it is not possible to identify which consumption point will result from trade. Thus, in figure 2.2 post-trade consumption may take place at a point such as D, which was not attainable by either country without trade and which may be mutually preferable to any point within the rectangle ABEC. The possibility that other points within the wedge of newly feasible consumption bundles created by specialization and trade may be superior to the points which are strictly superior to the autarchy consumption points does not invalidate the conclusion that potential gains from trade exist, but it does prevent any prediction of the size or distribution of these gains.

The production function represented in the PPFs of figure 2.1 is also rather simplified. There is likely to be more than one factor of production and, although this could be resolved by defining the output levels per unit of composite input, it would mask the probability of diminishing marginal productivity (for example, of land as grain output is expanded). The assumption of a single factor of production operating at constant returns to scale in each activity is responsible for the linear PPFs, which in turn generate the unrealistic conclusion that the gains from trade are maximized by complete specialization (at least in the smaller trading partner).

In the next chapter a model is developed which overcomes these two weaknesses of the simple classical model by introducing demand and by allowing PPFs to be nonlinear. It is, however, important to note that these weaknesses do not interfere with the fundamental proposition that as long as opportunity costs differ there are potential gains from trade. Even if costs are not constant there are potential gains *at the margin* if the two countries' PPFs do not have identical slopes at the pre-trade consumption price. Since this is invariably the case for some pairs of goods, the principle of comparative advantage provides an extremely general explanation of why countries trade with one another.

Further Reading

The classic reference is Ricardo (1817), Chapter 7. Dornbusch, Fischer, and Samuelson (1977) analyze the classical model with many goods.

3

A General Equilibrium Model of International Trade

In the previous chapter a simple model was used to establish the existence of gains from international trade as long as there are differences in the opportunity costs of producing any good at the autarchic output levels of two countries. This is a strong conclusion and, because it requires few assumptions, a robust one. The simple classical model, however, says little about the pattern of trade and nothing about the distribution of gains from trade. In this chapter an alternative model, which overcomes some of the shortcomings of the classical model, will be developed.

The neoclassical model is essentially the analytic framework of modern microeconomic theory (applied to international trade it is sometimes referred to as the Heckscher–Ohlin–Samuelson model, after three major contributors to this application). The assumptions made in this chapter are:

- the state of technology and consumer preferences are given and satisfy certain conditions (more technically, isoquants and indifference curves are concave)
- product and factor markets operate perfectly competitively
- factor supplies are fixed for each country
- there are no transport or information costs, and no government intervention

Most of these assumptions will be relaxed in subsequent chapters, but for the moment we will begin by deriving results from the model in its most abstract form. One difference from the simple classical model is the absence of any assumption about production functions differing from country to country, and an important neoclassical result is that even with identical production functions gains from trade can arise from international differences in tastes or in factor endowments.

3.1 Closed Economy Equilibrium

This section provides a concise summary of the neoclassical theory of resource allocation in a closed economy. It presupposes knowledge of this theory, and is intended as a revision exercise, highlighting the tools which will be most useful for analyzing international trade issues. It finishes with the standard neoclassical conclusion that, given "well-behaved" production and preference functions, perfectly competitive markets lead to a unique equilibrium output and consumption of all goods with a single set of equilibrium prices.

A production function indicates the minimum quantity of inputs needed to produce any output level of a good or, to reword the problem, the maximum output obtainable from any quantity of inputs. These technical relationships are assumed to be exogenously determined. Restricting the number of inputs to two primary factors of production, labor and capital, the production function for a good can be represented by an isoquant map (figure 3.1). Each isoquant is labeled by an output level and traces out all the

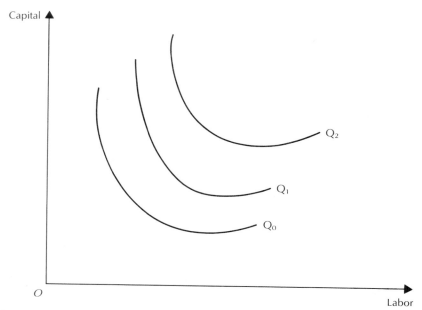

Figure 3.1 An isoquant map.

combinations of labor and capital which could be used to produce that output level. Combinations of labor and capital to the northeast of any isoquant
could be used to produce that isoquant's output level, but such combinations
would be inefficient (not least cost), while using any combinations to the
southwest of an isoquant would be infeasible for producing that output level.
The isoquants in figure 3.1 are smooth, which implicitly assumes the two
inputs to be continuously substitutable, and curved because the marginal
rate of technical substitution diminishes (the more labor is used relative to
capital then the less capital has to be substituted for a one-unit reduction in
labor input in order to maintain a constant output level).

Each isoquant traces out the combinations of inputs which could be used
to produce one output level efficiently. The combination which will actually
be used depends upon the relative price of inputs. For any total amount to be
spent on producing a good the constraint can be represented by an isocost
line, the slope of which is the input price ratio. In figure 3.2 the isocost line
represents a situation in which $100 is to be spent and the prices of capital
and of labor are $20 and $10 respectively; its slope is P_L/P_K or one-half. The
triangle of which the isocost line forms the hypotenuse contains all the input

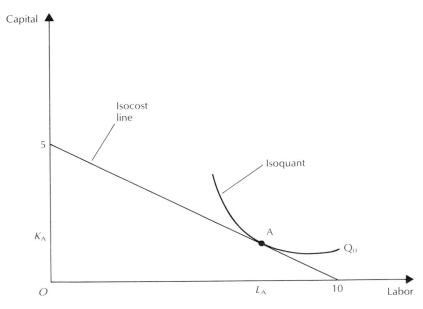

Figure 3.2 The optimal combination of inputs. K_A and L_A represents the least-
cost combination of inputs to produce output Q_0 when $P_K = \$20$ and $P_L = \$10$.
With these input prices Q_0 is the maximum output which can be produced with
an outlay of $100.

combinations which could be used, given the budget constraint. Given the shape of the isoquants, production will take place at point A, because any other possible output level would be lower (on an isoquant to the left of that drawn in figure 3.2). At the tangency point A the slopes of the isoquant and of the isocost line are equal; that is, the marginal rate of technical substitution is equal to the factor-price ratio (in this numerical example the MRTS of labor for capital at A must be 2).

Different goods have different production functions and thus for any isocost line they will have different efficient input combinations. In figure 3.3 production of good Y takes place at the tangency point B which is to the left of point A, the production point for good X. Since, in this model, the isoquant map is the defining characteristic of each product, figure 3.3 offers a short-hand way of labeling products: Y is the capital-intensive good and X is the labor-intensive good. As long as the isoquants for the two products only intersect once, this ranking holds for any set of factor prices.

If X and Y are the only two goods to be produced, then the output mix depends upon factor supplies and relative factor prices. This is best illus-

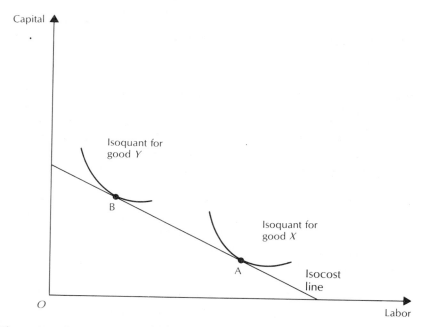

Figure 3.3 Comparing factor intensity of two goods. X is the labor-intensive good because the capital : labor ratio at A is lower than that at B. Y is the capital-intensive good because, faced with the same factor prices as producers of X, its producers adopt a higher capital : labor ratio.

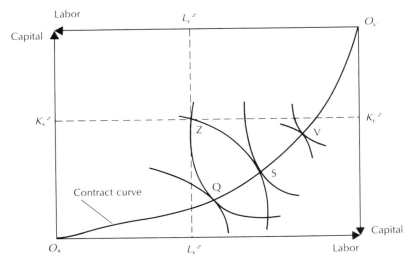

Figure 3.4 Allocation of inputs between activities (the Edgeworth Box). Each point in the Edgeworth Box represents an allocation of the economy's labor and capital between the two activities X and Y. For example, at Z activity Y employs L_y^z and K_y^z, while activity X employs L_x^z and K_x^z. The dimensions of the box are set by the total availability of each factor; that is, the total labor force is $L_x^z + L_y^z$ and the total capital stock is $K_x^z + K_y^z$.

trated by drawing an Edgeworth Box, a rectangle encompassing all available labor and capital combinations (figure 3.4). The isoquant map for each product can be drawn from one of the origin points; in figure 3.4, O_X is set at the bottom left and O_Y at the top right of the Edgeworth Box. If labor and capital are allocated between the two activities in the quantities defined by point Z, then the maximum possible output of X and Y is given by the two isoquants which intersect at Z. This point is suboptimal because, by reallocating labor and capital, the economy could reach point Q (at which the same amount of X is produced and more Y) or point S (at which more X and the same amount of Y is produced). Thus an efficient resource allocation implies being at a tangency point such as Q, S, or V. The locus of these tangency points is the contract curve, which in figure 3.4 bulges downward because X is the labor-intensive good. At each point on the contract curve $MRTS_X$ is equal to $MRTS_Y$. Which of these points represents the best allocation of resources depends upon relative factor prices, because for any given factor prices only one point will satisfy the optimizing condition that $MRTS = P_K/P_L$. Thus, given production functions and factor supplies, there is a single optimum output mix associated with any factor-price ratio *or* for any output mix there is a single equilibrium factor-price ratio.

The Edgeworth Box analysis can be directly related to the production possibility frontier. Each point on the contract curve corresponds to a point on the production possibility frontier, and vice versa. Thus, for point Q in figure 3.4 the output values of X and Y can be read off the two isoquants and the point marked in commodity, instead of factor, space. Following the same procedure for S, V, and all other points on the contract curve traces out the production possibility frontier (figure 3.5). All points in the Edgeworth Box which are off the contract curve correspond to points within the production set but inside the production possibility frontier, for example Z.

The production possibility frontier in figure 3.5 is convex to the origin, unlike the linear PPF in figure 2.1. Convexity follows from the assumed shape of isoquants, that is from assuming diminishing MRTS; as greater quantities of X (the labor-intensive good) are produced more and more demand is placed on increasingly scarce labor resources, raising the opportunity cost (in terms of foregone Y production) of producing additional units of X. The degree of convexity is greater if there are diminishing returns to scale, but this is not a necessary condition; increasing returns to scale, however, offset the factor-substitution effect and may imply a concave PPF (at least over some range).

The point on the PPF at which production will actually take place depends upon relative goods prices. With a price line R'R (the slope of which is P_X/P_Y) production occurs at point Q; at any other point the total value of

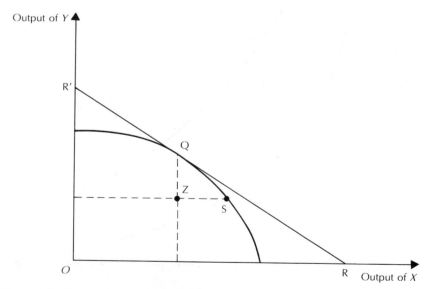

Figure 3.5 The production possibility frontier and the optimum output mix.

production could be increased by changing the output mix (for example at point S by producing more Y and less X). The intercepts of the price line provide alternate measures of total output; R′ measures total output in units of Y, and R measures total output in units of X. Since any goods price ratio implies a unique optimum output mix, then it also implies a unique optimum point on the contract curve and a single equilibrium factor-price ratio. Similarly, any given factor-price ratio can only be associated with one equilibrium goods price ratio. Thus, although in both figures 3.4 and 3.5 the relevant price ratio was introduced exogenously, only one price ratio can be determined independently. The model will now be closed by showing how relative goods prices are determined.

Relative goods prices are set by the interaction of demand and supply, so the analysis now turns to the demand side. The underlying forces here are consumer preferences, which can be represented by indifference curves shaped as in figure 3.6. Higher indifference curves represent higher utility levels. Individual curves are smooth (because of substitutability) and concave (because of diminishing marginal rates of substitution in consumption). Since we are concerned with the operation of the national economy, we will

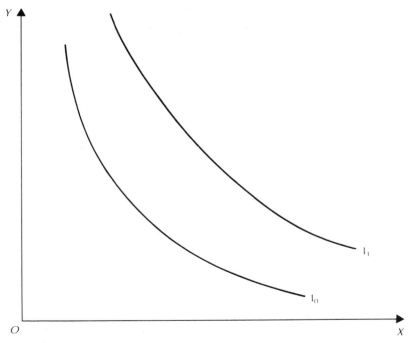

Figure 3.6 Community indifference curves.

be more concerned with community indifference curves than with individuals' indifference curves. The community indifference curve is a summation of all individual indifference curves and as such may be expected to retain the same shape. There is, however, a serious problem insofar as the community curve is a kind of average. If the MRS is 3, then the nation's citizens will, on balance, be prepared to give up three units of Y for an extra unit of X, but if that tradeoff is actually made some consumers will be happy and others unhappy – and who is to say that they are on balance "indifferent" to the change? Thus there is a problem in using community indifference curves with their implicit interpersonal utility comparisons, and especially so if trade changes the distribution of income (which it does in the neoclassical model). Nevertheless, the community indifference curve is a useful way to represent demand-side considerations, relating them to underlying consumer preferences. In the next chapter the analysis is repeated by going directly to demand and supply curves, and we will see that the general conclusions are the same but that different features are highlighted.

Within a closed economy· production and consumption of each good must match. The highest attainable utility level is at the point at which a community indifference curve is tangent to the production possibility frontier. At this point there is no possibility of raising the output of one good without reducing output of the other good, and any such tradeoff (that is, movement along the PPF) will lead to a lower level of community utility. The tangency point can be supported by a single equilibrium price ratio; that is, a price line tangent to both the indifference curve and the PPF so that the relative price ratio is equal to both the marginal rate of substitution in consumption and to the marginal rate of transformation in production. Corresponding to this goods market outcome is a unique allocation of factors between the X and Y industries and a single equilibrium factor-price ratio. If all individual producers seek to maximize profits, factor-owners maximize income, and consumers maximize utility, then perfectly competitive markets lead to the community-welfare-maximizing outcome described in this paragraph.

3.2   The Gains from Trade

The closed economy model can easily be extended to show once again the gains from trade. For the moment assume that the autarchic country just described opens itself up to trade and faces a given world price ratio, leaving until section 3.4 the question of how world prices are determined. In figure 3.7 R'R is the relative price ratio in autarchy, and C is the consumption (and production) point described in the previous paragraph, yielding the utility

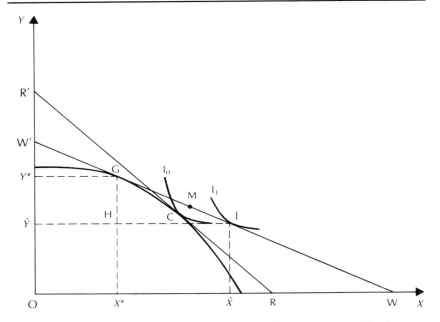

Figure 3.7 The gains from trade with given world prices. At world prices the country produces OX^* and OY^* and consumes $O\hat{X}$ and $O\hat{Y}$.

level associated with community indifference curve I_0. The world price is W'W, the slope of which differs from that of R'R – which is the sufficient condition for there to be gains from trade.

In figure 3.7 W'W is flatter than R'R; that is, the opportunity cost of buying X domestically is higher than the opportunity cost of importing X, so the country benefits from specialization by comparative advantage in the production of Y. The optimal output mix is at point G, where the marginal rate of product transformation is equal to the world price ratio; this realizes the maximum possible output level measured in world prices. The country's consumers can now enjoy any combination of X and Y bounded by the line GW, and will maximize utility by consuming at J, the tangency point between GW and a community indifference curve. Since the indifference curve on which J lies must be to the right of the autarchy indifference curve I_0, then the society benefits from international trade.

This diagram will be used frequently in the remainder of the book, so it is worth spelling out some of its features in more detail. As drawn, opening up to trade is associated with a fall in the relative price of X and the output mix is unambiguously shifted in the direction of more Y and less X (if W'W were steeper than R'R, then the opposite would be true). Consumption of the import good (X) will increase, but consumption of the export good, although discouraged by the higher price, may rise or fall depending on the strength of the income effect. The extent of international trade is measured by the triangle GHJ, the shorter sides of which measure imports (HJ) and exports (GH); the world price ratio, or terms of trade, is measured by the slope of the trade triangle's hypotenuse, GH/HJ. If the world price line becomes still more different from the autarchy price line (in figure 3.7 W'W becomes flatter) then the terms of trade have improved, but if it pivots to become more similar in slope to the autarchy price line then the terms of trade have deteriorated.

A final point to note about figure 3.7 is the key role which the community indifference curves play in permitting welfare conclusions to be drawn. Without the community indifference curves there would be indeterminacy; people consuming above-average amounts of Y suffer from the relative price changes and some producers of X lose out because they have to change jobs, so that under the surface lie distributional issues which can only be resolved by imposing an explicit criterion for measuring social welfare. The link between goods and factor markets described in the previous section points to another distributional matter; if goods prices change with the opening up to trade then the equilibrium factor-price ratio must change too (in figure 3.7 since the capital-intensive good is being exported this price change will be in favor of capital and against labor). These issues will be taken up in subsequent chapters, and it is one of the merits of the neoclassical model that it yields strong results about the relationship between international trade and the functional distribution of income. The problem of assessing whether society's welfare has improved in the presence of such distributional changes will prove less tractable.

Agnosticism about the income distribution effects accompanying international trade is not incompatible with the conclusion in the opening paragraph of this section that there are gains from trade. Producing at point G in figure 3.7 and exporting good Y enables the society to consume some combinations of X and Y involving more of both goods than at the autarchy point C (for example, point M in figure 3.7 yields unambiguous gains from trade). Point J in figure 3.7 is analogous to point D in figure 2.2; consumption of this combination of goods is only feasible with international trade and it may be superior to consumption at a point such as M, but that can only be shown if interpersonal utility comparisons are made (for example, by constructing community indifference curves). The adjustment costs to displaced labor and capital in the import-competing activity are assumed away in this simple model by the existence of perfectly competitive factor markets; this assumption is relaxed in the appendix.

3.3   *The Pattern of Trade (The Heckscher–Ohlin Theorem)*

In a two-country world gains from trade arise whenever the autarchy prices differ between the two countries. Such a divergence may be due to differences in either the community indifference curves or in the production possibility sets or both. In practice neoclassical trade theorists have tended to emphasize one source of differences in production possibilities: differing factor endowments.

In the $2 \times 2 \times 2$ model (two countries, two goods, two factors) developed above, assuming similar tastes and similar production functions in the two countries leaves differences in factor endowments as the sole basis for trade. In figure 3.8 the PPF in country I is flatter than the PPF in country II because country I is more poorly endowed with capital and hence is less well able to produce the capital-intensive good (Y). The capital-abundant country (II) is less well endowed with labor and hence less well able to produce the labor-intensive good (X). By specializing and trading each country can reach a community indifference curve which was unattainable under autarchy.

The specialization pattern illustrated by figure 3.8 can be generalized. Trade encourages specialization toward those activities requiring factor inputs in proportions similar to a country's endowment bundle. In a two-country setting the factor proportions explanation of trade, or the *Heckscher–Ohlin theorem*, can be expressed more succinctly: countries will have a comparative advantage in producing the good using their abundant factor relatively intensively, and each country will export its abundant-factor good in return for imports of the good which uses its scarce factor relatively intensively.

3.4   *Determination of International Prices (Offer Curves)*

Just as goods prices in the autarchic economy are determined by the interaction of demand and supply, "world" prices are determined in the same way. Figure 3.8 already provides a hint of this process; in a two-country world the trade triangles must be of equal size because each country's exports are the other country's imports and vice versa. In a many-country world the same identity between total imports and exports must characterize the equilibrium set of world prices. A useful tool for identifying those prices is the offer curve, which traces out the quantity of goods a country will want to export and to import at any set of world prices. Offer curves can be derived for every trading nation, and their interaction will determine the set of world prices at which world demand and supply for each product are equalized.

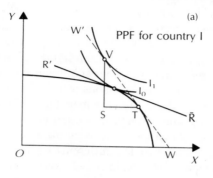

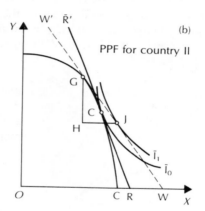

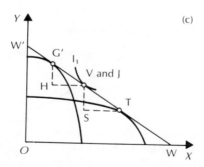

Figure 3.8 Equilibrium trade between two countries (the Heckscher–Ohlin theorem): (a) PPF for country I; (b) PPF for country II; (c) both countries' PPFs together. Note that in (c) it is assumed that both countries are of the same size (that is, both have a post-trade GNP equal to OW units of X); this is not necessary for the Heckscher–Ohlin theorem. In a two-country world the trade triangles must be equal: GHJ = VST.

The basic idea that world prices are determined by reciprocal demand and supply has been accepted since the mid-nineteenth century, but was only really formalized in the early 1950s by James Meade. Meade's approach is complicated but it follows directly from figure 3.7. Corresponding to the community indifference map is a trade indifference map representing combinations of imports and exports among which the country is indifferent. The derivation of the trade indifference map is given in figure 3.9. The trade indifference curve passing through the origin (T_0) contains all the import/export combinations which yield the same utility as the autarchy production/consumption level. All trade indifference curves to the northeast of T_0 represent import/export combinations yielding higher utility, and can only be reached by some international trade. The import/export combination which maximizes national utility depends upon world prices. At the world price ratio R'R nothing better than autarchy is available, but at higher relative prices for Y (for example, W'W or Z'Z) higher trade indifference

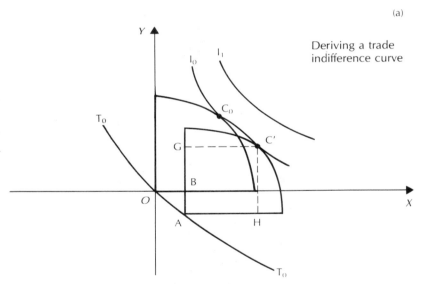

(a)

Deriving a trade indifference curve

Figure 3.9 Meade's derivation of the offer curve.
(a) Deriving a trade indifference curve. Consumption point C' yields the same community utility as the autarchy consumption point C_0. The C' combination can be obtained by producing AG of Y and AH of X, and then exporting AB units of Y in return for OB units of X; that is, point A identifies an import/export combination yielding the same utility as the no-trade combination. Other points on the trade indifference curve T_0 are found by sliding the production possibility block along

curves can be reached. Joining the utility-maximizing import/export combinations at each set of world prices yields the offer curve.

An alternative method of deriving the offer curve is to work directly with the trade triangle in figure 3.7. By aligning the trade triangle with its horizontal side at the origin (as in figure 3.10), the highest point represents a point on the offer curve, the utility-maximizing import/export combination associated with world price ratio W'W. Repeating this for all world price lines flatter than R'R, the highest points trace out the offer curve. This method is simpler than Meade's method, but it brings out less clearly the fact that points on the offer curve represent higher utility levels as they get further away from the origin. Indirectly, it is apparent in figure 3.10 that points further away from the origin are associated with world price ratios further removed from the autarchy price ratio, but in figure 3.9 the utility relationship is a direct one as movements away from the origin are on to ever higher trade indifference curves.

The offer curve analysis is symmetrical in the sense that there is always a

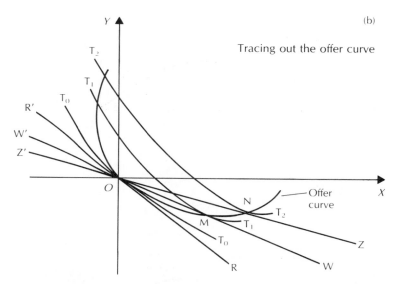

(b)

Tracing out the offer curve

I_0. Repeating the procedure for community indifference curves to the northeast of I_0 traces out higher utility trade indifference curves.

(b) Tracing out the offer curve. For each set of world prices the preferred trading point will be the tangency point on the highest attainable trade indifference curve; for example, O, M, or N. The offer curve is the locus of these tangency points.

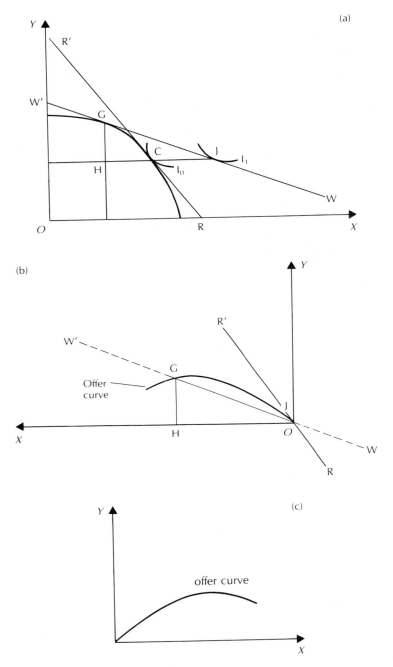

Figure 3.10 Deriving the offer curve from trade triangles: (a) deriving a trade triangle (figure 3.7); (b) tracing out the offer curve; (c) redrawing the offer curve in positive space. Note that the offer curve always bends toward the axis of the import good (X in this example).

second quadrant in which world prices induce the other good's exportation. The important point here is that comparative advantage can never be determined by looking at a single economy in isolation – it is a relative concept. In practice, however, we treat only one quadrant as relevant and always draw the offer curve so that exports and imports are both read in positive space; that is, from left to right and from bottom to top. The offer curve's slope depends upon the underlying production possibility set and consumer indifference map. It is likely to bend backward at some stage, because real income rises with movement away from the origin and eventually the import good becomes so cheap and plentiful that consumers will only accept more imports if they can also consume more of the export good (the quantity available for export has to fall).

The offer curve indicates the quantity of imports demanded and the quantity of exports supplied at any set of relative prices *if* a trading partner can be found. In a two-country world the point at which exchange actually occurs is the intersection of their two offer curves (figure 3.11). At points nearer the origin each country is willing to offer more units of its export good than the other requires to be induced to sell a unit of its own export – thus

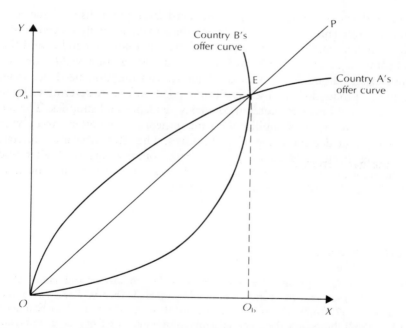

Figure 3.11 Equilibrium in a two-country model. In equilibrium, country A exports O_a units of Y and imports O_b units of X. Given the production functions and consumer preferences in the two countries, no other level of trade could be supported by a price equating demand and supply for both goods.

trade expands. At points beyond E neither country is willing to part with additional units of its export good in return for the quantity of imports being offered by the other – thus trade does not take place. At the intersection point E, the equilibrium price ratio is established as the slope of OP (that is, O_a/O_b).

Any change in either country will shift its own offer curve, and therefore move the equilibrium exchange point and alter world prices. Thus an open economy is inherently less stable than a closed economy in the sense that changes in faraway places will have repercussions via changes in world prices which require domestic adjustment, even though nothing has changed at home. On the other hand, by being part of a larger market domestically induced shocks may be dampened; for example, a bad harvest will be less disastrous if resources can be shifted into producing exports which can be traded for food imports or if domestic consumption of exportable goods can be reduced.

3.5   Summary and Conclusions

In closed economy microtheory the standard assumptions listed at the beginning of this chapter yield the conclusion that, given normally shaped production functions and indifference curves, there is a unique general equilibrium outcome in autarchy. Relaxing the no-trade assumption yields the same conclusion, although in this case domestic consumption need not match domestic production and the equilibrium goods prices are determined by the interaction of home and foreign countries' demands and supplies. The only novel tool for readers familiar with microtheory is the offer curve, which illustrates the determination of world prices. The offer curve also illustrates the gains from trade (in figure 3.11 both countries are on higher trade indifference curves at E than at O) and the way in which the distribution of these gains depends on the world price ratio.

Further Reading

Bertil Ohlin (1933) emphasizes the role of factor proportions and James Meade (1952, 1955) sets out the geometry of neoclassical trade theory. These two authors shared the 1977 Nobel Prize in Economics for their contributions. Paul Samuelson (1939, 1962) shows how the potential gains from trade arise from the unambiguous expansion of society's consumption frontier, even though the actual post-trade situation cannot be proved superior to the autarchy situation. Samuelson also received the Nobel Prize in 1970 for "raising the level of scientific analysis of economic theory." Ron Jones (1965) provides a neat algebraic version of the general equilibrium trade model. Michael Mussa (1974) combines the Heckscher–Ohlin and specific factors models by assuming some factors may be specific in the short run and mobile in the long run.

Appendix: the Specific Factors Model

In section 3.2 it was mentioned that some producers of the imported good may suffer from the opening up of international trade because they have to change occupation. The extent of this loss depends upon the degree of factor mobility. If factors are freely mobile from one activity to any other, as is assumed in models of perfect competition, then there are no adjustment costs. The other polar case, totally immobile factors, can be analyzed with the specific factors model developed by Samuelson (1971) and Jones (1971).

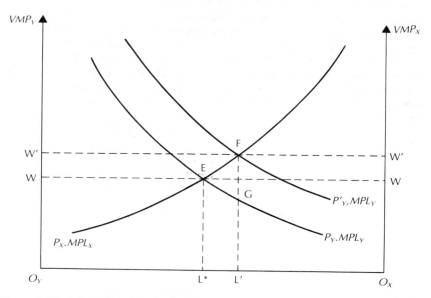

Figure 3.12 Labor allocation in the specific factors model. At the original prices P_X and P_Y the equilibrium wage rate is W, and $O_Y L^*$ units of labor produce good Y and $O_X L^*$ produce good X. After the price of Y increases by an amount FG (to P_Y') the equilibrium wage rate is W' and now $O_Y L'$ units of labor produce good Y and $O_X L'$ produce good X.

Suppose that production of good Y requires labor and capital and production of good X requires labor and natural resources; perhaps the two sectors of the economy are industry and agriculture. Labor is perfectly mobile between the two sectors, so there is a common wage rate. The other two factors are sector-specific, and have no use outside their current employment.

The allocation of labor between the two sectors depends upon the value of the marginal product (VMP) of labor in each sector. Equilibrium is where $VMP_Y = VMP_X$, and these will both be equal to the nominal wage rate (w). Point E in figure 3.12 illustrates such an equilibrium. Now what happens if relative prices change? If the price of good Y increases, then the VMP curve shifts vertically by this amount. The new equilibrium is at F, with more labor producing Y and less labor producing X, and a higher nominal wage. The effect on real wages is uncertain because the wage rate has risen by less than the price of Y but by more than the price of X, which is assumed to be unchanged. Capitalists are, however, unambiguously better off; more Y is being produced, and the price received per unit of Y has increased more than the wage cost per unit (the difference between price and wage cost is the capitalists' income per unit sold). Conversely, owners of natural resources are unambiguously worse off. In general, owners of factors specific to export sectors will benefit from international trade, while owners of factors specific to import-competing sectors will suffer.

In England, when Ricardo was writing against the Corn Laws, landowners wanted restrictions on grain imports because land was specific to food production and they would suffer from cheap imports. More recently, the specific factors model explains the regional problems of Texas, Oklahoma, and Louisiana when oil prices fell in 1986, despite the fact that the US, as an oil-importing country, benefited from this price change. Labor often has some degree of sector-specificity in the short run but is not totally immobile, so workers may suffer from import competition to the extent that they have to personally bear the cost of retraining and of physical relocation.

4

A Partial Equilibrium Model of International Trade

The offer curve analysis illustrates how international prices are determined by reciprocal supply and demand forces in all countries participating in international trade. A more direct approach is to use domestic demand and supply curves to establish world demand and supply curves; at any price the existence of excess domestic demand represents a demand for imports, and excess domestic supply represents a supply of exports. This approach is simpler and more operational than the production possibility frontier/ community indifference curve analysis of the previous chapter, but only really suitable for analyzing trade in a good which does not form a large part of total trade. Hence the partial equilibrium model developed in this chapter will turn out to be a useful complement to the general equilibrium model of the previous chapter; they focus on different aspects of trade, all of which are relevant, but the more insightful approach in any case will depend upon the specific questions to be answered.

Panels (a) and (b) of figure 4.1 contain the domestic demand and supply curves in the two countries A and B for a single good, X. In autarchy the price of X (in terms of "all other goods") is higher in country A than in country B, so that the opening up of trade will see B exporting good X in return for a bundle of imports from A. In a two-country setting, then, the world demand for imports is given by the excess demand in A. The import demand curve, D_m, is traced out in the middle panel of figure 4.1; the intercept is A's autarchy price and at prices below P_A world demand is the horizontal distance between A's domestic demand and supply curves. The world supply of exports of this good, S_x, is equal to country B's excess supply and can be readily plotted in figure 4.1. At the intersection point E world demand equals world supply, and the corresponding price, P_w, is a stable equilibrium.

In the remainder of this book reference will often be made to the special case of a country that is too small to affect world prices by its actions in international markets. This special case can be defined in terms of the partial equilibrium approach; a "small" country faces a perfectly elastic import supply curve and a perfectly elastic export demand curve (figure 4.2). The

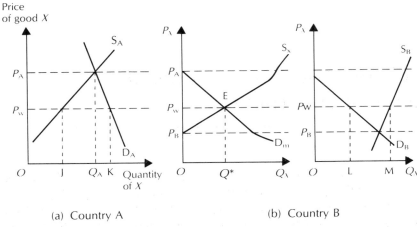

(a) Country A   (b) Country B

Figure 4.1 Determination of world price. At point E the equilibrium price is P_w and the amount traded is OQ^*, which is the amount imported by country A (quantity JK) and the amount exported by country B (quantity LM). Note that at prices above P_A both countries would be exporters and at prices below P_B importers – these prices are outside the relevant range if B is the rest of the world.

economic significance of the assumption is much clearer in this context than in its general equilibrium setting, where a "small" country is one facing a linear rest-of-the-world offer curve. In the remainder of the book the term "small country" will be used without inverted commas, but always in the technical sense defined in this paragraph.

The disadvantages of the demand and supply curve approach reflect the superficiality of these curves. Without knowledge of what underlies the domestic demand and supply curves, it is not possible to predict shifts in the curves as a result of more fundamental changes. More importantly, there is no indication of second-order effects of price changes. For example, in figure 4.1(a) what happens to the factors of production no longer used in the X industry and how does this affect factor prices, with what indirect impact on the X industry? Most fundamentally among these second-order effects, if the country's trade was balanced before trade in X commenced, then country A has a trade deficit when it begins to import X. This omission may be trivial if the X industry is small and its impact on the trade balance (and on factor markets) is minimal. In such a case the benefits from the partial equilibrium approach exceed the costs, although it must be borne in mind that, however minor they are, the general equilibrium effects will always exist.

The main advantage of this approach to the determination of world prices and trade patterns is its reliance on the more directly observable domestic demand and supply curves, rather than on production possibility

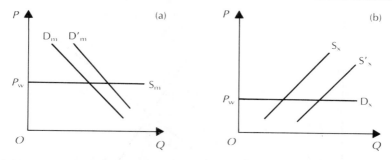

Figure 4.2 Demand and supply curves for (a) imports and (b) exports of a small country. In a small country a change in the demand for imports (for example, from D_m to D_m') or in the supply of exports (for example, from S_x to S_x') has no effect on price.

frontiers and community indifference curves. A further advantage is that it sheds light upon the distribution of the gains from trade within countries. In figure 4.1 the impact of a lower price for X in country A is felt by both consumers and producers:

1   Consumers of X pay less for what they were already buying in autarchy and may now decide to buy additional units. These gains may be represented by the change in the area between the price line and the domestic demand curve – an increase in consumer surplus.
2   Producers of X receive less revenue for each unit sold and may decide to cut back output. These costs may be represented by the reduction in the area between the price line and the domestic supply curve – a reduction in producer surplus.

Both of these welfare effects (the changes in consumer surplus and in producer surplus) can be measured if the pre-trade price and output (P_A and Q_A), the world price, P_w, and the domestic elasticities of demand and supply are known. These data requirements are not too onerous, and this technique has been frequently used to measure the welfare gains from freer trade (see chapter 13).

Figure 4.3 presents a simple numerical example, illustrating the general conclusion that if each unit is given equal weight the increase in consumer surplus exceeds the reduction in producer surplus. Suppose that without trade a shirt sells for two bananas, 50 shirts are produced and consumed, and the elasticity of demand is -0.4 and the elasticity of supply is 1.2. The world price is one banana per shirt and this country's entry into the world market

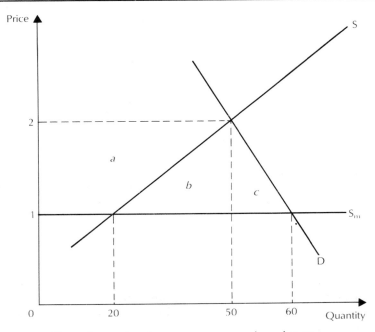

Figure 4.3 Welfare effects of trade on consumers and producers.

will have no effect on shirt prices (it is a small country, S_m is horizontal). The fall in price from the autarchy price (two) to the world price (one) benefits consumers and harms producers of this good; consumer surplus is increased by the area $a + b + c$, while producer surplus is reduced by the area a. In this example $a = 35$, $b = 15$, and $c = 5$, so consumers gain 55 and producers lose 35 (the units depend upon the way in which price is being measured; in this case in bananas, but it could be in "all other goods" or in money). Giving equal weights to a unit of consumer surplus and to a unit of producer surplus, the net gain from trade is 20. This gain consists of: (i) the benefit of specializing in production and importing those units of the good for which the world price is less than domestic marginal cost, measured by area b; and (ii) the benefit of being able to consume those units which consumers value at more than the world price but less than the pre-trade domestic price, measured by area c.

Figure 4.3 provides, once again, evidence of gains from trade, but the distributional issue is highlighted; the gainers and losers may be different people (the shirt-consumers in this example may work in the shirt industry or they may not), and any statement of national gains from trade implicitly or explicitly involves an interpersonal utility comparison. At first sight (and as a working rule of thumb) equal weights, or one dollar–one vote, is an attractive principle, but trade policy debates often focus precisely on the question of whether it is always the best principle.

5

The Core Propositions of Neoclassical Trade Theory

The theory of international trade developed in the previous two chapters is a powerful tool. Not only does it resolve some of the logical difficulties of the simple classical model (for example, the determination of world prices), but it also yields some testable propositions. Apart from the demonstration of the gains from trade, the core propositions of neoclassical trade theory are four. The Heckscher–Ohlin theorem about trade patterns has already been mentioned in section 3.3. The other core propositions concern the functional distribution of income (that is, relative factor rewards) and the relationship between growth and trade.

5.1 International Trade and the Functional Distribution of Income

From the one-to-one correspondence between goods market and factor market equilibrium in the general equilibrium model, it follows that any change in goods prices after the opening up of a country to international trade will be associated with changes in income distribution. If the export good is capital-intensive, then the movement along the contract curve will be to a new equilibrium associated with a higher price of capital relative to the price of labor. If world prices do not change as a result of this adjustment (this is a small country), then the new factor-price ratio favors capital more than the old ratio. What if the capitalists consume disproportionate amounts of the new higher-priced export good? Is it possible to say that capitalists are unambiguously better off in this case?

The Stolper–Samuelson theorem states that the real return of the factor used relatively intensively in the production of the good whose price has risen will unambiguously increase. In the example of the previous paragraph, capitalists will be better off relative to workers, irrespective of the two groups' consumption patterns. There is a magnification effect which ensures that in the 2 × 2 case the price of the abundant factor increases relative to the price of either good, and the price of the scarce factor decreases relative to the price of either good.

The Stolper–Samuelson theorem applies equally to a closing off of international trade. In their original formulation Stolper and Samuelson assumed a trade barrier which did not affect world prices, and demonstrated that the scarce factor gained unambiguously. Metzler subsequently pointed out the possibility that, if world prices are allowed to change, the trade barrier may depress the world price of the imported good sufficiently far that its tariff-inclusive domestic price falls, in which case it is the abundant factor whose real return rises. To encompass the Metzler paradox, modern formulations of the Stolper–Samuelson theorem simply refer to a change in relative prices of commodities, for whatever reason. Nevertheless, the normal interpretation remains that an opening up of trade benefits the abundant factor and a closing down of trade benefits the scarce factor of production.

Since the Stolper–Samuelson theorem applies to any change in relative goods prices, a simple proof can be based on an arbitrary relative price movement. Suppose the price of good Y increases by 10 percent and the price of good X is unchanged. The increase in P_Y can be divided into the higher costs of labor and capital employed in Y production. These costs cannot, however, have risen equally because the factor-price ratio, P_K/P_L, has increased.

If both P_K and P_L have risen by more than 10 percent then so must P_Y, and, if both P_K and P_L have risen by less than 10 percent, then P_Y must have risen by less than 10 percent. Therefore, since P_Y increased by 10 percent, the increase in P_K must exceed 10 percent and the increase in P_L must be less than 10 percent. A similar argument with respect to P_X establishes an increase in P_L of less than zero and an increase in P_K greater than zero. Therefore, there is a strict ranking of the proportional changes in factor and goods prices:

$$\uparrow P_K > \uparrow P_Y > \uparrow P_X > \uparrow P_L$$

This is the magnification effect referred to above, which establishes the Stolper–Samuelson theorem. With more than two factors, the same method could be used to prove that for this change in relative goods prices one factor price must increase by over 10 percent and one factor price must increase by less than zero (that is, must fall).

Figure 5.1 illustrates the Stolper–Samuelson theorem in an Edgeworth Box diagram. Suppose a capital-abundant country allocates its two factors, capital and labor, such that it is at point A before it begins to trade. Opening up the economy and responding to the higher relative price of good Y shifts the equilibrium point on the contract curve from A to B. The economy now produces more of the capital-intensive good Y and less of the labor-intensive

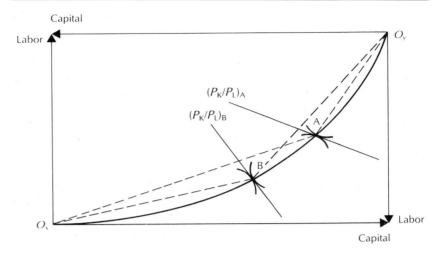

Figure 5.1 The Stolper–Samuelson theorem. Point A is the pre-trade equilibrium and point B the post-trade equilibrium. At B the price of capital relative to
that of labor is higher (indicated by the steeper factor price line) and the
capital : labor ratio is lower in both activities (indicated by the flatter dotted lines
from O_x and O_y) than at A.

good X. At point B the equilibrium factor-price line, which is tangential to
the two isoquants, is steeper than the factor-price line at point A, indicating
an increase in the relative price of capital. Since the capital : labor ratio
(measured by the slope of a straight line from the origin to the equilibrium
point) has fallen in both industries, the productivity of capital has increased
and the real return to capital must be higher.

In recent economic history, there are cases of the Stolper–Samuelson
process working in favor of labor and other cases where it favored capital. In
the nineteenth century, the opening up of Thailand to international trade led
to the export of rice (a labor-intensive good), which benefited small-scale
farmers. In Japan, too, the pre-1900 export mix of silk and tea meant that the
opening up to trade probably benefited rural low-income households, at least
with respect to their pre-tax income. In Chile, by contrast, the dominant
position of nitrates in her exports meant that capitalists, mainly American
and British investors, were the chief beneficiaries. A similar outcome arose
in countries entering into international trade as oil exporters. Application of
the Stolper–Samuelson theorem to analysis of trade barriers will feature in
part III, but nineteenth-century American history illustrates the point. In
the US, where land was plentiful and capital scarce, landowners in the South
and the West favored free trade while the capital owners in the Northeast
lobbied for trade restrictions.

The Stolper–Samuelson theorem is both robust and powerful. It is robust because the assumptions required are only a subset of those underlying the entire general equilibrium model. It does not depend on conditions outside the country being analyzed, so there is no need to assume, for example, identical production functions or identical consumer preferences across countries. It is powerful because of the clarity of its message – international trade policy inevitably involves domestic distributional conflicts. There are gains from trade so the abundant factor gains more from trade than the scarce factor loses, but without compensation arrangements the latter will see its income share fall and will be worse off with trade than in autarchy.

5.2   Factor-price Equalization

In a two-country world the movement in relative factor prices in one country will be accompanied by changes in the opposite direction in the other country. Thus, the increased price of capital relative to that of labor described in the previous section will be accompanied by a fall in the price of capital relative to the price of labor in the (relatively labor-abundant) rest of the world. For how long will this process continue? With identical production functions and consumer preferences, and in the absence of transport costs or other restrictions on the international movement of goods, the process will continue until factor prices are identical in both countries.[1]

The factor-price equalization theorem will not be formally proven here. Intuitively, the proposition can be seen in terms of the relative costs proof used in the previous section. With no restrictions on the movement of goods, international trade must lead to the goods price ratio (P_Y/P_X) being equalized across countries, which means that relative costs must be the same. Equality of relative costs can only be achieved by directing so much capital into Y production in the Y-exporting country that its capital-abundance is reflected entirely in higher output of the capital-intensive good; as long as capital-abundance is reflected in a lower relative price of capital, there are untapped gains from trade.

The factor-price equalization theorem encountered some reactions of incredulity when first proven by Samuelson in the 1940s. After all, factor rewards are clearly not equal in different countries. There is, however, no

---

[1]The process may be forestalled if a country becomes completely specialized before factor prices are equalized. This possibility is ignored in the remainder of this section because complete specialization is rare, and it does not explain the absence of factor-price equalization in the global economy.

doubting the theorem's logic, given the neoclassical assumptions. It is a reaffirmation of the point made in section 3.1 about there being only one degree of freedom in the neoclassical model. In applying this model to international trade the focus has been on the immobility of factors across national boundaries, but as long as goods can freely cross these boundaries the equilibrium outcome is equivalent to having unified factor markets. It follows equally from the model's structure that, if factors were freely mobile, trade in goods would be unnecessary; Mundell (1957) proved that, with mobile factors, goods price equalization occurs with utility maximized at the same level as with immobile factors and free trade in goods.

The factor-price equalization theorem is logically impeccable, but less robust than the Stolper–Samuelson theorem. It requires the full range of assumptions to hold absolutely, and if there are any differences in production functions, then factor-price equalization does not hold. Moreover, in the real world, transport costs and other trade barriers hinder the free movement of goods (and there are even greater barriers to the international movement of factors), so that a wedge between national factor prices is inevitable. Nevertheless, the factor-price equalization theorem does point to long-term tendencies in international factor-price comparisons; goods trade helps to even out disparities in demand relative to supply of factors at the national level and hence to diminish the variance in factor returns across countries.

The empirical record is inevitably difficult to interpret in this area. Factor-price equalization is incomplete, despite a long history of international trade: just how incomplete is a matter of dispute, with some writers dismissing the theorem as being without any empirical basis because of large international income differentials, while others (such as Krueger, 1968) argue that *per capita* income differences are mostly explained by differences in resource endowments (especially human capital), so that the situation may not be far removed from factor-price equalization. Moreover, there is some evidence that trade reduces factor-price differentials; for example, in the postwar period wage differentials among industrialized countries (and even more so between the newly industrializing countries and the old industrialized countries) have narrowed.

There is also evidence that when trade barriers are erected to stop this process, factor flows replace goods flows; for example, the labor inflows from low-wage countries into northwest European textile and clothing industries or the investment in low-wage countries by transnational corporations. Such evidence is, however, far from conclusive and, particularly in the trade of less-developed countries, other considerations have swamped any tendencies toward factor-price equalization. Nevertheless, the factor-price equalization theorem, together with Mundell's theorem, provides some basis for believing that reductions in barriers to the international movement of goods or factors would be significant steps toward reducing global income inequality.

5.3   Economic Growth and International Trade

The analysis so far has been concerned with international trade at one point in time. What effect does economic growth have on this analysis? First let us consider the small-country case, where the growing country has no effect on world prices. Then we will drop this assumption to permit shifts in the country's offer curve to affect world prices. Throughout this section growth will be assumed to occur exogenously (represented by an outward shift of the production possibility frontier); the causal relationship between trade and economic growth will be discussed in section 16.2.

The fundamental small-country result is that growth always raises welfare in a small open economy. The outward shift in the production possibility frontier permits the country to trade along a world price line further from the origin (that is, parallel to and northeast of W'W in figure 3.7) and hence to consume at a point on a higher community indifference curve.

Is growth in a small open economy associated with more or less international trade? The answer depends upon the shape of the community indifference map and the nature of the outward shift in the production possibility frontier. Figure 5.2 is a simplified version of figure 3.7 with the newly attainable world price line marked as $\overline{W}'\overline{W}$. If post-growth consumption takes place at B then the consumption mix is unchanged; the country's demand for imports and supply of exports increases in proportion to the growth in output. Consumption bundles on $\overline{W}'\overline{W}$ to the left of B represent a greater increase in Y consumption than in X consumption, and since Y is the export good these points reflect an anti-trade bias. Similarly, points to the right of B involve a pro-trade bias, with the demand for imports and supply of exports growing more than proportionately to output. In the extreme cases in which demand for the export good or for imports actually falls (that is, points to the right of U or to the left of V) there is an absolute increase or decrease in self-sufficiency, and growth is ultra anti-trade- or ultra pro-trade-biased. The net trade bias also depends upon how the production possibility frontier shifts. If the frontier shifts uniformly (in the sense that along any ray from the origin the point on the new PPF is the same percentage further out than the point on the old PPF) then there is no production-side trade bias, but if the shift is not uniform (because of biased technical change or unbalanced growth in factor supplies), then a taxonomy of production-side trade biases similar to those for the consumption side can be drawn up.

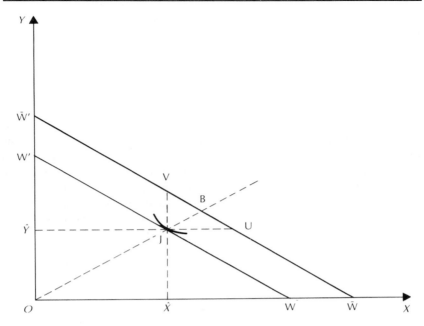

Figure 5.2 Growth and trade in a small economy. Because of an outward shift in the production possibility frontier (not drawn) the economy can consume on a higher world price line ($\bar{W}'\bar{W}$ instead of W'W); that is, GNP measured at world prices has increased from OW to $O\bar{W}$ units of X. If consumption is to the right of point B, the share of the export good Y in gross national expenditure has fallen (there is a pro-trade bias) and if it is to the right of U there is an absolute fall in domestic consumption of Y (an ultra-pro-trade bias).

When growth is due to increased supply of a single factor of production, then a strong result about the ensuing trade bias holds. The Rybczynski theorem states that unbalanced growth in factor supplies leads, at given commodity prices, to larger asymmetric changes in output. In the 2×2 model, growth in one factor leads to a decline in the output of the good using the other factor relatively intensively. Thus, growth due to expansion of a single factor must be ultra pro-trade- or ultra anti-trade-biased.

Analytically, the Rybczynski theorem is closely related to the Stolper–Samuelson theorem (the former refers to quantities and the latter to prices) and a similar proof can be employed. Suppose that the labor force increases by 10 percent. If goods prices are unchanged, then the equilibrium factor prices do not change. With two goods, output of both goods (X and Y) cannot increase by more than 10 percent because that would require additional capital, nor can output of both goods increase by less than 10 percent because that would leave labor unemployed. Thus one good's output must increase by over 10 percent, and this must be the labor-intensive good (X). Expansion of X output with constant capital supply and factor prices must involve reallocation of capital away from Y production, and since the capital : labor ratio will not change (because factor prices are constant) output of Y must fall.

The Rybczynski theorem can also be neatly illustrated using an Edgeworth Box diagram (figure 5.3). An increased labor force elongates the box in one direction; for example, shifting the Y origin from O_Y to O_{Y}'. With constant factor prices the capital : labor ratio in each activity, represented by a ray from the origin, remains unchanged. The equilibrium points on the old and new contract curves (E and F) are the intersection points of the relevant rays, and F must involve absolutely less Y production than point E.

The Rybczynski theorem points to a magnification effect on the quantity side. There is a strict ranking of the proportional changes in factor supplies and output of goods:

$$\uparrow X > \uparrow L > \uparrow K > \uparrow Y$$

that is, the output mix must change by more than the factor endowment mix. Like the Stolper–Samuelson theorem, this result does not depend on

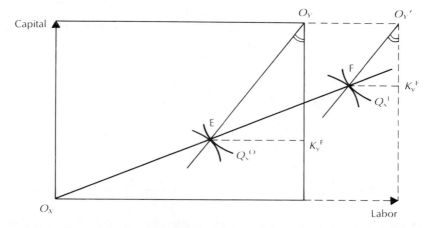

Figure 5.3 The Rybczynski theorem. After an increase in the labor force, output of the labor-intensive good X increases; that is, isoquant Q_x^1 represents a higher output level than Q_x^0. Since the amount of capital allocated to Y production has fallen, from K_y^E to K_y^F, and the capital : labor ratio is unchanged, output of the capital-intensive good Y must fall.

conditions outside the country being analyzed; that is, technology and consumer preferences may differ across countries.

In sum, growth in a small open economy increases welfare but can have any impact on the level of trade, depending on the nature of the production possibility frontier's outward shift and on the shape of the community indifference map. Only in specific cases, for example if the export good is known to be an inferior good or if growth is due to expansion of a single factor, are further generalizations about the trade bias possible. Dropping the small-country assumption, the impact of growth on the terms of trade depends upon the trade bias of the country's growth.

Anti-trade-biased growth shifts the growing country's offer curve downwards; for example, from OA to OA'' in figure 5.4. If conditions in the rest of the world are unchanged then the growing country enjoys improved terms of trade, and fewer units of its export good (Y) are required to buy a given quantity of the import good X. In this case the induced change in world prices reinforces the welfare-improving aspect of economic growth.

Pro-trade-biased growth shifts the growing country's offer curve outward; for example, from OA to OA' in figure 5.4. The country suffers a

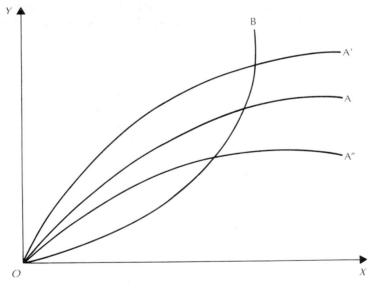

Figure 5.4 Growth and the offer curve. Ultra-anti-trade biased growth shifts country A's offer curve from OA to OA''; less of its export good Y is offered at any set of world pieces, so that the relative price of Y increases and the rest of the world moves to a lower utility point on its offer curve OB. Otherwise, growth has the opposite effect, with A's offer curve shifting from OA to OA'.

deterioration in its terms of trade. This opens up the possibility of immiserizing growth; that is, the adverse welfare effect of the change in world prices may leave the country worse off with economic growth than without growth. Immiserizing growth is illustrated in figure 5.5, where expansion of the factor used relatively intensively in production of the export good (Y) is associated with a larger trade triangle at constant world prices; that is, pro-trade bias. With the new steeper world price line (V'V) the equilibrium consumption point is on community indifference curve I_1; which is not only below the indifference curve I_3, which a small open economy would reach after the same economic growth, but is even below the indifference curve I_2 on which pre-growth consumption took place.

How likely is immiserizing growth? There are three major conditions:

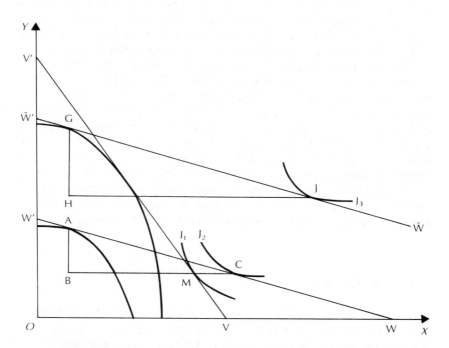

Figure 5.5 Immiserizing growth. Here, economic growth is pro-trade biased; at constant world prices the trade triangle becomes GHJ instead of ABC. For a large country, the relative price of the export good Y will fall; that is, the world price line becomes steeper. If the price of Y falls far enough, for example as indicated by V'V, then post-growth consumption, M, may be on a lower indifference curve than pre-growth consumption; that is, economic growth has left the country worse off.

1   Growth must have a pro-trade bias, either because of consumption patterns or the nature of the growth.

2   Foreign demand for the export good should be quite price inelastic, so that increasing the amount of Y being offered by the growing country leads to a substantial fall in its relative price.

3   The growing country must depend heavily on trade for the welfare effect of deteriorating terms of trade to offset the gains from producing more.

A frequently cited example of immiserizing growth is Brazilian coffee-based growth in the 1930s, but the hypothesis has not been quantitatively tested. In general, the conditions seem more plausible for less developed than for more developed countries; for example, for countries with fast-growing labor forces who export labor-intensive goods the Rybczynski theorem points to an ultra pro-trade bias, while the demonstration effect which makes import demand income elastic reinforces this bias. On the other hand, individual developing countries have small shares of the world market for labor-intensive goods. The complicated relationship between international trade and economic development will be taken up in greater detail in chapter 16.

The immiserizing growth phenomenon depends upon relaxing the assumption of perfectly competitive markets; if all countries are price-takers, then they cannot experience immiserizing growth. It is an example of the theory of second-best, which states that if one of the conditions for a welfare optimum is absent then changes which would be welfare-improving in the unconstrained general equilibrium model need not necessarily be so. Thus, imperfect competition in world markets opens up the prospect of para-doxical outcomes such as immiserizing growth. As with all second-best outcomes the paradoxical result is a possibility, not a certainty, and the conditions necessary for immiserizing growth to occur are sufficiently strin-gent to make it unlikely in contemporary world market situations.

5.4   Conclusions

This chapter has been concerned with developing the logical implications of the general equilibrium model of international trade set out in chapter 3. Because the model identifies countries by their factor endowments and defines goods by the relative intensity with which they use factor inputs, the key results are concerned with the interaction between quantities and prices of goods and factors. The four core propositions are the Heckscher–Ohlin theorem, the Stolper–Samuelson theorem, the factor-price equalization theorem, and the Rybczynski theorem.

It is appropriate to end part I by emphasizing what has been omitted.

The strict validity of the core propositions depends upon restrictions on the production technology (for example, no joint products and no factor intensity reversals – on the latter point see section 6.2.1) and on consumers' tastes. Their validity outside of the 2×2 case has also been given short shrift; in general, they do hold for some cases of higher dimensionality, but not all. On the positive side, the simple model can usefully be extended to include, say, a nontraded good or factors specific to a single sector of the economy: in these extensions three of the core propositions generally remain valid (the factor-price equalization theorem is the exception). Correcting these omissions would require a book in itself, and a different level of technical analysis than the present book; the decision to leave them out in favor of more extensive treatment of the topics covered in parts II and III indicates the relevance of both opportunity costs and comparative advantage to the writing of economics books.

Further Reading

The core propositions are discussed in Ron Jones (1987). The original contributions referred to in the text were Stolper and Samuelson (1941), Samuelson (1948, 1949), Jones (1965) on the magnification effect, and Rybczynski (1955). Johnson (1955) develops the taxonomy of trade biases, and immiserizing growth was analyzed by Bhagwati (1958).

Part II

Extensions and Modifications to the
Basic Model

6

Empirical Tests of Simple Trade Theories

To what extent are the theories of part I consistent with international trade flows in the real world? This is not an easy question; for a variety of reasons, few of the propositions are amenable to rigorous testing. Casual empiricism suggests that the gains from trade are indeed pervasive; no country engages in zero international trade – and even Albania, the nearest case to autarchy in the postwar world, appears to be recognizing the foregone gains from trade. It is also obvious that factor-price equalization has not occurred, but this scarcely brings down the neoclassical model because it is an easy task to enumerate frictions preventing this outcome.

Serious empirical work has tended to focus almost entirely on the commodity pattern of trade: Do countries' export and import bundles reflect comparative advantage and disadvantage, and are they related to factor endowments as the Heckscher–Ohlin theorem implies? This chapter surveys the most influential attempts to answer these questions. Tests of the Heckscher–Ohlin theorem have been unsuccessful in proving or refuting the theorem, but they were important in providing guideposts for useful modifications of the general neoclassical model to account for real-world phenomena.

6.1 Explaining the Commodity Pattern of Trade

The first serious empirical study of whether trade patterns are determined by comparative costs was made by MacDougall. He used data for British and American exports to third countries of 25 manufactured goods in 1937. Observing that US wages were approximately double British wages, he hypothesized that the US would dominate export of goods for which output per worker in the US was more than double output per worker in the UK, and that Britain would be the dominant exporter when the ratio of outputs per worker was less than two. The hypothesis was supported for 20 of the goods, and among these each country's dominant position tended to become

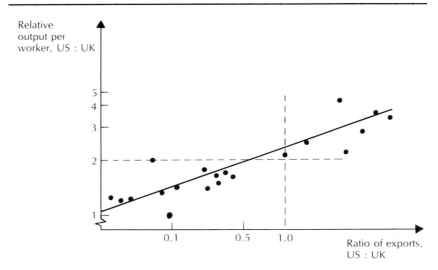

Figure 6.1 MacDougall's results.
Source: adapted from MacDougall (1951)

stronger as its comparative advantage was more pronounced. Figure 6.1, adapted from MacDougall (1951), illustrates the positive relationship. Similar studies by Balassa and Stern using postwar data confirmed MacDougall's results. Altogether, this work provides strong evidence in support of the classical model described in chapter 2.

MacDougall's results provide little guidance to the underlying determinants of comparative advantage. For example, figure 6.1, is consistent with the Heckscher–Ohlin theorem, but is no test of the theorem. He tried a simple test using horsepower per worker as a proxy for the capital : labor ratio and found no evidence that the UK exports had consistently lower capital : labor ratios than the US exports; this is not hopeful for the Heckscher–Ohlin theorem, but horsepower is a very rough measure of capital. A more serious challenge to the theorem came from a series of studies published by Leontief in the mid-1950s.

Leontief (1953) aggregated US industries into 50 sectors, 38 of which were directly involved in international trade. Depending upon the sign of the net trade balance in 1947, he divided the latter into export and import-competing industries. The capital : labor ratio for the export industries was $14,010 per man–year and for the import-competing industries $18,180 per man–year. Since the US appeared to be the most capital-abundant country in the world, this result directly contradicted the Heckscher–Ohlin theorem and became known as the Leontief Paradox.

The Leontief Paradox generated an enormous literature, and the next section will consider the various attempts to reconcile Leontief's results with the Heckscher–Ohlin theorem. One reaction was to question the accuracy or appropriateness of Leontief's data and choice of year. Subsequent studies by Leontief himself and by Baldwin, using more disaggregated data from later years, confirmed that the Leontief Paradox still characterized US trade in the 1950s and early 1960s. Moreover, similar paradoxes emerged from studies of Japanese trade (Tatemoto and Ichimura, 1959) and Canadian trade (Wahl, 1961), while other studies (such as Stolper and Roskamp, 1961, on East Germany) found nonparadoxical results. Bharadwaj's work on India found her exports to be more labor-intensive than her imports (no paradox), but her exports to the US were more capital-intensive than her imports from the US (paradox!). Such a mixture provides little support for the Heckscher–Ohlin theorem – a theorem which is only right part of the time, and in an apparently random fashion at that, is of little value!

6.2   Explanations of the Leontief Paradox

During the 1960s the empirical basis of the Leontief Paradox was generally accepted and great energy was applied to its explanation. The major explanations can be divided into four groups, of which the last two, involving additional factors of production, are the most convincing.

6.2.1   Factor Intensity Reversals

The production-side assumptions upon which the neoclassical trade theory is built were glossed over in chapter 3 by simply drawing isoquants of the required shape. In the late 1950s several economists pointed to the possibility that these assumptions may be inappropriate in certain cases, and the Heckscher–Ohlin theorem may not be valid. Several implicit assumptions are involved (such as no joint products, and non-increasing returns to scale), but most attention was drawn to factor intensity reversals.

If the isoquants for two products intersect more than once, then it is no longer possible to define one of the goods as capital-intensive and the other as labor-intensive in all situations. In figure 3.1 good Y was the capital-intensive good at all sets of factor prices. In figure 6.2, however, Y is the capital-intensive good at some sets of factor prices (such as $P_1'P_1$), and the labor-intensive good at others (such as $P_2'P_2$). When factor intensity reversals such as this are present, no unique ranking of goods by factor intensities exists and the Heckscher–Ohlin theorem becomes meaningless. For example, if the two price lines in figure 6.2 apply to two different countries, of

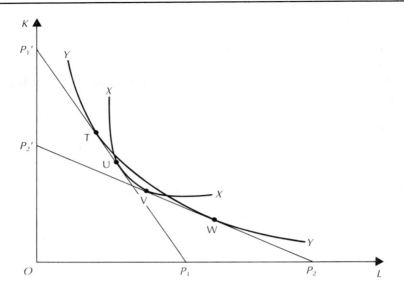

Figure 6.2 Factor intensity reversal. With the factor-price ratio $P_1'P_1$ good Y is produced with the combination T and good X with the input combination U, so that Y is the capital-intensive good. With factor-price ratio $P_2'P_2$, however, good Y is produced with combination W and good X with V, so that Y is the labor-intensive good.

which country 1 is relatively well-endowed with capital, the Heckscher–Ohlin theorem implies that country 1 should export its capital-intensive good and that country 2 should export its labor-intensive good – but these are the same good (Y is capital-intensive in country 1 with factor prices $P_1'P_1$ and labor-intensive in country 2 with factor prices $P_2'P_2$).

Since factor intensity reversals undermine the Heckscher–Ohlin theorem, their presence could explain the Leontief Paradox. Using Indian production coefficients which reveal agriculture to be highly labor-intensive, it would be strange for her to be importing food. American agriculture is capital-intensive, so the presence of grain among US exports to India is less surprising from that perspective. The point, however, is that the Heckscher–Ohlin theorem can provide no guide to agriculture trade flows between India and the US if production is characterized by a factor intensity reversal.

How frequent are factor intensity reversals? Minhas (1962) studied 24 industries in 19 countries and found factor intensity reversals in five industries. Also, making a bilateral comparison of 20 industries in the US and Japan he found a low correlation between capital : labor ratios in the two countries. Minhas concluded that factor intensity reversals were sufficiently frequent to explain the Leontief Paradox. Leontief himself himself questioned Minhas's conclusions, and subsequent empirical work (especially by Lary) failed to support Minhas. More recently little interest has been shown in this topic; the existence of factor intensity reversals is not disputed, but they are uncommon and insufficient to explain much of the Leontief Paradox.

6.2.2 Taste Differences

Even if all the assumptions of the neoclassical model are satisfied, trade patterns need not be determined only by factor endowments. If production functions or consumer preferences differ across countries, then they provide alternative explanations of trade patterns which could dominate the influence of factor endowments.

The existence of production function differences is to some extent a semantic issue. A sufficiently broad definition of factors of production would allow inclusion of every conceivable influence on output as a factor input, in which case the production function relating inputs to output would be the same for all countries. However, this is tautological, and empirical economists have used a more limited definition (but broad enough to include the additional factors covered in the next two subsections). Under a more limited definition of factors the possibility of production function differences cannot be excluded, and the Heckscher–Ohlin theorem is unlikely to be a sufficient explanation of international trade. The relative importance of the Heckscher–Ohlin and "classical" explanations has not been formally tested, but I will return to this point in chapter 9.

International differences in consumer preferences pose a more distinct challenge to the Heckscher–Ohlin theorem. If American consumers' tastes tend to favor capital-intensive goods more than do other countries' citizens' tastes, then trade may reduce the relative price of the capital-intensive good (relative to the US autarchy price) leading to increased US output of the labor-intensive good, which would be exported. In the extreme case of two countries with identical production possibility frontiers and different community indifference maps, trade will be determined solely by taste differences. Dropping the simplifying assumption of identical tastes does not invalidate the Heckscher–Ohlin theorem; rather, it introduces an alternative determinant of trade patterns which may complement or counteract the Heckscher–Ohlin influence. In principle, this joint determination of trade patterns could account for the Leontief Paradox.

In practice, few economists have argued that taste differences are a major explanation of the Leontief Paradox. The empirical evidence provides support for the hypothesis that, at least at aggregation levels similar to those employed by Leontief, household expenditure patterns do not differ much across countries (Houthakker, 1957). The only economist to pursue this issue has been Linder, who theorized that producers are myopic in the sense that they first supply their domestic market and then export to markets with demand patterns that are similar to those of their home country. Linder's theory is consistent with the high levels of trade among the richest countries (the factor endowments of which do not differ greatly), but empirical tests of the theory at a more specific level have been unconvincing.

6.2.3   Natural Resources

The two-factor, two-goods model used in chapter 3 to derive the Heckscher–Ohlin theorem is an abstraction from the more complex reality of more goods and more factors. Introducing more factors does not necessarily invalidate the Heckscher–Ohlin theorem, but it does cast doubt on Leontief's two-factor test of the theorem. An obvious omission from the two-factor test is natural resource inputs; indeed, many 2×2 expositions of the Heckscher–Ohlin theorem label their two factors labor and land!

During the twentieth century the US has become an increasingly heavy importer of resource-intensive products. Vanek (1959) estimated the natural resource content of American exports to be approximately one-half of the natural resource content of American imports. Assuming strong complementarity between natural resources and capital, Vanek concluded that the US, although capital-abundant, imported capital-intensive goods because of their natural resource content. For example, minerals and petroleum can only be efficiently obtained with highly capital-intensive techniques, so that the US as a net importer of copper, chrome, coal, oil, and so on is importing capital-intensive goods. This argument might also explain why Canadian exports to the US are more capital-intensive than her imports from the US, despite America's greater capital abundance; hydroelectricity, minerals, and other natural-resource-intensive goods which involve capital-intensive production techniques bulked sufficiently large in this bilateral trade flow during the 1950s to plausibly explain the paradoxical result.

More recent empirical studies tend to support Vanek's findings. In activities which are not natural-resource-intensive (which could be roughly identified with manufacturing), a Leontief Paradox is rarely to be found. There is, however, some variation in results depending on how "natural-resource-intensive" is defined. This is another manifestation of the definitional problem of what is a factor and what is part of the functional relationship between inputs and outputs.

6.2.4   Human Capital

Leontief's own explanation of his paradox was that American labor was in some way more efficient that labor elsewhere, so that the US must in fact be labor-abundant. This explanation is unconvincing. It appears as an after-the-test rationalization; the Heckscher–Ohlin theorem posits trade patterns as a result of relative factor endowments, whereas Leontief's explanation deduces factor endowments from trade patterns – and then explains the trade patterns in terms of the deduced endowments! Moreover, if the greater effectiveness of US labor reflected better management and superior organization (as Leontief suggested), then these US advantages should also increase the effectiveness of capital; no explanation is given of this bias in entrepreneurial impact in factor productivity, and thus Leontief's explanation found little favor.

A more promising line of reasoning is to question the homogeneity of the "labor" factor or the completeness of Leontief's measure of "capital." Skilled labor differs from unskilled labor in its contribution to output and in its price. Alternately, the education and training needed to produce skilled labor could be seen as a source of capital formation, sacrificing present output for future output; Leontief's measure of capital included only physical capital (buildings, machinery, and equipment), and ignored America's endowment of human capital.

The hypothesis that the US exports goods using skilled labor relatively intensively was tested by Keesing (1966) and others. These studies found that the export : output ratio of US industries was positively related to the skill level of their labor force measured by educational qualifications, professional grades, and so forth. Skill levels are of course difficult to measure with any precision and some studies used expenditure on research and development (which requires skilled labor) as a proxy, finding that industries with higher ratios of R&D expenditure to output tended to be net exporters.

A similar hypothesis is that US capital abundance consists of both physical and human capital. Kenen (1965) estimated the US human capital stock by capitalizing the wage differential between skilled and unskilled labor, and found that the Leontief Paradox then disappeared. This procedure is dependent on definitions of skilled labor and on the discount rate used to capitalize the wage differentials, and other studies have been less conclusive; for example, Baldwin (1971) found that including human capital weakened the Leontief Paradox but, by itself, was insufficient to reverse the paradox. All variables proxying skills or human capital are open to criticism, but almost invariably they have some explanatory role with respect to US trade patterns. In particular, R&D, which is relatively easily measurable, retains significance in multiple regression analysis of US trade patterns for many years and industry classifications – it is a robust explanatory variable.

6.2.5   Summary and Conclusions

Leontief's empirical work had a tremendous influence on international trade theory. One reaction was to examine more thoroughly the assumptions upon which the Heckscher–Ohlin theorem was based. On an empirical level, however, the possibility of factor intensity reversals or of taste differences determining trade patterns appears to be insufficiently important to reverse Leontief's findings. A more promising route was to question the relevance of the 2×2 trade model to actual trade patterns. The introduction of additional factors, such as natural resources or human capital, seems sufficient to explain Leontief's and other paradoxical results. With more than two factors, however, the Heckscher–Ohlin theorem loses its simplicity because a unique ranking of goods by their relative factor intensities requires further assumptions. One reaction to this problem was to develop new theories of international trade to supplement the Heckscher–Ohlin theorem, especially for goods the production of which demands large inputs of skilled labor. This development is the subject of the next chapter.

Even with two factors of production, extending the neoclassical trade model to more than two goods and two countries poses problems for Leontief's study. With many countries the appropriate measure of factor abundance is whether a country's share of the global capital stock is greater or less than its share of the global labor force. Leamer (1980) has shown that with many commodities the ordering of exports and imports by their capital : labor ratios only bears an unambiguous relationship to factor abundance if the net export of labor services has the opposite sign to the net export of capital services. In Leontief's study the US was a net exporter of both labor and capital services, in which case the appropriate test of the Heckscher–Ohlin theorem is whether or not the capital : labor ratio embodied in net exports exceeds the capital : labor ratio in domestically consumed goods. Leontief's own data can be used to show that this was the case in 1947, so the Heckscher–Ohlin theorem is not refuted. Leamer concludes that: "There is no paradox if the conceptually correct calculations are made." To rub in his critique he also asks why Leontief's original data indicate the US to have such a large trade surplus; the answer is because Leontief excluded noncompeting imports (tea, coffee, jute, and so on) which all appear to be labor-intensive, and thus their exclusion biased his study against the Heckscher–Ohlin theorem.

Accepting the Leamer critique, the whole Leontief Paradox appears to be much ado about nothing. The literature remains important, however, because many of the contributions have relevance beyond being comments on Leontief's work. Leamer himself has added to this positive literature in a book which analyzes in some detail the relationships between trade flows and eleven measurable immobile resources (physical capital, unskilled labor, two categories of skilled labor, and seven natural resource categories) for a large number of countries. He emphasizes that he is not formally testing the Heckscher–Ohlin theorem (*inter alia*, there is no competing trade theory against which it can be tested), but concludes that the theorem "comes out looking rather well" in the sense that the main currents of international trade are well understood in terms of the abundance of a remarkably limited list of resources (Leamer, 1984, p. xvi).

In sum, the empirical literature on trade patterns provides support for the trade theories developed in part I. Countries trade with one another and trade flows do reflect differences in comparative costs. Emphasis on factor abundance and factor intensities as the primary determinant of trade patterns is justified; neoclassical assumptions about technology and the cross-national similarity of production functions and tastes are reasonable bases for trade theories. In the complex real world there are of course more than two goods or two factors, but this can be accommodated by introducing additional factors, of which the most important are varieties of natural resources and human capital.

Further Reading

The Leontief Paradox literature has been surveyed by Stern (1975) and by Deardorff (1984).

7

Technology-based Trade Theories

The most popular new trade theories during the 1960s focused on technology. This was a satisfying reaction to the Leontief Paradox because it was consistent with the recurring empirical finding that US trade patterns were related to R&D expenditures. Technological gap theories emphasized that innovating firms enjoy a temporary monopoly at home and in foreign markets. If the US was a particularly successful product innovator, then this could explain her export mix without regard to the capital : labor ratio in new goods.

Hirsch (1967) combined the technological gap approach with Linder's theory to provide an explanation of the strong trade links among high-income countries, despite the similarity of their factor endowments. Innovations are designed with the home market in mind, and reflect consumer preferences and income levels in that country. The first export markets will thus be found in countries with similar consumer tastes and income levels. If continuous innovative activity is fuelling a substantial part of international trade, then we might expect particularly heavy trade flows among the higher income countries.

The location of innovative activity is not random. Innovation, improvements in a new product, and marketing all require highly skilled labor, so that new goods will tend to be produced in the most skill-abundant country. As the product matures, its demands for skilled labor in production and marketing become less pronounced, until the product becomes standardized, and comparative advantage is determined by other considerations (perhaps by physical capital and unskilled labor endowments). Vernon (1966) developed the idea of a product cycle, in which trade patterns depend upon countries' relative skill endowment and the age of each product.

The possible evolution of international trade balances over the product cycle is illustrated in figure 7.1. The horizontal axis, measuring time, has its origin at t_0, the date when the new product is first produced in the skill-abundant country (let us assume it to be the US). At time t_1, exports from the innovating country to other developed countries begin. Over time, however, the importing countries begin to produce the good domestically, reducing

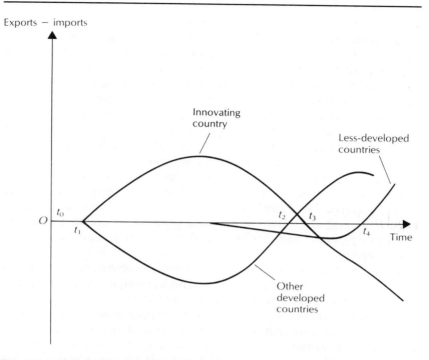

Figure 7.1 The product cycle. Note that the diagram represents trade in a single product; that is, world net exports sum to zero.

their demand for American exports. Also, with increasing product maturity, demand in lower-income countries develops and is supplied first by the original innovator and then by imitators (perhaps producing less sophisticated models) in other high-income countries. Eventually the second-generation producers become net exporters of the by now mature product (at time t_2), and the innovating country becomes a net importer (at time t_3). Later still, the less-developed countries may become net exporters (at time t_4) if the standardized product is unskilled-labor-intensive. The details vary from product to product and may involve any number of overlapping cycles.

A long-term example of the product cycle's impact on trade patterns is provided by cotton textiles. These goods were Britain's leading export after her Industrial Revolution of the late eighteenth century. As the knowledge of mechanical production which had provided Britain's technological edge spread to western Europe, that region began to replace imported British cotton textiles by domestically produced cotton textiles. Britain continued to be the dominant exporter to non-European markets until after Japan adopted the by now standardized technology at the end of the nineteenth century;

with far lower labor costs than European producers, Japan expanded her cotton textile exports rapidly in the early twentieth century, and the British export surplus diminished during the inter-war years. The other western European nations might have reverted to being net importers of cotton textiles had they not raised their trade barriers to keep out Japanese goods – a situation which re-emerged in the mid-1950s after Japan's recovery from wartime destruction got under way. The postwar period has seen further cycles as Japan herself has faced competition from still-lower-wage countries such as Hong Kong, Taiwan, and South Korea, which transformed the Japanese textile trade balance from surplus to deficit; and then the newer suppliers in turn have faced competition from still-lower-wage countries (mainly because export success itself bid up wages in Hong Kong, Taiwan, and South Korea, who shifted their product mix out of textiles and into more skill-intensive goods). The current trade patterns in cotton textiles are affected by pervasive trade barriers, but the long-term picture illustrates the product cycle.

Many examples of the product cycle could be described, each with its own special features. Automobiles, for example, illustrate the importance of product differentiation, after-sales service, and so on in slowing down the shift in production location over the standardization process. American car makers, who first perfected the mass-produced automobile and dominated international car exports in the 1920s, were on the defensive in the 1950s and 1960s against European producers. By the 1970s the automobile had become a standardized product, but Japan was the only country to emerge as a major new exporter. Once the Japanese industry established itself it enjoyed a strong competitive advantage, but it required substantial investment in physical capital and in creating a dealer and after-sales network (all activities with economies of scale) plus a time lag to establish consumer acceptance. Several lower-wage countries have established domestic automobile industries, but often at great resource cost (the cars could be more cheaply obtained via import) and only South Korea and possibly Brazil and Mexico were on the horizon as serious new exporters by the end of the 1980s. In this case product cycle phenomena are apparent, but the number of actively participating countries is limited by the pronounced scale effects in production and marketing.

Case studies have documented trade patterns during the product cycle in industries as varied as synthetic materials and other chemicals, electronics, office equipment, films, and so on. Two interesting aspects from some of these studies are the role of raw materials and the possibility of multiple product cycles even in one country's trade. In the cases of synthetic fibers and petrochemicals (as well as in cotton textiles), the raw materials producers (Canada and Sweden for wood pulp and the OPEC countries for petroleum) never became major suppliers of the finished product; exports came first from the "high-tech" countries and then from low-wage countries (or occasionally capital-abundant countries) as the technology became standardized. In general, natural resource endowment plays little role in determining comparative advantage in manufactured goods; primary product inputs can be traded and it is the relative factor intensity of the processing activity, not of the manufactured product, which is important.

A single product may pass through a series of product cycles if repeated innovations occur. Figure 7.2 provides a stylized picture of postwar trade patterns in radios, as represented by US and Japanese net exports. Initially, the technological gap in vacuum tube radios favored the US. As the product matured, Japan emerged as the major supplier and US net exports declined. Instead of following the figure 7.1 pattern, however, the US was able to reverse her decline by developing a new technology based on transistors. The second cycle mirrored the first in shape, and it too was reversed by a technological innovation in the US (the silicon chip). In passing, we can note that the product cycle theory is extremely difficult to test with standard trade data because the US was simultaneously importing and exporting radios (the imports were low-priced, old-technology radios, while the exports were high-tech, state-of-the-art radios); using net imports or net exports to

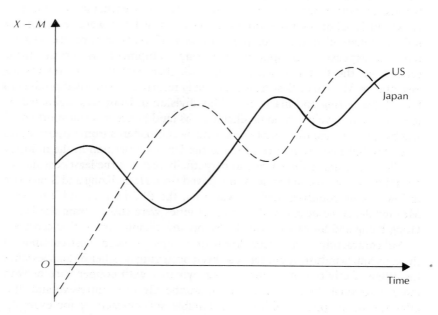

Figure 7.2 Stylized product cycles for radios since the late 1940s.

determine whether the US had a comparative advantage in radios would be misleading.

The cycles in figure 7.2 had an obvious message for US corporate executives. Since the Japanese upswings were a result of higher US wages, why not lower costs by shifting assembly activities to low-wage countries, thus lengthening the period during which the US firm would maintain its competitive advantage? When Japanese firms began to produce and export transistors in the late 1950s, two US firms pursued different reactive strategies. Philco invested heavily in automated production processes to offset the high US wage rates, and enjoyed disastrous losses because of rapid obsolescence of their expensive equipment. Fairchild reacted by setting up in 1961 a manufacturing affiliate in Hong Kong for assembling US-made components for re-export to the US, and the strategy was so successful that it was quickly copied. Such arrangements, whether involving wholly owned subsidiaries, independent local firms, or joint ventures, became known as international subcontracting.

Semiconductor technology was ideally suited to subcontracting. Production involves four discrete steps: design, chip fabrication, assembly, and testing. Design requires highly skilled labor and soon became concentrated in small pockets where such labor conglomerated, of which Silicon Valley in California was the prototype. Fabrication is very capital-intensive, requiring state-of-the-art machinery. Assembly can be automated, but seldom is because of short production runs due to rapid obsolescence; manual assembly is extremely labor-intensive (in 1976, 54 years of labor were required per million dollars of output, compared to only 35 years in apparel). Testing requires expensive, computerized testing equipment. American firms carried out the first two steps in the US, then sent the components for assembly in Mexico or East Asia, and finally returned the finished product to the US for testing and marketing. This division of labor was facilitated by the high value : weight ratio of silicon chips (and hence low transport costs) and by tariff reform to exempt the US-made components from import duties when the finished product returned to the US. Competition in the industry was fierce enough to force firms to perpetually seek out the least-cost site for assembly operations, so that location moved from Hong Kong and Singapore to lower-wage countries such as Malaysia, the Philippines, and Thailand. Meanwhile, some design and testing activities were shifted from the US to Hong Kong and Singapore, which also became regional marketing centers.

Subcontracting of different production steps has been most common in the electronics industry, but has also been occurring in other industries since the 1960s. Activities involving sewing, whether with copper wire or with more traditional threads, have proven stubbornly labor-intensive and thus offer the major opportunities for profitable subcontracting; for example, pre-cut US denim is sent to Malta to be sewn into jeans for the European market, baseball mitts are stitched in Haiti, and athletic shoes are stitched up in many low-wage countries (all of these activities – not just the last! – are known as "footloose" industries because they require little fixed capital and can readily shift location if labor conditions change). The possibilities of dividing production into steps located in different countries are, however, present in many industries; for example, German cameras have long been assembled in Singapore, British books are typeset in India, and the automobile industry is becoming increasingly involved in producing components in different locations (see box 7.1).

The footloose nature of many subcontracting activities has been a source of concern for host country governments. They fear that the foreign firm facing a choice of locating in many low-wage countries will reap most of the gains from trade, and if gains do accrue to the host country in the form of rising wage rates then the firm will switch location to another low-wage country. In practice, however, there are few documented cases of footloose activities being relocated with sufficient rapidity to justify host country fears of exploitation or economic instability. The preferred locations for subcontracting depend on the product, and the search has rarely led to the lowest-wage countries because firms may require some level of labor skills and acceptance of factory discipline, as well as being concerned about political stability, labor market legislation, and so forth. Bulkier products or activities requiring close supervision tend to be subcontracted to geographically closer locations, so that northern Mexico has been popular with American firms and the Mediterranean region with European firms. Taking all considerations into account, the firm seeking a location for subcontracting activities may find few ideal locations and may have a strong ranking of preferences among these, so that neither the degree of footlooseness nor the bargaining strength of the firm *vis-à-vis* host countries are as strong as they might appear at first sight.

When the "footloose" activities do shift location this is usually part of a more general change in the mix of a country's economic activities. Thus, the changes in activities carried out in Hong Kong and Singapore by electronics firms reflected the changing factor endowments of these locations. The eventual departure of unskilled labor-intensive activities did not reverse the benefits from having had those activities, and the local knowledge obtained during the earlier period encouraged the international firms to locate more skill-intensive activities in these places. This process of moving to progressively more skill-intensive activities is often likened to a ladder, with the developing countries on the bottom rung, the newly industrializing countries on the next rung, and so forth. Subcontracting can help a country climb off the bottom rung by developing the more rudimentary skills needed in a modern economy.

BOX 7.1   *Internationalization of Production in the Automobile Industry*

In the mid-1980s the Ford Escort was assembled in England and in the Federal Republic of Germany, but its components were obtained from a global network of suppliers, some of whom were part of Ford Motors while others were independent. The following diagram illustrates the component network:

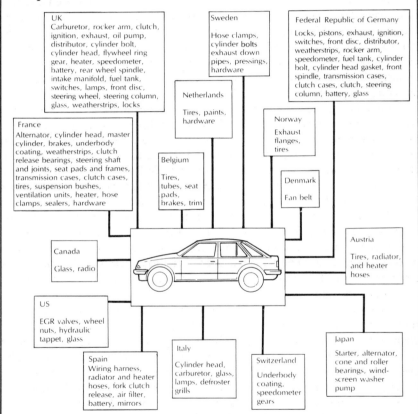

Such a network raises a question: Of what nationality is a Ford Escort? This became important during the late 1980s when Japanese car manufacturers hopped over trade barriers by setting up assembly plant in Europe and in North America, while domestic producers argued that products of these "screwdriver" plant were still Japanese.

Source: *World Bank,* World Development Report 1987, p. 39

Subcontracting again illustrates the practical difficulty of testing explanations of trade patterns in manufactured goods. The exported components may belong to the same category of goods as the imported assembled goods, so that without detailed investigation the trade data may present an inscrutable trade pattern. Subcontracting is consistent with the product cycle model, although it will speed up the cycle as the shift in location of production activities is accelerated. Ultimately, however, if the innovator seeks out the least-cost location for each activity from the start, then there is no product cycle explanation of trade patterns.

Vernon himself conceded by the late 1970s that, although the product cycle explained much international trade in the 1950s, this would no longer be true in the 1980s because of the increased global scanning capability of transnational corporations. Table 7.1, taken from Vernon's own work at Harvard Business School, reports the number of subsidiaries of 316 transnational corporations and indicates the dramatic globalization of these corporations; in 1950 only 62 had subsidiaries in more than five countries, while by 1975 this number had risen to 276. Greater global presence has meant that these companies can plan production of a new good on a global basis to minimize costs. Thus, recent new products such as disposable razors and digital watches were produced with assembly at low-wage locations and marketed on a world scale from the beginning; no product cycle existed in their trade patterns.

The internationalization of production just described represents a strengthening of factor endowments as the basis for international trade. The Heckscher–Ohlin theorem focuses on the relationship between factor endowments and factor intensities when economic decision-makers are trying to maximize the gains from trade, but the same analysis leads to the theorem as a condition for minimizing costs. If trade patterns do not reflect factor endowments then firms are not minimizing costs, presumably because of some market imperfections. The transnational corporation and other subcontracting arrangements have evolved as institutional arrangements to

Table 7.1   The global spread of large corporations

Number of countries in which subsidiaries are located	181 US-based corporations		135 European-based corporations	
	1950	*1975*	*1950*	*1975*
Less than 6	138	9	116	31
6–20	43	128	16	75
More than 20	0	44	3	29

Source: Vernon (1979)

overcome some imperfect markets (especially for knowledge and intangible property rights such as secret formulas, trademarks, and so on) and, meanwhile, falling transport costs have increased the feasibility of splitting up production activities geographically. If labor at various skill levels remains relatively immobile internationally, then the geographic allocation of production activities will reflect their factor intensity and relative factor endowments in potential locations, although transport costs, political stability, and government policies will also enter into the decision. Testing the Heckscher–Ohlin theorem becomes more complex because imported and exported components at different stages in the production process may enter a country's trade statistics under the same heading. Nevertheless, the growth of subcontracting and global scanning can be expected to have reinforced the relevance of the Heckscher–Ohlin theorem as an explanation of trade patterns.

Further Reading

In addition to the references in the text, Posner (1961) and Hufbauer (1966) were also landmark studies in the technology-based trade theories. Flamm (1985, especially pp. 48–54, 68–79) describes the semiconductor industry's trade.

8

Economies of Scale, Imperfect Competition, and Intra-industry Trade

Two empirical phenomena have played key roles in setting the agenda for postwar trade theorists. The Leontief Paradox stimulated re-examination of the assumptions underlying the Heckscher–Ohlin theorem, and a search for new trade theories incorporating additional factors of production. Explanation of intra-industry trade had a similar effect in the 1970s and 1980s in stimulating research on the implications of imperfectly competitive markets for international trade theory.

The statistical evidence on intra-industry trade is presented in section 8.1, together with some uncontroversial explanations of the phenomenon. The econometric literature is surveyed in the next section, and an explanation consistent with the results is provided. Section 8.3 considers the implications of scale economies for the theory developed in part I of this book. Finally, some recent trade theories, which relax the assumption of perfect competition and which introduce scale economies and product differentiation as key elements, are examined in section 8.4.

8.1 Measuring Intra-industry Trade

In the trade models of part I, international variations in production functions, factor endowments and consumers' preferences determine in which goods a country's comparative advantage and comparative disadvantage lie; trade patterns follow, in that exports come from the former group and imports from the latter. There is no room for simultaneous import and export of the same good. However, economists had been noting since at least the 1930s the presence of such two-way flows in international trade statistics. This phenomenon was highlighted after the formation of the European Economic Community because, contrary to the predictions of inter-industry specialization (for example, that French wheat would be traded for German machinery), much of the subsequent specialization and trade was within industries (for example, French cars were traded for German cars).

In a series of articles, collected in their 1975 book, Grubel and Lloyd documented the pervasive importance of intra-industry trade in the trade flows of the major trading nations. They measured the share of intra-industry trade in a country's total trade of a good by the expression:

$$B = \frac{X + M - |X - M|}{X + M}$$

where X is exports and M is imports. The numerator is intra-industry trade; that is, the difference between total exports plus imports and the absolute value of net exports or net imports (the lines around $X - M$ indicate that the sign of this expression is to be ignored). The value of B varies between one (when $X = M$ and all trade is intra-industry) and zero (when X or M is zero and no intra-industry trade occurs). Using data for three-digit Standard International Trade Classification (SITC) groups from ten industrialized countries, Grubel and Lloyd calculated that B averaged just under 0.5; thus almost half of these countries' trade was intra-industry trade. This finding both posed a challenge to traditional trade theories which predicted only inter-industry trade, and cast doubt on Leontief-type tests which, by defining industries in terms of net exports or net imports, were using only half of a country's trade flows to test general trade theories.

How is intra-industry trade to be explained? Some intra-industry trade is border trade related to high transport costs; for example, if British Columbia exports coal to Washington State and Pennsylvania exports coal to Ontario, the US and Canadian statistics will record simultaneous import and export of coal. There is also seasonal trade due to high storage costs; for example, fruit and vegetables with different growing seasons in different parts of the world may appear in a country's annual trade statistics as both imports and exports. For a few nations entrepôt trade, that is, acting as a transshipment point, may be important. All of these types of intra-industry trade exist, but their significance is much too slight to account for the magnitude of intra-industry trade calculated by Grubel and Lloyd. The reasons for these types of intra-industry trade are for the most part obvious and require only minor revisions to more general trade theories; most can be seen as a kind of aggregation phenomenon; for example, daily or monthly instead of annual data would eliminate intra-industry trade based on seasonality.

There is also a more general aggregation problem due to the difficulty of defining an industry, a difficulty which everybody recognizes but about whose significance there is a major disagreement.

International trade data are organized into categories, the criteria for which vary (for example, some are based on similarity of end-use, and some on the primary material input, while others are miscellaneous catch-all categories) and which can be accessed at various aggregation levels. The most common classification system, the Standard International Trade Classification (SITC),[1] identifies ten major classes (0 is food, 1 beverages and tobacco, 2–4 raw materials, 5 chemicals, 6–8 manufactures, and 9 other), each of which is broken down into up to ten subclasses, which in turn can be divided into up to ten groups, and so on; the SITC three-digit level contains 182 groups, while the six-digit level contains over 2,000 categories. Grubel and Lloyd selected the three-digit level for their calculations on the grounds that SITC three-digit groups correspond most closely to what are normally thought of as "industries," although they recognized this to be a subjective matter. At finer aggregation levels measured intra-industry trade declines (as long as at least one of the subgroups has net exports and at least one has net imports, then intra-industry trade must be smaller when calculated at the subgroup level and summed up than when calculated at the group level). Grubel and Lloyd illustrated this by recalculating their Australian measure using six-digit instead of three-digit SITC data and found that intra-industry trade fell from 20 percent to 6 percent of Australian trade, which they offered as evidence that intra-industry trade remains substantial even when highly disaggregated data are used.

Controversy over the importance of the aggregation problem centers on two issues: the definition of an "industry" and how much intra-industry trade is "substantial." Some three-digit SITC groups do indeed correspond to common perceptions of industries; for example, SITC 781 (passenger motor vehicles except buses) has attracted considerable interest because of the readily observable intra-industry trade within western Europe. Other three-digit SITC groups are, however, equally obviously heterogenous; for example, SITC 793 (ships and boats) runs from kayaks to supertankers. In truth no SITC aggregation level corresponds to common perceptions of an "industry," but it is prohibitively expensive to reorder trade data into more appropriate categories, even if there were agreement on how to define these categories (for example, to test the Heckscher–Ohlin theorem industries should be defined by input structure, but most common usage defines them in terms of cross-elasticities of demand). The controversy is unresolved; in my view, so many three-digit SITC groups are heterogenous (especially in SITC categories 5–9) that intra-industry trade measured at this level is largely picking up the phenomenon of dissimilar products being placed in the same group.

Measured at the six-digit SITC level intra-industry trade tends to be less than 10 percent of total trade, which raises the question of whether this small

---

[1] The SITC was first devised under United Nations auspices in 1950, and was revised in 1960 and 1974. The revisions mean that the categories have differed slightly over time.

component of total trade is worth bothering about. There is always likely to be some intra-industry trade as soon as we define "industries" to include more than a single transaction; intra-industry trade in functionally homogenous goods occurs because of border trade, and so on, as described above, and in differentiated goods because of different vintages of models (as in the product cycle explanation in the previous chapter) as well as because of some obvious special cases (for example, *The Times* is sold in Paris and *Le Monde* in London). These are all readily explicable phenomena, but if their total impact amounts to less than one-tenth of international trade flows should we worry much about them?

The issues discussed in the previous paragraphs are crucial for deciding whether the high intra-industry trade ratios calculated by Grubel and Lloyd represent a substantive economic phenomenon or a statistical artefact. Grubel and Lloyd themselves believe both that SITC three-digit groups are the appropriate aggregation level and that, even if this were incorrect, intra-industry trade remains substantial with more disaggregated data. Thus, intra-industry trade demands an explanation since it is not consistent with existing models' predictions of inter-industry trade. For Grubel and Lloyd scale economies and product differentiation were the crucial forces; scale economies restrict the number of varieties which can be produced domestically, so minority interests are satisfied by imports and minority demand elsewhere for popular varieties here are serviced by exports. They present some anecdotal supporting evidence for automobiles and cigarettes, and the automobile case has been examined in more detail by Hocking (1980), who found that western European countries specialized in producing cars in the model range for which domestic demand was strongest.

The automobile industry provides an example of an imperfectly competitive industry, in which economies of scale and product differentiation are important. None of these characteristics fit into the trade theories of part I, which assume no scale economies and perfect competition everywhere. Thus, Grubel and Lloyd's work stimulated new thinking about imperfectly competitive markets and international trade, which will be reviewed in the final section of this chapter. The automobile example does not, however, prove that scale economies and product differentiation provide an explanation of the high levels of measured intra-industry trade. During the 1960s and 1970s, the automobile industry was a rather special case of a shift in comparative advantage from Europe to Japan which was slow-moving due to the high barriers to entry and was delayed even more by huge government assistance for major European producers (without which Britain, for example, would have had larger imports and little intra-industry trade in automobiles by the 1970s). Whether the scale economy/product differentiation hypothesis explains intra-industry trade more generally requires cross-sectional testing across the whole range of industries.

8.2   *Explaining Intra-industry Trade*

Intra-industry trade indices have now been calculated for many countries and some empirical regularities have emerged. The level of intra-industry trade is positively related to *per capita* income levels, both across countries and over time. It is much higher in the manufacturing sector than in primary activities (roughly SITC 0–4). Weaker relationships seem to exist with respect to distance and to trade liberalization; closer neighbors have more of their bilateral trade in the form of intra-industry trade, and reducing trade barriers increases the ratio of intra-industry trade to total trade.

Since the mid-1970s a number of econometric studies have sought to explain variations in intra-industry trade from industry to industry in terms of industry characteristics. The results of these studies, most of which use three-digit SITC groups as their definition of industries, have been unconvincing. In particular, despite various formulations there has been little support for the hypothesis that intra-industry trade should be greater in industries characterized by economies of scale and extensive product differentiation. While measurement problems associated with these two variables make it impossible to regard any test of this hypothesis as conclusive, the accumulated evidence does cast doubt on the generality of Grubel and Lloyd's explanation of intra-industry trade at the three-digit SITC level in terms of product differentiation and scale economies.

How then is the intra-industry trade phenomenon to be explained? Intra-industry specialization is nothing more than increased division of labor which, as Adam Smith pointed out, is dependent on the size of the market. As countries have grown economically and become more integrated into the world economy, they have faced a larger market which has permitted further division of labor. Vertical specialization, that is the location of different stages of production in different countries, underlies the growth and current preponderance of intermediate goods in international trade, as well as the phenomenon of subcontracting described in the previous chapter. Since goods traded at different production stages are often recorded under the same SITC heading, a country participating in any but the first stage of production will have intra-industry trade. The intra-industry trade literature has tended to focus more on horizontal intra-industry trade involving finished products such as automobiles, but here too expansion of the market permits finer specialization. Ricardo may have been content with categories such as shoemaker and hatmaker, but the footwear industry now includes ski-boots and running shoes (and among running shoes there are both sophisticated high-tech models and basic canvas and rubber models); there is no reason to expect these subgroups to have the same input structure, and the presence of intra-industry trade may be consistent with the Heckscher–Ohlin theorem.

Explaining growing intra-industry trade in terms of increased division of labor due to expanded market size has several testable implications. The most developed countries will have taken the division of labor furthest, while less-developed countries are likely to have simpler export mixes. With economic growth and falling transport costs, intra-industry trade will tend to increase over time. Trade liberalization plays a similar role to falling transport costs in encouraging finer specialization. Adding that the opportunities for further division of labor seem to be intrinsically greater in most manufacturing activities than in agriculture or other primary activities, the Adam Smith explanation of intra-industry trade is consistent with all of the strong empirical regularities found in the calculated intra-industry trade ratios. This explanation does not rest upon scale economies or product differentiation within an industry. It is, however, consistent with the sometimes considerable reduction in intra-industry trade when calculated with more disaggregated data.

In sum, the phenomenon of intra-industry trade does not pose a serious challenge to the trade theory developed in part I. It does however, pose a problem for empirical work which, if it is to avoid any risk of aggregation bias, must operate at ever-increasing levels of disaggregation; this is both costly and clumsy insofar as the results are difficult to digest or interpret if they cover thousands of separate industries or goods. To present a table of trade flows, barriers to trade, and so on at the industry level, the SITC three-digit groups will normally provide as large a number of entries as readers are prepared to go through, but the intra-industry trade literature has shown that these groups are so heterogenous that a single figure for each group may have little meaning.

8.3   Economies of Scale

Economies of large-scale production have long been recognized as a determinant of international trade, and it is rather obvious that their presence may permit additional gains from trade. Scale economies have, however, not featured prominently in international trade theory because their presence makes trade patterns indeterminate. This inherent arbitrariness of trade patterns holds whether scale economies are external or internal to the firm, although in the latter case the additional problem of imperfectly competitive markets arises.

Before the 1970s, the treatment of scale economies was usually based on the assumption that they are external to the firm. For example, individual farmers' average cost curves may be flat or rising at all but very low output levels, but expansion of total agricultural production may reduce farmers' average costs by permitting production of specialized machinery, fertilizers, and so on, as well as better transport, handling facilities, and so forth. Scale economies external to the firm are not inconsistent with perfect competition, and thus this assumption permits the consequences of increasing returns to scale to be isolated from those of imperfectly competitive markets.

Figure 8.1 illustrates how each of two identical economies characterized by scale economies in the production of two commodities can gain from international trade. With no trade both countries produce and consume bundle A; with trade each specializes in producing one commodity and consumes bundle B. This simple example illustrates two general propositions: scale economies are a reason for international trade (because they are a source of gains from trade) and the pattern of trade based on scale economies alone is arbitrary (which country produces X and which produces Y is a matter of chance).

Chance is not a satisfying explanation of trade patterns. One response is to accept the presence of scale economies but only as a subsidiary reason for trade; for example, Ohlin in his 1933 book referred to in chapter 3 noted that,

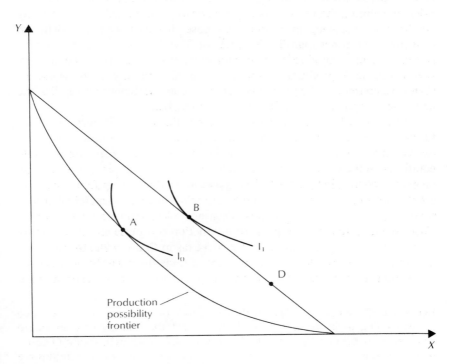

Figure 8.1 International trade with economies of scale.

while scale economies offered extra scope for gains from trade, the basic patterns were determined by factor endowments. This is perhaps correct (see the concluding remarks to chapter 6), but there are some industries where scale economies are important and chance has played a role. Seagrams became the best-selling whiskey in North America because the Canadian manufacturer had stocks of aged whiskey, denied to US producers, when the US abolished Prohibition. In financial services, the pre-eminence of London and, to a lesser extent, Luxembourg in Europe depended on historical factors. Once one company or location had a head start, its advantage became cumulative. Even if trade patterns initially reflect factor endowment or tastes, they can become fossilized in the presence of scale economies and cease to reflect current locational considerations; for example, the establishment of the agricultural machinery industry in the American Midwest and Ontario gave firms such as John Deere, International Harvester, and Massey-Harris a long-term comparative advantage even when large markets for such products opened up elsewhere.

Figure 8.1 presents a special situation of identical economies, each of which receives the same post-trade consumption bundle regardless of which good it specialized in producing. In general, this will not be so because the price line joining the two complete specialization points will not necessarily be the market-sharing price ratio. Suppose that each country wishes to consume at D rather than B. The price of X will increase and the country specializing in X production will gain more from trade than the country specializing in Y production. The latter country could even be worse off than with no trade, if the price line were to become sufficiently steep that the new tangency point lies on an indifference curve below I_0.

Thus, not only the trade patterns but also the sign of the welfare effects for each country are unpredictable in the presence of scale economies. In a two-country setting, world prices may be indeterminate; there are multiple equilibria, some of which are unstable. Take, for example, the price line tangent to point A in figure 8.1: A is a possible production equilibrium but so are the two total specialization points, at each of which the marginal cost of producing the commodity of specialization is less than its relative price. Corresponding to the three possible production equilibria are three trading equilibria; that is, points on the offer curve (as in figure 8.2(a) for the price line T'T). In general, for any given terms of trade there will be one, two, or three points on the offer curve. With two identical countries, the production

Figure 8.2 Offer curve analysis with economies of scale. (a) The offer curve corresponding to figure 8.1: at world prices T'T the country may specialize completely in Y (point H) or in X (point J) or remain in autarchy (point O corresponds to A in figure 8.1). (b) International equilibrium: at L both countries are completely specialized, at M neither country is, and at N one is completely

(a)

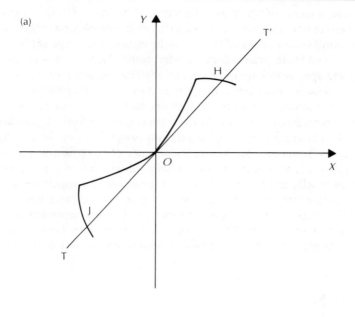

(b)

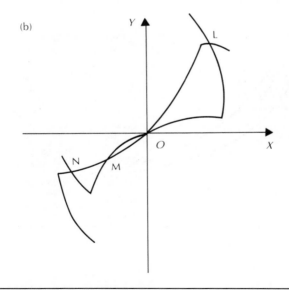

specialized and the other is not. Assuming that producers rather than consumers respond first to domestic disequilibrium, points L and N are stable equilibria and M is unstable.

possibility frontiers of which are characterized by figure 8.1, the offer curves may intersect one, two, or three times (figure 8.2(b) illustrates the last case) and the equilibrium terms of trade may lie outside the range set by the two countries' pre-trade price ratios. Under some dynamic assumptions, all incomplete specialization equilibria are unstable, which repeats the importance of a head start in determining production and trade patterns.

Scale economies internal to the firm are more difficult to handle because they are inconsistent with perfectly competitive markets. If average and marginal costs are falling over the relevant range for firms in an autarchic economy (as in figure 8.3), then in the absence of government intervention the industry will become monopolized with a single firm producing quantity Q_d which it sells at price P_d. If the world market is competitive after this country enters into international trade, then any world price below P_d will yield welfare gains as the increase in consumer surplus outweighs the reduction in monopoly profits. This is not a rare occurrence, because domestic monopolies are frequently successful in setting up barriers to imports, and

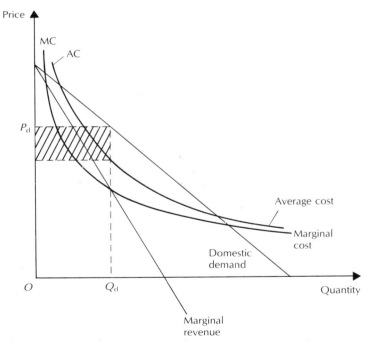

Figure 8.3 Price and output decision of a profit-maximizing monopoly. To maximize profits the monopolist produces output level Q_d, where MR = MC. Profits are equal to the shaded area.

removal of such barriers is then an effective antitrust policy. If world markets are not competitive because scale economies or other entry barriers are important at the world level, then this beneficial conclusion may not hold. Domination of the world market by a single foreign firm may lead to elimination of the domestic producer and subsequent return to a price which leaves domestic consumers no better off than before, while the monopoly profits now accrue to foreigners. If the world market is not a monopoly, then the outcome depends on the specific market structure; some possible outcomes will be analyzed in the next section.

8.4   Imperfect Competition

Scale economies internal to the firm received scant treatment by trade theorists before the late 1970s. In part this reflected the analytic dilemmas posed by scale economies in general, and the market structure implications of scale economies internal to the firm in particular. Neglect could also be attributed to the casual observation that, although agglomeration effects consistent with scale economies external to the firm are apparent in the world economy, global markets do not seem to be characterized by small numbers of participants and high barriers to entry. The intra-industry trade literature challenged this observation by identifying an empirical phenomenon which was claimed to be a result of pervasive scale economies and product differentiation. Although this claim does not appear to be well-founded (see section 8.2), it had the effect of stimulating theoretical work on imperfectly competitive international markets.

The most popular approach has been to work within the monopolistic competition framework, which permits scale economies and product differentiation; but by retaining the assumption of free entry it is consistent with any number of firms. The precise outcome depends upon the specification of cost and utility functions but, typically, firms are assumed to be equal-sized and thus the equilibrium number of firms (and therefore of product varieties, since each firm is associated with a differentiated product) is endogenous. The characteristic result that in equilibrium each firm has excess capacity highlights the dilemma posed by scale economies between diversity and quantity, both of which are desirable if indifference curves are convex and more is preferred to less; in the presence of scale economies it may be optimal to produce less than the minimum average-cost output of each variety in order to have more varieties.

The essential elements of the monopolistic competition model are shown in figure 8.4. The representative firm faces a downward-sloping demand curve for its product, which is differentiated from the products of other

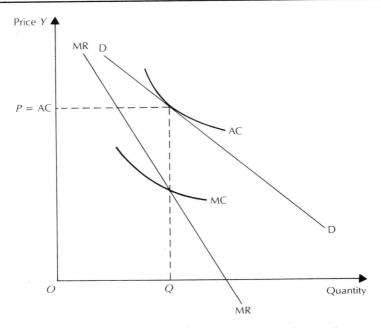

Figure 8.4 Price and output decision of the representative firm under monopolistic competition. DD is the demand curve facing the individual firm. If all firms are identical then in equilibrium total demand is equal to nQ, where n is the number of firms in the industry (that is, the number of firms is equal to the total market size divided by Q).

firms, and hence sales do not depend solely on price. In a closed economy the number of firms is determined by total demand for the industry's product and the profit-maximizing output of the individual firm; that is, the number of firms is equal to the former divided by the latter if all firms are equal-sized. Opening up the economy to international trade flattens each firm's respective demand curves, because there is more overall demand but there are also closer substitutes to its differentiated product. Some firms may go out of business, but those remaining will be operating at lower average costs, and the free entry condition ensures that price will be lower. Thus, domestic consumers benefit from lower prices and from the greater variety available.

Paul Krugman has derived these conclusions more rigorously by applying to international trade a monopolistic competition model, based on an additive utility function in which all goods enter symmetrically, and on a simple cost function with a fixed term. Total output and the number of firms depends on the quantity of a single input – labor. With international trade there is larger output, because of scale economies in the varieties produced, and greater variety, because the number of differentiated products available for consumption depends upon the size of the total market. Both of these changes increase the welfare of the representative consumer, so that "economies of scale can be shown to give rise to trade and to gains from trade even when there are no international differences in tastes, technology of factor endowments" (Krugman, 1979, p. 477). In this setting the volume of trade is determinate but the pattern of trade is not; that is, it is arbitrary which goods are produced in which country.

In his 1980 article Krugman imposed stricter conditions on the utility function to show that each country specializes in the good for which it has the larger home market. This is, however, a rather fragile result requiring strong assumptions, and one for which the evidence is mixed. As mentioned in section 8.1, there is some support from the car industry, but in other industries firms from small countries have established global markets with a minimal home market base (for example, Philips in electronics, Nestlé in food, and Electrolux in refrigerators are all household names far beyond the Netherlands, Switzerland, and Sweden).

Other writers have introduced product differentiation in alternative ways to Krugman's view of consumers loving variety for its own sake. Each consumer may have a preferred variety of the product, but consumer preferences are varied. More difficult to work with is vertical differentiation; that is, where quality varies. The reassuring point, however, is that the various demand specifications all yield similar results with respect to intra-industry trade, while numerous producers can coexist in the international market.

Setting monopolistically competitive industries in a general equilibrium model with perfect competition in some activities allows both intra- and inter-industry trade to coexist, and variations in factor endowments then permit determination of some trade patterns along lines familiar from part I. The other core propositions continue to hold despite the presence of imperfect competition. The relative importance of inter- and intra-industry trade depends in part upon the degree of difference in factor endowments; that is, between similarly endowed economies trade will be mainly intra-industry trade. Since intra-industry trade involves smaller adjustment costs than inter-industry trade (one requires factors to relocate within the industry, while the other requires them to find an occupation in another industry), we might expect continued expansion of international trade to proceed more smoothly among similarly endowed economies. Thus, for example, the great postwar dismantling of the 1930s trade barriers promoted trade among industrial countries more than North–South trade.

A second branch of the imperfect competition literature has focused on oligopoly. With respect to intra-industry trade the added contribution of small-numbers models has been to show that intra-industry trade may occur even with nondifferentiated products. Such results are, however, dependent on assumptions about blocked entry or market segmentation, because in the equilibrium with intra-industry trade there are incentives for arbitrage. Excluding arbitrage activities is more plausible when trade barriers exist, and we will examine these models in the next part of the book. More generally, product differentiation works with scale economies to produce results reminiscent of the large-numbers cases, although in oligopoly models the outcome depends crucially on how firms believe their rivals will react to their output or pricing decisions.

It is difficult to assess the flourishing of trade theories based on imperfectly competitive markets. Theoretical developments have outpaced empirical work, and none of the specific models has been subjected to rigorous testing against data from international markets. Most of the theories do provide a rigorous underpinning for Grubel and Lloyd's emphasis on scale economies and product differentiation as the forces behind intra-industry trade, but I have argued earlier (section 8.2) that this phenomenon can be explained otherwise. Some world markets are obviously oligopolistic with high barriers to entry (such as civilian jet aircraft), but there has been no systematic evaluation of how prevalent oligopoly is at the global level. Despite these empirical reservations the imperfect competition literature has gained wide acceptance, particularly in offering new justifications for trade barriers, which will be discussed in section 12.2.

Further Reading

Balassa (1966) and Grubel and Lloyd (1975) brought attention to the phenomenon of intra-industry trade. Greenaway and Milner (1986) survey the issues and the literature, while Pomfret (1986) provides an alternative view. Kemp (1964, pp. 110–31) deals with scale economies. The imperfect competition models were initiated by Krugman (1979, 1980) and Brander (1981), and are given a unified treatment in Helpman and Krugman (1985).

9

Intermission

After stressing in the opening chapter that national policies give significance to the study of international trade, it may seem strange to have assumed the nonexistence of governments in the next seven chapters. Analyzing the "no-government" case provides a useful guide to the essence of international trade: why trade occurs, and what goods and services will be traded if producers and consumers are left to their own devices. In this analysis pre-trade situations have been compared with post-trade situations, although the sequential setting is only a convention; the more interesting comparison is between trade and no trade *ceteris paribus*; in other words, with/without comparisons are analytically more relevant than before/after comparisons. The two extreme cases of no trade and free trade provide useful yardsticks for evaluating trade policies, because although policy debates often involve various restrictions of trade, the two polar cases will normally be amongst the set of possible options.

What conclusions can be drawn from the "no-government" analysis? First of all, the economic case for some trade being superior to no trade is extremely strong. For any pair of countries, any difference between opportunity costs yields potential gains from trade. Since such differences are pervasive there are strong pressures for international trade, and the infrequency of autarchy is unsurprising. The positive assessment of trade over no trade does, of course, depend on the assumed maximand, that is, the social welfare function from which the community indifference map is derived, and if distributional effects are not compensated for or if the structural change and irrevocably altered lifestyle are undesirable then the assessment may be negative. Even with these caveats the pro-trade argument is very strong.

The pro-trade argument carries over from static analysis to dynamic analysis, at least in the simple growth setting of chapter 5. The small open economy always benefits from growth, although it may trade more or less of its output over time. A large open economy can experience mixed benefits from growth because its terms of trade may deteriorate as a result; only in the exceptional and unlikely case of immiserizing growth will the country actually be made worse off by growth, which suggests scope for government intervention but not a justification for cutting off international trade completely.

Explaining trade patterns is related to the question of why countries trade, because it involves finding the sources of opportunity cost differences (that is, of comparative advantage and disadvantage). Four main explanations have been highlighted. They have been introduced as competing theories (because new theories are usually presented as challenges to existing theories), but they may be complementary, applying to different sets of goods. The primary products in SITC categories 0–4 (and some of SITC 5) are "Ricardo" goods, the production functions of which vary from country to country, while trade in manufactured goods is explained by the product cycle model (for new goods) or the Heckscher–Ohlin theory (for mature goods), or occasionally by scale economies. Arguably, the factor endowments approach, including human capital and natural resources, is a more general explanation than such an eclectic approach, but the search for a general explanation of trade patterns has been an elusive one, and in the empirical literature case studies of a single industry have usually been more convincing than the aggregative Leontief (or Leamer) type of study.

In the remainder of the book the assumption of no government interference in international trade will be dropped. Both the tools and the analytic conclusions developed so far will prove useful for analyzing and assessing government policies. In particular, the argument in favor of trade over no trade also provides a general presumption in favor of free trade, certainly from a cosmopolitan perspective and usually from a national perspective. Nevertheless, recurring arguments are made in favor of barriers to trade, and it is important to determine which are valid, which are based on sectional interests alone, and which are without merit.

Part III

Trade Policies

10

Economic Effects of a Tariff

The remainder of this book will be concerned with international trade policy. This chapter analyzes tariffs (taxes on imported goods). The analysis is then extended in the next chapter to other trade barriers.

10.1   General Equilibrium Analysis of a Tariff

Application of the general equilibrium model of chapter 3 to analyzing a tariff is straightforward and yields powerful conclusions. The tariff opens up a wedge between international and domestic prices, with the imported good now being more expensive in the domestic market by the size of the tariff. The change in relative prices encourages increased domestic output of the imported good, reducing specialization and the gains from trade at the existing world prices. If the country's shrunken trade triangle affects world prices, then the benefits from improved terms of trade may offset the losses from reduced specialization.

Figure 10.1 is the familiar two-good general equilibrium model, with free trade production at P_0 and consumption at C_0. A tariff on the imported good, X, increases the domestic price of X, so that the domestic price line DD is steeper than the world price line WW. At the tariff-inclusive domestic prices, production takes place at P_1. For a small country world prices are unchanged, so trade can occur along a world price line P_1W' parallel to WW. The consumption pattern will be determined by domestic, not world, prices and thus will be at a point on P_1W' tangential to a line. In figure 10.1 consumption is at parallel to $D'D'$ point C_1.

The with-tariff production point must lie between the nontariff production point, P_0, and the nontrade production point (not marked) to the right of P_1. The output mix consists of more X and less Y than under free trade, and at least as much Y and no more X than under no trade. If the tariff is prohibitive, then at P_1 a community indifference curve is tangent to the production possibility frontier and no international trade takes place. For tariffs above

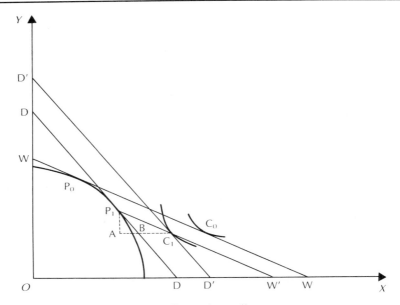

Figure 10.1 General equilibrium effects of a tariff.

the prohibitive level the domestic price ratio (and the output mix) will be that associated with the prohibitive tariff; the additional tariff margin is "water" with no economic effect.

The with-tariff consumption point must lie on a lower world price line than the no-tariff consumption point C_0. Total consumption, measured at world prices, is lower with the tariff, but the consumption mix depends on the shape of the indifference curves; the relative price change encourages substitution of Y for X, but the income effect is unknown *a priori*. A point such as C_1 must exist for a nonprohibitive tariff; at P_1 the indifference curve's slope is greater than that of DD (the indifference curve is steeper than DD), while at C_0 the indifference curve's slope is less than that of DD (the indifference curve is flatter than DD), so that somewhere in between the P_1W' line must contain a point at which an indifference curve has a slope exactly equal to that of DD. The point C_1 must be on a lower indifference curve than C_0, so that the small country always suffers a welfare loss from imposing a tariff.

The with-tariff trade triangle is P_1AC_1. This will be smaller than the free trade triangle, the hypotenuse of which is P_0C_0, because imports are less with the tariff than without it. Total imports are AC_1, of which AB exchange for the exports AP_1 at the domestic price ratio and BC_1 accrues to the government as tariff revenue. The tariff rate, BC_1/AB, defines the difference in slope between the domestic and world price lines. The tariff revenue is assumed to be redistributed in such a way as not to hinder achievement of the constrained utility maximum at C_1.

The small country's welfare loss from imposing a tariff has two components, a production effect and a consumption effect. Responding to domestic rather than world prices producers reallocate resources to producing import-substitutes, the domestic production of which has a higher opportunity cost (in terms of foregone Y in figure 10.1 between P_0 and P_1) than imports of the same quantity would have. Thus the country is foregoing some of the gains from trade demonstrated in the classical model of chapter 2; possible consumption bundles lie along P_1W', and the best attainable bundle must be inferior to the free trade consumption point C_0 in figure 10.1. Meanwhile, consumers, by also responding to domestic rather than world prices, will fail to attain the best (that is, utility-maximizing) consumption bundle along P_1W'. Consumers could enjoy higher utility at points to the right of C_1, with the country exporting more Y and importing more X at world prices, but at domestic prices they are unwilling to pay the amount of Y required for additional units of X beyond C_1. Thus, even given the losses from insufficient specialization involved in producing at P_1 rather than P_0, there is a further loss from failing to realize all the potential gains from exchange in world markets in order to reach the highest attainable community indifference curve.

Before leaving figure 10.1, note that the same diagram can be used to analyze an export tax. The export tax reduces the price received by domestic producers of the export good so that their revenue per unit sold and the price charged in the domestic market will be less than the world price by the amount of the tax. The wedge between world and domestic prices is identical to that between WW and DD in figure 10.1, and the analysis of production, consumption, and welfare effects is identical to that for an import tax. In practice, export taxes are far rarer than import taxes (for reasons to be discussed in chapter 14), but it is interesting to note their analytic equivalence in the general equilibrium model. After this digression, let us return to the tariff.

If the tariff-imposing country is large enough to affect world prices by its action, then the analysis must be taken a step further. By changing the trade triangle associated with any set of world prices, the tariff shifts the country's offer curve from OA to OA' in figure 10.2. The size of the shift is determined by the tariff rate; for example, GH/OG in figure 10.2. The tariff-imposing country enjoys an improvement in its terms of trade (from OE to OE'); the world price line in figure 10.1 becomes flatter, permitting consumption on a higher community indifference curve than C_1 and possibly on a higher indifference curve than the free trade point C_0.

The impact on the rest of the world in figure 10.2 is unambiguously negative. Movement toward the origin of the unchanged offer curve OR

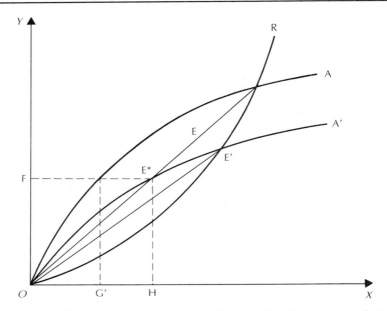

Figure 10.2 Offer curve analysis of a tariff. Note that if country A here is the country analyzed in figure 10.1, then $OF = P_1A$, $GH = BC_1$ and $OG = AB$, and the slope of OE is the same as that of WW and P_1W'. The movement from E^* to E' represents the unambiguously beneficial terms of trade effect on A.

places the rest of the world on a lower trade indifference curve than before the tariff was imposed.

Whether or not the tariff-imposing country benefits, global welfare must be lower in the presence of a tariff than under free trade. If domestic prices differ across countries, then some opportunities for increasing world output are being missed because the opportunity cost of producing the marginal unit of any good will be higher in the country where the relative price of that good is higher. Similarly, some opportunities for mutually beneficial exchange between consumers in different countries are being missed.

The terms of trade impact of a tariff will be analyzed in more depth in section 12.1, but for the moment consider the conclusions from the simple general equilibrium model. A small country always loses from imposing a tariff, whereas a large country may gain or lose, but if it gains then this will be at a cost to its trading partners. In all cases the with-tariff global welfare is lower than the free trade global welfare. These conclusions are based on the simplifying assumptions of chapter 3, which will be relaxed in the following analysis, but the general conclusions do turn out to be remarkably robust.

10.2 Partial Equilibrium Analysis of a Tariff

A tariff can also be analyzed within the demand and supply framework of chapter 4. This framework is especially useful in looking at a tariff imposed on imports of a single good by one country in a multi-country world, and it is a highly practical technique because trade policy debates are often over such microeconomic decisions and because the effects of a tariff are readily quantifiable within this framework. For these reasons the partial equilibrium model will be prominent in the remainder of the book, but it is often necessary to recall the drawbacks of omitting secondary effects on factor markets and on the terms of trade (or the exchange rate in a monetary setting). These secondary effects can be important, if the tariff affects a large trade flow or if many tariffs are changed simultaneously, and can only be analyzed within a general equilibrium framework such as that of the previous section.

Figure 10.3 represents the imposition of a tariff, equal to $P_d - P_w$, on a homogeneous imported good. The perfectly elastic import supply curve

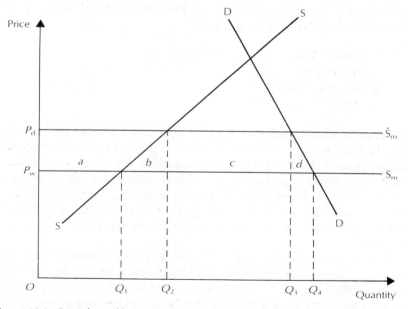

Figure 10.3 Partial equilibrium analysis of a tariff imposed by a small country. S_m is the import supply curve with no tariff; $\hat{S}_m$ is the import supply curve with a tariff equal to $P_d - P_w$.

indicates that the country is "small." The homogeneity assumption means that the domestically produced units of output sell at the same price as imported units, and after imposition of the tariff domestic consumers have to pay P_d for all units of the good. At the higher price consumption falls from OQ_4 to OQ_3, domestic production increases from OQ_1 to OQ_2, and imports decrease from Q_1Q_4 to Q_2Q_3.

Consumers of the good lose: first, they pay a higher price for the OQ_3 units which they continue to consume and, second, they are deprived of the utility derived from consuming the units which they no longer consume (Q_3Q_4). The loss in consumer surplus is measured by area $a + b + c + d$ in figure 10.3. Domestic producers of the good gain from the higher price, which yields a windfall gain of $P_d - P_w$ per unit produced without the tariff (OQ_1), and which offers a surplus equal to P_d minus marginal cost (the area between the supply curve and the domestic price line) on the Q_1Q_2 additional units produced with the tariff. The gain in producer surplus is measured by the area a in figure 10.3. The government obtains tariff revenue of $P_d - P_w$ multiplied by Q_2Q_3; that is, area c in figure 10.3.

In sum, there are gainers and losers from imposition of a tariff, and the net welfare effect depends upon how interpersonal utility comparisons are made. The simplest criterion is to give equal weight to each unit of all the components of the welfare change, in which case simple arithmetic indicates a net welfare loss from imposing a tariff:

$$
\begin{aligned}
\text{consumers' loss} &= a + b + c + d \\
\text{producers' gain} &= a \\
\text{government's gain} &= c \\
\text{net loss} &= b + d
\end{aligned}
$$

The two "welfare triangles" b and d in figure 10.3 measure the net social loss. The two triangles are analogous to the production and consumption effects of a tariff, described in the previous section. Area b captures the loss to society from producing quantity Q_1Q_2 domestically at a higher opportunity cost than that of obtaining this amount by importing. Area d captures the loss from not consuming quantity Q_3Q_4, whose marginal valuation by domestic consumers exceeds the cost of purchasing these units from foreign suppliers.

The partial equilibrium analysis thus restates the proposition that a small country suffers a net welfare loss from introducing a tariff. The size of this loss is readily measurable from observed variables such as output, imports, and the change in domestic price, unlike the loss in the general equilibrium analysis, which is defined in terms of unobserved community indifference curves. Even if one wants to assess a proposed policy change, such as the introduction or removal of a tariff or a change in its value, this can be done on the basis of demand and supply elasticities (from which post-policy quantities can be calculated, as in chapter 13).

The partial equilibrium analysis highlights the distributional conflicts inherent in trade policy. The net welfare gains from having no tariffs mean that potential gainers should be able to compensate potential losers sufficiently that the tariff can be removed; for example, in figure 10.3 consumers should be willing to accept a tax of $a + c$ (of which the first portion is transferred to producers) in return for removal of the tariff, since they will remain better off by $b + d$. Thus, the existence of distributional conflicts does not preclude the possibility of strong conclusions about the superiority of removing tariffs; if some people can be made better off while nobody becomes worse off as a result of tariff removal accompanied by appropriate compensation payments, then surely it can be accepted as a beneficial policy change. As a practical matter, however, the losers may fear that compensation payments will not actually be made and the gainers may be unwilling to make them, so that the decisions end up being taken in a political rather than an economic marketplace, where equal weights may not be given to equal units of producer and consumer surplus and government revenue.

The distributional conflict between producers and consumers of the imported good is only one of the conflicts arising from tariffs. Other conflicts are, however, hidden in the partial equilibrium framework. With a tariff the quantity imported is less and to maintain trade balance a floating exchange rate would lead to appreciation of the currency, harming exporters who receive less domestic currency for their export receipts. With a tariff, domestic output increases, raising demand for inputs and (as we know from the Stolper–Samuelson theorem) shifting the distribution of income in favor of the factor used relatively intensively in this industry. These indirect effects on export industries and through factor markets may be small, and they are camouflaged by their indirectness, but they are nevertheless present and should be considered when tariffs reduce imports by a significant amount.

There may also be other indirect effects of a tariff which limit its consequences, so that figure 10.3 overstates the impact of trade policy. A tariff on a single good encourages a shift to substitute products, which may be greater than is recognized in the pre-tariff demand curve; for example, high, long-lasting and well-publicized barriers to cotton textile imports into the US and western Europe during the 1960s helped to stimulate the development of man-made fibers, which reduced the loss to consumers from the cotton textile trade barriers. When the tariff is on an intermediate good, adjustments in end-use industries may shift the demand curve; for example, trade barriers on steel imports may make domestic automobiles more expensive because they now use higher-priced inputs, and reduced automobile sales will feed back as reduced demand for steel. In many situations the most serious undermining of the tariff arises from the incentive for illegal action to avoid paying duty whether by smuggling, bribery of customs officials, false invoicing (so that the duty paid is less than that legislated), or more innovative responses. All of these, and other similar points, illustrate the need for careful analysis of any actual tariff if its consequences are to be foretold with any precision. The simple models described in this and the previous section provide a guide to the main qualitative effects, but they may induce exaggerated conclusions about the efficacy of trade barriers in practice.

10.3   Tariff Structure

In the foregoing models the tariff appears as a simple tax on imports. Modern tariff schedules are, however, enormously complicated, with thousands of separate entries and different ways of assessing the import tax. This section considers whether the form and structure of a country's tariffs matter for analytic or empirical purposes; important questions for assessing both the relevance of the simple models and the quantitative measures of trade barriers' effects described in chapter 13.

Tariff rates may be *ad valorem* (a percentage of the imported goods' price), specific (a fixed payment), or compound (for example, 10 percent plus $2). The balance varies across countries; specific duties account for about one-third of US tariffs, one-tenth of the European Community's common external tariff, and the entire Swiss tariff schedule. Specific duties are easier to administer because they are less easily circumvented by false invoicing and intra-firm pricing decisions, but their impact is eroded by inflation; for this last reason newer tariffs tend to be *ad valorem*. Specific duties are regressive because, say, a $2 duty on shirts falls more heavily on cheap shirts than on fancy designer shirts, so that poorer consumers are more heavily taxed, and imports from poorer countries, catering for the lower-quality end of the market, are often more heavily restricted. The distinction between specific and *ad valorem* duties poses no analytic or empirical problems, however, because at any moment a specific duty has an *ad valorem* equivalent and vice versa. The analysis of figure 10.3 applies equally to a specific duty of $P_d - P_w$ or to an *ad valorem* tariff of $(P_d - P_w)/OP_w$.

A more worrying empirical problem arises from the multitude of individual tariff rates in national tariff schedules. It would be tedious to estimate changes in consumer and producer surplus for each individual rate in order to find the overall cost of tariff barriers, so a frequent problem is how to aggregate individual tariff rates. Consider the example in table 10.1 for a country with four separate rates on different categories of road vehicles. Taking a simple average the tariff on road vehicles is 20 percent, but this is

Table 10.1 Hypothetical tariff rates for road vehicles

Tariff (percent)	Category	Imports (value)	Share of domestic consumption of road vehicles (percent)
10	Automobiles	35,000	60
50	Trucks	0	15
15	Bicycles	10,000	15
5	Motorbikes	5,000	10

Average tariff using import weights is $(10 \times 0.7) + (50 \times 0) + (15 \times 0.2) + (5 \times 0.1) = 10.5$ percent, which could also be calculated by dividing the duty collected (5,250) by the value of imports (50,000).

misleading because not all of the categories are equally important; in the example, the high tariff on trucks is probably giving an upward bias. If the individual rates are weighted by imports the average tariff is 10.5 percent, but this is an understatement because the prohibitive tariff on trucks receives zero weight. The shares in domestic consumption are better guides to the relative importance of individual categories, but they still impart a downward bias because higher tariffs lead to higher prices and lower consumption; weighted by consumption the average tariff in table 10.1 is 16.25 percent. Thus, in this simple example three plausible calculations of the average tariff give 20 percent, 10.5 percent and 16.25 percent – a wide range if we wish to measure the costs of tariffs on road vehicles. Of the three procedures the first is usually rejected as too arbitrary and the third as too difficult (because consumption data tend to be classified differently to trade and tariff data), so that the obviously downward-biased weighting by imports is the most common averaging procedure.

The import-weighted average is often used to measure changes in a country's tariff level over time, or to compose tariff levels across countries or across sectors. Figure 10.4 illustrates US tariff history since 1821. Here the average tariff is computed by dividing actual customs duties collected by the value of dutiable imports, which is a quick way to measure the import-weighted average tariff. Table 10.2 lists the average tariff for a variety of countries. For the developed countries in table 10.2 the first column is the import-weighted average MFN tariff after the Tokyo Round had been implemented in the 1980s. Dividing customs duties collected by total dutiable imports yields lower figures (column 2) because some imports face lower tariffs as a result of the various preferential trading agreements described in chapter 15. The numbers in table 10.2 are downward-biased, perhaps by about 40 percent (Laird and Yeats (1988) reached this conclusion after computing average tariffs for the European Community, Japan, and the US according to different procedures), but the downward bias applies to

(a)

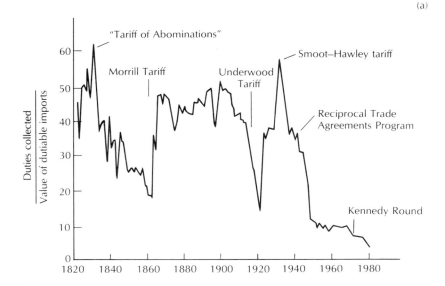

(b)

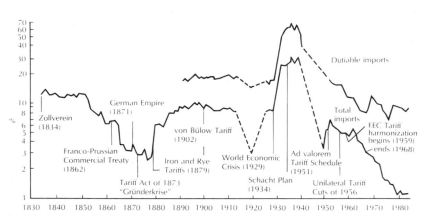

Figure 10.4 US and German tariffs. (a) US tariff, 1821–1980: duties collected as a percentage of the value of dutiable imports. (b) German tariff, 1830–1984 (West Germany after 1949); duties collected as a percentage of the value of imports. (Weiss et al., 1988).

Table 10.2 Average tariffs in selected countries (percent)

Developed countries			Less-developed countries	
	MFN	Actual		
Australia	12.4	8.2	Bangladesh, 1983	68.8
Austria	9.9	2.0	Egypt, 1981	24.2
Canada	6.5	4.5	India, 1984	44.8
EC[a]	4.2	2.5	Indonesia, 1980	23.0
Finland	4.8	1.0	Ivory Coast, 1980	34.9
Japan	3.5	3.0	Malaysia, 1981	11.6
New Zealand	13.6	10.9	Mexico, 1984	20.0
Norway	4.8	1.0	Pakistan, 1982	43.4
Sweden	3.5	0.8	Singapore, 1983	1.3
Switzerland	3.0	1.0	Thailand, 1981	14.5
USA	3.9	3.8	Yugoslavia, 1980	10.0

[a] The tariff averages for the European Community are based on the EC's external trade and do not count trade within the customs union. The large gap between MFN and actual tariff rates for the European countries is especially due to the EC–EFTA free trade area, which is most important for the EFTA countries.

Source: Laird, Sam and Yeats, Alexander 1987: *The Uruguay Round: A Handbook.* World Bank, p. 92

all the figures, and the ranking across countries provides a useful guide to relative tariff levels.

Once it is recognized that the average tariff hides a range of individual tariff rates we should also ask whether the tariff structure, and not just its average level, matters. The answer is clearly yes; a tariff on an industry's inputs shifts its supply curve to the left, reducing domestic output and increasing imports of the final good. To take account of the fact that tariffs on inputs matter as well as tariffs on outputs, economists have developed the concept of the effective rate of protection (ERP), which is the percentage by which a country's trade barriers increase the value-added per unit of output. The ERP is much better than the nominal tariff as a measure of the tariff protection granted to firms because value-added is what matters to them, and hence ERPs provide a better guide to the resource allocation consequences of a country's tariffs.

The ERP concept is best illustrated by a numerical example. Suppose the coffee beans for a jar of instant coffee cost $8 at world prices and are the only intermediate input, and with no trade barriers the price in New Zealand of instant coffee is $10 per jar. Domestic producers can meet import competition as long as their value-added is no more than $2. Introduction of a 30 percent tariff on instant coffee would allow the domestic price to increase to $13, and domestic firms would be competitive with value-added of up to $5 per jar, two and a half times as high as the value-added of foreign producers; that is, the domestic firms can enjoy a much higher producer surplus or be much less efficient than their competitors. In this example the ERP is 150 percent. If a tariff were also imposed on coffee beans the ERP would be lower, but as long as the tariff on the input were lower than the tariff on the output, the ERP would be greater than the nominal tariff on instant coffee of 30 percent; for example, a 5 percent tariff on coffee beans would mean an ERP for instant coffee producers of 130 percent.

The ERP has so far been defined as the difference between the actual value-added (VA_a) and free trade value-added (VA_{ft}), divided by the free trade value-added:

$$ERP = \frac{VA_a - VA_{ft}}{VA_{ft}} \qquad (10.1)$$

More usefully, by substituting for VA_a the expression $[1 + t_0] - [\Sigma a_i (1 + t_i)]$, the formula can be expressed in terms of the tariff on the output t_0, and the tariff on each input t_i weighted by its share of the value of the finished product at world prices a_i, all divided by the free trade value-added $[1 - \Sigma a_i]$:

$$ERP = [t_0 - \Sigma t_i a_i] / [1 - \Sigma a_i]. \qquad (10.2)$$

In the last example of the previous paragraph t_0 is 30 percent, t_1 is 5 percent, a_1 is 0.8 and, because there is only one input, Σa_i is also 0.8, so that the ERP is $(30 - 4)/0.2 = 130$ percent. Expression (10.2) shows that the ERP is determined by the tariff structure and by the share of value-added in total output. If tariffs are uniform the ERP is the same as the nominal tariff, but if tariffs are higher on outputs than on inputs then the wider the spread the larger the numerator of the second ERP formula. The effect of any spread between input and output tariffs will be magnified the smaller is the share of value-added in the price of the final good. Thus, on items such as instant coffee or rubber tires, where a raw material on which tariffs are typically very low constitutes a large part of the total cost, modest tariffs can offer high levels of effective production.

Tariff structures typically cascade; that is, tariffs are low or zero on raw materials, higher on intermediate goods, and highest on finished products (table 10.3). Thus, ERPs are almost always higher than nominal tariffs, especially for finished manufactures. The New Zealand instant coffee calculations given above are simplified but approximate the current situation where the tariff on coffee beans is zero, the tariff on coffee extracts is 31 percent, and the ERP has been estimated at 137 percent. Common areas for high ERPs are processed foods, chocolate, wood and paper products, cotton,

Table 10.3 Average MFN tariffs by sector, selected countries

	Australia	Canada	EC	Japan	New Zealand	US
Fuels	0.0	1.4	0.1	1.5	0.2	0.4
Chemicals	5.4	6.4	8.4	5.5	6.7	3.7
Other manufactures	17.7	7.0	8.1	5.7	22.6	5.6
leather	17.8	3.8	10.2	11.9	20.9	4.2
textiles	15.3	9.4	17.3	8.6	16.2	10.6
clothing	49.3	12.6	19.9	15.0	93.0	20.3
footwear	43.9	11.9	22.5	14.2	40.3	11.7

Source: Laird, Sam and Yeats, Alexander 1987: *The Uruguay Round: A Handbook*. World Bank, pp. 94–5

leather, vegetable oils, and tobacco products. This helps to explain why developing countries may experience problems penetrating markets for manufactured exports and, specifically, why raw material producers may not be able to profit from processing their materials and exporting the finished product (for example, Brazil with instant coffee and Malaysia with rubber tires). It should, however, be recalled from part II that this failure may also reflect lack of comparative advantage in the processing stage.

In a few cases ERPs turn out to be negative. European producers using inputs protected under the EC's Common Agricultural Policy must buy their inputs at above world prices. Steel-users in countries where the steel industry is heavily protected may find that even with a tariff on their output their value-added is less than it would have been with free trade. Automobile manufacturers in the US and the EC may have suffered in this way, although they have usually been sufficiently influential to obtain offsetting increases in nominal protection for their finished product. Secondary industry in many developing countries with inefficient steel industries has been less fortunate, and thus been penalized by a trade policy ostensibly aimed at promoting industrialization.

The ERP concept is complementary to the analysis in the previous section of this chapter. If the demand and supply analysis were carried out in terms of ERPs and value-added, it would give a fuller guide to the welfare effects of a country's tariffs, because the ERP indicates the net discrimination against imports and hence determines the change in imports which underlies the welfare calculations. Resources move between economic activities; therefore to evaluate the resource allocation effects of a country's tariffs one must calculate the rate of protection for each activity – a point described as the main message of ERP theory by Corden (1966). Using effective rather than nominal tariff rates would not alter the qualitative conclusions from figure 10.3, but it would alter the magnitude of the various welfare effects.

Further Reading

James Meade (1955 – the geometric appendix has been published separately) provided a thorough exposition of the general equilibrium model. The partial equilibrium or "welfare triangles" model was pioneered by Corden (1957) and Johnson (1960). Baldwin (1982) analyzes the efficacy of trade policies. Corden (1971) contains the most thorough treatment of ERP. Preeg (1970, pp. 273–81) gives a clear account of the practical difficulties behind tariff averaging.

11

Nontariff Barriers to Trade

Tariffs remain the most common form of government intervention in international trade, although during the postwar period tariff levels have fallen substantially as a result of international negotiations. This trend has highlighted the importance of other trade barriers, a process often likened to the draining of a swamp, which reveals all the stumps and other obstacles to cultivation. Moreover, agreements not to raise tariffs have also been a cause of increased resort to other instruments of trade policy, as countries have adopted nontariff barriers (NTBs) to trade when, for whatever reason, they have wished to restrict trade without breaking the letter of international commitments.

11.1 Quantitative Restrictions on Imports

Quantitative restrictions on imports, usually known as import quotas, are the simplest nontariff barriers to trade. The usual administrative procedure is to prohibit imports without a license, and then restrict the issue of licenses to a predetermined limit. The operation of an import quota can readily be compared to that of a tariff, the former operating on quantity, the latter on price. The most appropriate framework for such a comparison is partial equilibrium analysis with demand and supply curves, because import quotas typically apply to a specific product. Measures to restrict the aggregate quantity of imports will be analyzed in part IV.

In figure 11.1 the free trade level of imports is Q_aQ_f. Introduction of an import quota restricting the quantity imported to Q_aQ_b creates excess demand for the good (equal to Q_bQ_f) at the world price, P_w. The domestic price will be bid up by consumers unable to obtain the good, and will continue to rise until the excess demand is eliminated at price P'.

Figure 11.1 looks similar to figure 10.3, the partial equilibrium analysis of a tariff. If the import quota were set at the same level as the imports occurring with a given tariff, then we could refer to this as the equivalent

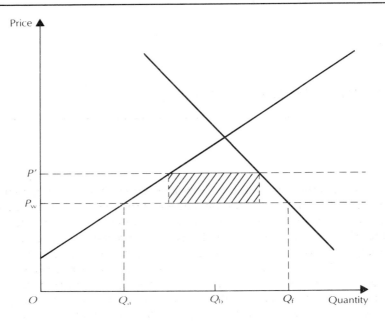

Figure 11.1 An import quota. The shaded area, equal to Q_aQ_b multiplied by P' P_w, measures the rent on import licenses.

tariff; for example, if Q_2Q_3 in figure 10.3 is the same as Q_aQ_b, then $P_d - P_w$ is the tariff equivalent to this quota. In the two cases the domestic price, production, consumption, and imports are the same with the trade barrier in place. The welfare analysis of an import quota is the same as that of the equivalent tariff, with one important difference: the changes in consumer and producer surplus are identical, but there is no tariff revenue. The shaded area in figure 11.1, equal to area c in figure 10.3, measures the rent on import licenses; holders of import licenses purchase imports at the world price and sell at the higher domestic price. Thus, comparison between a quota and the equivalent tariff requires information about what happens to this quota rent.

What happens to the quota rent depends upon how import licenses are allocated. If the licenses are sold in a competitive auction, then their price will be bid up to $P' - P_w$ per unit of imports; at any lower price there would be excess demand for licenses because there would be riskless profit opportunities, and nobody would offer a higher price because it would involve importing at a net loss. At the equilibrium price the revenue accruing to the government from the sale of import licenses, that is, $P' - P_w$ multiplied by Q_aQ_b, is exactly equal to the revenue from the equivalent tariff. In this case, the welfare consequences of tariff and quota are identical.

A second allocation mechanism is to give away import licenses freely by government fiat. If there are no application procedures, then the license recipients incur no costs in obtaining permission to import and reap a windfall gain equal to the entire quota rent (see the shaded area in figure 11.1). American oil import licenses between 1959 and 1973, which were distributed to oil companies in proportion to their 1959 outputs, were an example of freely allocated licenses. In such cases the net welfare effect is identical to that of a tariff, but the distribution of gains is different because license-holders benefit instead of the government.

Thirdly, potential importers may be required to follow resource-using procedures in order to obtain permission to import. At its simplest level, this may involve merely filling out forms, or queuing to clear one's imports before an annual limit is reached, or discovering which officials need to be approached for a license and whether to bribe them. The time spent in these activities yields no additional welfare to the community, but there is a private return, because acquiring an import license brings to its holder the quota rent. More complex allocation procedures may waste additional resources. If import licenses are allocated on the basis of domestic production capacity or previous year's imports, then there are incentives to build excess capacity or to import more than is really wanted in order to stake claim to future quota rents. If the quota is filled on a first-come basis, then there will be a rush to import in January even if this incurs additional storage costs because the imported items are not wanted until later in the year; this "greyhound" system also favors imports from geographically closer trading partners, incurring potential costs of discriminatory trade barriers (see chapter 15). With all of these procedures potential importers will be encouraged to incur as many costs as are necessary to obtain the import licenses as long as the costs work out at no more than the quota rent (that is, in figure 11.1 no greater than $P' - P_w$ per unit imported). Thus, part or all of the shaded area in figure 11.1 will be dissipated in directly unproductive activities, increasing the net welfare loss from restricting trade.

In sum, a quota and its equivalent tariff may have identical welfare effects, if import licenses are auctioned competitively. In practice, this may be difficult to implement if licenses apply to imports of narrowly defined goods and few bidders have accurate knowledge of the size of the quota rent. With many bidders for a homogeneous good (as in US Treasury Bill auctions) the competitive outcome is probable, but attempts to sell foreign exchange by auctions in Zaire, Zambia, Jamaica, and other countries encountered difficulties in reaching the competitive outcome because of thin markets and incentives to withhold truthful revelation of preferences by underbidding. The only experience with auction quotas for imports has been in Australia and New Zealand during the 1980s, and there only for a limited number of products; practical problems were quickly eliminated, although complaints about uncertainty, speculation, and unfair pricing behavior were heard. The government can avoid these problems, and still maintain the same net welfare loss from a quota as from its equivalent tariff, if import licenses are freely distributed; in this case the distribution of benefits is altered in favor of the license recipients. Finally, the government may distribute licenses by resource-using procedures. This is the most common outcome, and often appears attractive because priority can be given to imports which are more socially desirable, or on the grounds that it is "fair" for larger end-users to receive proportionately more of an intermediate input, or for other similar reasons. The cost, however, is that applicants for import licenses have an incentive to use resources in trying to obtain part of the quota rent instead of in directly productive activities. Thus, the net welfare cost of the quota will be higher than that of the equivalent tariff, and any undissipated quota rent will be redistributed from the government to the importer (or to government officials if bribery is involved).

In situations of imperfect competition, the analysis of figures 10.3 and 11.1 will be different (for example, in the presence of uncertainty). The simplest, and probably most important, example is the case of a domestic monopoly. With free trade the domestic monopoly is forced to charge the world price, so that trade acts as a form of competition or antitrust policy (chapter 8). A tariff retains this benefit from trade because the monopolist is still constrained in its price-setting ability, but an import quota removes this constraint and the monopolist is able to increase profits by producing less and charging at a higher price than the world price plus the "equivalent" tariff. Figure 11.2 illustrates the argument. With an import quota, MQ, the demand curve facing the domestic monopolist shifts to the left by the horizontal distance MQ at all prices above P_w. Under competitive market conditions the equivalent tariff to the quota MQ would be $P' - P_w$ and the net welfare loss would be triangle $b + d$. The monopolist, however, maximizes profits when marginal revenue equals marginal cost so the firm gains from reducing its output to OQ^*, which can be sold for a price P^*. The shaded area in figure 11.2 measures the additional net social loss due to monopoly pricing; the horizontal width of this area is the number of units consumed under the equivalent tariff which are no longer consumed, while the height measures the difference between consumers' valuation of these units and their cost of production. There are also distributional consequences from the monopoly pricing policy insofar as consumers lose more while import license-holders and the domestic firm gain more than under competitive market conditions. Parenthetically, it may be noted that the last two groups would prefer an import quota to unrestricted trade even if the quota were set at the free trade level of imports, because, by removing the threat of additional imports at the world price, they permit exercise of monopoly power by the domestic firm (Pomfret, 1989).

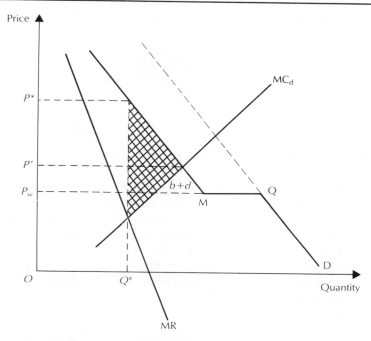

Figure 11.2 An import quota with a domestic monopoly.

Domestic producers often prefer an import quota to the equivalent tariff even when domestic markets are competitive. Because there are legislative or administrative rigidities limiting constant adjustment of trade barriers, the dynamic effects of changes in the size of the equivalent tariff are important. If domestic demand or costs are increasing or the world price is falling (all plausible characteristics of import-competing industries which have successfully obtained protective trade barriers), then the equivalent tariff of a fixed import quota is increasing over time. The domestic firms may then prefer to obtain protection from imports in the form of a quota rather than to make repeated requests for higher tariffs. The precise force of this argument rests, of course, on the institutional arrangements associated with establishing tariffs and import quotas in the importing country.

In sum, although import quotas and tariffs may be equivalent in their net welfare effects, economists faced with a choice between the two measures advocate the tariff because the nonequivalence cases involve additional costs from quotas. Import quotas are seldom auctioned off competitively or distributed freely, so that additional social costs are incurred. Domestic monopolies may be maintained behind the shield of import quotas, whereas nonprohibitive tariffs undermine the basis for monopoly pricing. Finally, import quotas tend to shield the domestic economy to a greater extent from dynamic changes in comparative advantage. All of these arguments also have distributional angles, so that some people gain more from an import quota than from the equivalent tariff, notably domestic producers, privileged holders of import licenses, and possibly the government officials making the license allocation decisions.

11.2   Voluntary Export Restraints

The fastest growing nontariff barriers to trade during the 1970s and 1980s have been agreements by exporters to voluntarily restrict exports of specified goods to a particular market. The agreements may be formally negotiated either on an *ad hoc* basis or within an umbrella framework establishing guidelines (such as the Multifiber Arrangement covering almost all textile and clothing exports from low-wage countries; see box 11.1), or be looser "gentlemens' agreements." Such arrangements currently cover most of world trade in automobiles and steel, the textile and clothing trade between rich and poor countries, and a host of individual items. Their full extent is unknown because many arrangements are unpublicized.

The consequences of a voluntary export restraint (VER) are in most respects similar to those of an import quota, but there are three differences which make the VER potentially inferior from the importing country's perspective. Firstly, the quota rent from a VER typically accrues to residents of the exporting country; that is, the shaded area in figure 11.1 is now lost by the importing country and in comparison with a tariff the government revenue accrues to foreigners (national net welfare loss of the importing country in figure 10.3 becomes $b + c + d$). Secondly, there is a general equilibrium effect in that the importing country now pays the full domestic price, rather than the world price, for its imports, so that its terms of trade deteriorate instead of improving (that is, in figure 10.2 the exporting country's offer curve OR moves to the left instead of the importing country's offer curve moving to the right). Thirdly, because VERs are usually discriminatory, applied only to the least-cost foreign suppliers, they may divert imports to higher-cost suppliers, increasing the importing country's import bill and misallocating the world's resources.

The exporting country may or may not prefer a VER to free trade, but it will usually prefer a VER to an import quota or the equivalent tariff imposed by the importing country. The first two of the costs to the importing country described in the previous paragraph involve benefits to the exporting country. Both the VER quota rent and the improved terms of trade due to the

BOX 11.1   History of the Multifiber Arrangement

Current restrictions on developed countries' textiles and clothing imports from "low-wage" countries have their origins in the US decision to negotiate a VER on cotton textiles with Japan in 1955. Restricting Japanese exports provided little protection for the US textile industry because other countries, notably Hong Kong, were ready to take Japan's place and further VERs had to be negotiated. In 1961 the US brought her cotton textile arrangements under GATT auspices; the Short Term Cotton Textile Arrangement was negotiated, and then replaced by a Long Term Arrangement (LTA) in October 1962. The LTA was a multilateral agreement, but it functioned by allowing importing countries to negotiate bilateral quotas on a country-by-country basis. During the long boom of the 1960s textile imports by the developed countries increased rapidly (especially on noncotton items not covered by the LTA), and when economic growth slowed in 1974 protectionist pressure led to the Multifiber Arrangement (MFA).

The first MFA broadened the LTA's coverage to include wool and synthetic fibers, but in return the supplying countries were guaranteed liberal minimum growth rates for their quotas (6 percent per year). When the MFA was renewed for 1978–82 it permitted more restrictive quotas, slower import growth and global ceilings on certain product categories. The third MFA (1982–6) introduced further restrictions to deal with import "surges," which were particularly aimed at medium-sized or new exporters. Nevertheless, imports from low-wage suppliers continued to grow, and in the fourth MFA (1986–91) additional fibers were included, specifically silk, linen, ramie, and jute. By the late 1980s the MFA encompassed thousands of bilateral product-specific quotas.

From being short-term measures to help temporary adjustment, arrangements to protect the industrial countries' textile and clothing producers have become ever more pervasive and have acquired an air of permanence. By using bilateral quotas to restrict individual suppliers the MFA first encourages new entrants, and then permits proliferation of quotas to cover the newcomers. Success in obtaining market share often depends on political considerations rather than on economic efficiency; for example, China as a new supplier was allowed considerable growth in exports to the US in the early 1980s while Bangladesh was not. Also, by being bilateral the MFA has leakages as a protectionist

BOX 11.1—*cont'd*

measure because some competitive suppliers may not be covered; the most competitive "high-wage" country, Italy, benefited from the MFA restrictions on its close competitors from East Asia to become the world's largest clothing exporter in the late 1980s. Finally, by applying to specific fibers the LTA and MFA have encouraged the use of new fibers, which are subsequently brought into the MFA; this is a process without justification in terms of global efficiency, but it benefits individual suppliers for as long as they are unrestricted.

Agreement	Period	Products	Regulations
STA	1961–2	Cotton products	Short-term quantity restriction on specific suppliers in case of "market disruption"
LTA	1962–74 (including two agreed extensions)	Textile and clothing products with 50 percent of cotton (in value)	1 New restrictions permitted where "market disruption" 2 Controls either unilaterally (Article 3) or bilaterally negotiated (Article 4) 3 Quota levels not below imports in preceding period 4 Minimum annual volume growth of 5 percent within quotas
MFA 1	1974–7	Coverage extended to all textiles and clothing of wool, cotton, or synthetic fibers	1 As in LTA but with more specifications of real or threatened market disruption 2 New provisions for base levels, annual growth rates (not less than

Agreement	Period	Products	Regulations	
				6 percent) and flexibility of quotas
			3	*Special provision for small and new suppliers and cotton textile exports*
			4	*Textile Surveillance Board to monitor bilateral agreements*
MFA 2	*1978–82*	*Same as MFA 1*	1	*As MFA 1*
			2	*A provision for "jointly agreed reasonable departures" which permitted derogation of MFA requirements (base levels, growth rates, and flexibility provisions*
MFA 3	*1982–6*	*Same as MFA 1*	1	*As MFA 1 ("reasonable departures clause" deleted)*
			2	*Introduction of "anti-surge" procedure to prevent "sharp and sustained" import growth within quotas*
MFA 4	*1986–91*	*Coverage extended to cover vegetable fibres (flax and ramie) and silk blends. MFA now excludes only hair fibers and other minor fibers (such as coir, sisal, and jute) already traded in substantial quantities*	1	*As MFA 1 ("reasonable departures" restored, albeit modified)*
			2	*Some tightening of Article 3*
			3	*Special treatment for "least developed" and wool textile exporters*
			4	*Commitment to scrap underutilized quotas*

VER are benefits to the exporting country, which can be compared with the costs of foregone gains from trade due to the existence of a trade barrier. The discriminatory aspect of a VER is not attractive to the exporting country, because it is penalized relative to other suppliers, but the extent of discrimination depends on the presence of substitute suppliers, and when it exists the importing country has an incentive to subject the substitute suppliers to equal treatment.

At first sight the existence of VERs poses a problem, because they are typically initiated by the importing country and yet they are inferior to other trade barriers from that country's perspective. The most plausible explanation of the problem is an institutional one: both tariff increases and import quotas are contrary to the General Agreement on Tariffs and Trade (GATT), and their introduction would bring bad publicity and the possibility of internationally sanctioned retaliation. To avoid these outcomes the importing country buys off the foreign suppliers by offering them the benefits of a VER. The exporting country is aware that the nonacceptance of such an offer will lead to unilateral action by the importing country, so that the relevant comparison is not between a VER and free trade but between a VER and an import quota or tariff; in the latter choice, the balance of advantages lies with the VER because of the quota rent and terms of trade effects.

In concentrated industries a VER may have additional attraction to participating firms. If administration of the VER leads to coordinated action on the exporters' part, then they could benefit from operating a cartel sanctioned by the consuming country. More importantly, the VER permits the firms in the importing country to practice monopoly pricing, secure in the knowledge that they will not be undersold by additional imports (as in figure 11.2); the quota rent on the fixed quantity of imports is then increased. Such motivation is consistent with Japanese decisions to continue VERs on automobiles to the US and on VCR exports to the European Community even after the importing country ceased to request further renewal of the agreement (in 1985 in both these cases). Here the main purpose of the VER from the firms' perspective is not so much to restrict trade but rather to allow the industry as a whole to move closer to the profit-maximizing level of supply and price in the importing country's domestic market.

11.3   Other Nontariff Barriers to Trade

Anything imposing differential conditions for foreign and domestic goods constitutes a barrier to trade. One consequence will be to open up a wedge between world and domestic prices, and the effects of this can be analyzed as comparable to the effects of an equivalent tariff. Most nontariff barriers, however, have other effects, which may be of greater importance than the trade effects and may make the barrier justifiable despite its trade-related costs. Generalizations are therefore difficult. Moreover, the trade-reducing aspect of nontariff barriers is often played down for fear of provoking retaliation, and the importance of individual NTBs is difficult to assess due to practical problems of estimating the equivalent tariff. In the jargon of economists, NTBs are opaque measures, which is itself a reason for preferring transparent trade barriers such as tariffs, which are more amenable to international negotiation. Thus, this section will offer examples of NTBs to give a flavor of the issues raised, rather than attempting the impossible task of cataloging all NTBs.

Customs valuation procedures are the easiest NTB to analyze. By valuing imports at a higher price customs officials increase the duty payable under the legislated *ad valorem* tariff rate. In the 1920s and 1930s, French customs officials used valuation procedures to ensure that French exports to Syria and Lebanon faced lower trade barriers than other countries' exports to these territories, which were obliged to levy nondiscriminatory tariffs under the terms of France's League of Nations mandate. The most notorious postwar example was the US practice of valuing certain chemical imports not at their invoice price (or any other "world price"), but at their "American selling price," which, as a wholesale price, was higher and thus led to higher customs duty payments; this procedure was abolished after the Tokyo Round. A variant on customs valuation procedures as an NTB is the imposition of bureaucratic delays in clearing customs, which increases the cost of importing just as a tariff does (but without raising revenue for the importing country government). The French decision to require all videocassette recorder imports to pass through the small inland customs station of Poitiers in 1982–3 is a famous example, but other countries have used customs go-slows to put pressure on their trading partners' exports when they want to provoke negotiations.

Local content regulations have been important in some developing countries' industrialization strategies. They have also figured in debates over automobile imports in Canada during the early 1960s and in the US during the early 1980s. Within the European Community, there is a major dispute over whether Honda and Nissan cars made in the UK have sufficient local content to be considered EC cars, or whether the British plants are just "screwdriver" operations putting the final nuts and bolts into what are essentially Japanese cars, in order to circumvent import quotas on cars. Local content may be difficult to measure (for example, should dealers' margins be counted and how should intra-firm traded imports be priced?), but the economic effects can be analyzed in a familiar way. Local content regulations protect the domestic producers of parts in a similar manner to an import quota defined as a share of the market, although there may be substitution effects if the final goods makers have flexibility in choosing which parts to source locally. The effect on the scarce domestic factor of production is as predicted by the Stolper–Samuelson theorem, because effective local content regulations force firms to carry out some activities domestically which could be done more profitably elsewhere. The impact on the final goods producers is more complex. Local content regulations discourage foreign investment rather than trade; they may even be trade-increasing if imports are not restricted by a binding quota, but then they will be efficiency-reducing because the goods are not being finished in the least-cost location.

Government procurement has always been a fertile area for discriminating between domestic and foreign suppliers, and as an NTB has grown in significance with the growth in government sectors. Tenders for public projects may be invited only from domestic suppliers or not be publicized to potential foreign suppliers and, even when bids are accepted from non-nationals, higher-priced domestic contracts may be accepted on security or some other grounds. In some countries explicit margins of preference for domestic tenders exist, while in others the government retains discretionary powers. In principle, the impact is as for a tariff, but without the tariff revenue. In practice, the tariff equivalent of discriminatory government procurement policies is difficult to measure, especially for large one-off projects, because there is no open market in which to observe world prices. An international code to regulate the use of government procurement as an NTB was agreed upon in the Tokyo Round, but given the intrinsic practical problems such agreements will always be difficult to enforce.

Governments may also use publicly owned retailing and marketing services to create barriers to trade. In Canada provincial liquor stores with a monopoly on wine sales set higher mark-ups on imported wines in order to encourage domestic wine sales; although this is a differentiated product, the pricing policy can be analyzed with figure 10.3, with P_d being set by the liquor store and area c being realized as trading profit rather than a tariff revenue. Compulsory marketing boards for primary products are used in many countries to tax exports by offering a domestic price below the world price (box 12.1 gives an example). All measures involving regulation of foreign exchange transactions are NTBs, requiring at a minimum bureaucratic delays and at a maximum total regulation of foreign trade, but these are better analyzed in the macroeconomic setting of part IV.

Technical NTBs are more difficult to assess because their trade aspects may be incidental. Differences in weights and measures or in national languages, for example, pose minor NTBs by requiring different packaging. More significant are national health, safety, environmental, and so on standards, which impose adjustment costs on foreign firms hoping to supply a market. Thus, US automobile firms will design their products and factories to comply with domestic safety and emission controls, while a foreign car maker that sends a small part of its output to the US market will have other design priorities and will make *ad hoc* adjustments to meet US standards on exports to the US (see box 11.2). Health, safety, and environmental protection are legitimate fields for government action, and criticism of such measures can encounter emotional reactions. Nevertheless, they are abused by governments; for example, by setting standards on packed meat quality or on pest control which (knowingly) exclude imports from certain suppliers, with little or no advantage in protecting public health. Despite agreement in the Tokyo Round that health, safety, consumer, or environmental protection measures should not create unnecessary obstacles to trade, many NTBs of this kind inevitably fall into a gray zone with respect to what is unnecessary and what is an unavoidable side-effect on trade.

Most problematic of all are policies which reflect differing national views of desirable government activity and which also affect trade flows. Governments which pursue "welfare state" policies, for example, provide some services which the private-sector employer may provide elsewhere, and which could be viewed as a subsidy for national producers. Subsidies to promote regional economic development may play the same role if a firm in a depressed region competes with imports or produces for export. Both of these issues have arisen in US–Canadian trade negotiations during the 1970s and 1980s; for example, a specific US complaint was against a European-owned tire factory located in Nova Scotia with Canadian government assistance, which the Canadians viewed as a subsidy for regional development and the Americans viewed as an export subsidy in disguise.

All of the NTBs described in this section will, to the extent that they reduce imports, have similar effects to the equivalent tariff. The protected domestic producers gain and consumers lose, and gains from trade are foregone. There is usually no "tariff" revenue, because the equivalent tariff is prohibitive or because this source of benefit is dissipated by resource-using requirements which increase foreign suppliers' costs. As trade measures these NTBs tend to be particularly obnoxious because their tariff equivalent is often high (and subject to arbitrary adjustment) and because additional losses are incurred. Their evaluation is, however, often complicated by the presence and possible dominance of nontrade considerations.

11.4 Conclusions

The variety of trade barriers is immense, and the precise form of a trade barrier determines its full range of consequences. Nevertheless, all trade barriers have as a common essential element the creation of a wedge between

BOX 11.2   The Proton Saga

Following the success of Japanese and South Korean car makers, the Malaysian firm Perusahaan Otomobol Nasional (Proton) began production in 1985. A key element in its strategy was, after supplying the relatively small domestic market, to achieve economies of scale by exporting. By 1989, although the Proton Saga was competing successfully in some foreign markets (Bangladesh, Sri Lanka, New Zealand, Jamaica, Malta, and Ireland), its planned entry into the US market had not materialized.

A key step in exporting automobiles to the US is homologation; that is, certification that the car meets standards for emissions, safety, and so on. In December 1986 Proton signed an agreement with a US agent who would obtain the necessary approvals by November 1988 and then act as distributor, importing a minimum of 30,000 cars during the first year. When the approvals had not been obtained Proton terminated the agreement in January 1989.

The cost of entering the US market was estimated by both Proton and the US agent to be $10 million in modifications needed to meet US standards and $20 million in promotion and advertising. On initial sales of 30,000 cars the standards modifications represent a tariff equivalent of $333 per car. This may be an overestimate insofar as subsequent sales would spread the once-and-for-all costs of homologation, but against this the $10 million are up-front costs paid before sales commence, whereas future sales revenue has to be discounted. Moreover, the modifications made for the US market have little spillover to other export sales because emission and safety requirements are quite different in, say, the UK market.

The effectiveness of the standards requirements as a trade barrier are, however, not fully measured by the tariff equivalent. Unfamiliarity with the bureaucratic process led Proton to deal through an American agent, who proved to be incompetent. By the time this was realized it was too late to enter the market with the original Saga model, which was becoming dated, and any exports to the US would have to await new models, which would not appear before the early 1990s. Thus, Proton's entry into the US market had been effectively delayed for at least four years by the need for homologation, even though the Saga was a competitive product and Proton were willing to make the necessary expenditures to meet US safety and technical standards.

domestic and international prices, which is captured in its purest form by the tariff analysis of chapter 10. Thus, analysis of trade policy can be carried out in terms of tariffs, with the knowledge that the general conclusions carry over to other policy instruments.

Beyond these general conclusions, NTBs typically have added consequences. The conditions under which an NTB is equivalent in effect to a tariff seldom hold completely in practical instances of NTBs, and almost invariably an NTB involves greater resource misallocation than a tariff. Some groups (such as domestic producers with potential monopoly power) may, however, gain more from an NTB than from its equivalent tariff, and use their political influence to lobby for an NTB rather than a tariff because of its added consequences, despite the negative impact of these consequences on national welfare. Policy-makers may also favor NTBs because they grant more discretionary power than do tariffs, the level of which is bound by international agreement, or because their opaqueness (the impact on domestic prices is less apparent than that of a tariff) may forestall opposition from groups negatively affected by trade restrictions. These distributional considerations are important in explaining the popularity of NTBs despite their inferiority to tariffs on cosmopolitan or national welfare criteria, and will be considered more fully in chapter 14.

12

Arguments Used in Support of Trade Barriers

The previous two chapters have revealed many negative consequences of trade barriers, and yet international trade is everywhere impeded to a greater or lesser extent by such barriers. A huge variety of arguments has been used to justify government restriction of international trade. The most frequently used of these arguments will be examined in the first seven sections of this chapter, and then a general assessment of their validity will be made in the final section.

12.1 The Optimal Tariff

Recalling from section 10.1 that a country may gain from imposing a tariff if the terms of trade effect offsets the resource misallocation effect, then a government may design its tariffs with this aim in mind. The tariff which maximizes the net benefits is conventionally referred to as the "optimal tariff." Less rigorously, the same argument could be applied to any attempt by a country to use a trade barrier to improve its terms of trade.

The optimal tariff is that which allows a country to reach its highest possible trade indifference curve. In the offer curve diagram, this is represented by a tangency point between the rest of the world's offer curve and a trade indifference curve of the tariff-imposing country. In figure 12.1 country A's optimal tariff is MX/OM, and at the equilibrium point (L) the trade indifference curve (and hence both the community indifference curve and the production possibility frontier) has the same slope as the domestic price line, SS'. There is also an optimal export tax OS/OY; note that OS/OY is equal to MX/OM because OKY and SLY are similar triangles.

The size of the optimal tariff is inversely related to the elasticity of supply of imports. For a small country, facing by definition a perfectly elastic supply of imports, the optimal tariff is zero. The small country faces a straight-line offer curve so the trade indifference curve reached under a free trade policy is the highest attainable. For a large country facing a less than

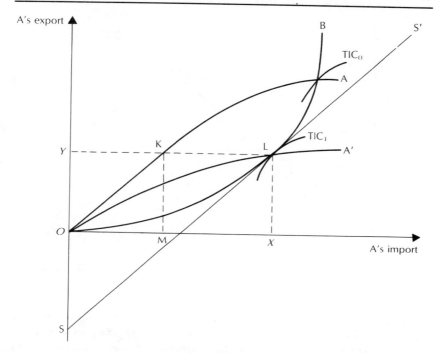

Figure 12.1 General equilibrium analysis of the optimal tariff. The optimal tariff shifts country A's offer curve from OA to OA', so that A reaches the highest feasible trade indifference curve (TIC_1) given the rest of the world's offer curve OB. The domestic price ratio in A is OY/OM, which is equal to the slope of SS'.

infinitely elastic import supply, the optimal tariff is greater than zero, but must be less than the prohibitive tariff because trade must take place for there to be a possible gain.

The relationship between the optimal tariff and the import supply elasticity can be seen in a demand and supply diagram. In figure 12.2 domestic demand and supply curves have been combined into a demand for imports curve, D_m. A tariff opens up a wedge between domestic and world prices $(P_d - P_w)$, imposing a net loss on the importing nation's producers and consumers represented by area $c + e$ (e is equal to the deadweight loss triangles $b + d$ in figure 10.3) and yielding tariff revenue equal to area $f + c$. The nation gains if f is greater than e, and the optimal tariff maximizes $f - e$. The more inelastic the S_m curve is, then the larger the optimal tariff. In the small country case, where S_m is flat, area f disappears, so the optimal tariff is that which minimizes area e; that is, a tariff of zero, which makes e zero. With steeper S_m

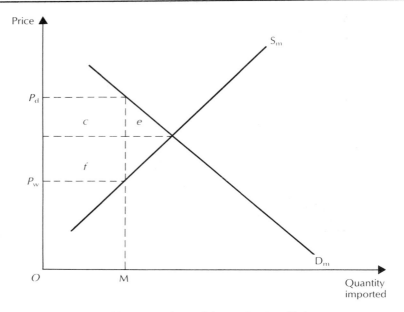

Figure 12.2 Partial equilibrium analysis of the optimal tariff. Area $c + e$ measures the difference between the loss in consumer surplus and the gain in producer surplus resulting from the increase in price from the free trade equilibrium to P_d. Area $c + f$ is the same as area c in figure 10.3, area e combines the two triangles $b + d$, and area a is suppressed because D_m measures the difference between domestic demand and supply at any price.

curves, higher and higher tariffs can be levied in order to transfer a larger portion of the world price to the importing country's government.

Within the simple models of chapter 10, the optimal tariff emerges as a logical argument for improving national welfare. In practice, however, the argument is not commonly heard. One reason is that in a two-country model the optimal tariff is inevitably greater than zero, but in a many-country world few importers have significant market power, and one country's tariff may have little impact on world prices. Nevertheless, as long as a country is not perfectly "small" there is some scope for realizing terms of trade gains by imposing a trade barrier.

The most important drawback to levying the optimal tariff is that the tariff-imposing country's gain is at the rest of the world's expense. Terms of trade effects are purely distributional, so that one country's gain is another's loss. In figure 12.1 country B's best response to A's optimal tariff is to levy its own optimal tariff, leading to a trade war because, facing B's tariff-inclusive offer curve, country A's own optimal tariff changes and probably will now be higher than MX/OM; successive shifts in the two offer curves are likely to reduce total trade, imposing a loss on both participants relative to the free trade equilibrium.

The retaliation threat is a major constraint, perhaps the major constraint, on countries' use of trade barriers. Any trade barrier, even if it is not justified by the optimal tariff argument or even if terms of trade gains are not intended, can have an impact on world prices to the detriment of trading partners. Thus, the trading partner may be pushed to retaliate, setting in motion a trade war. The post-retaliation equilibrium will not be a no-trade situation (recall that the optimal tariff is never prohibitive), but the experience of pre-1939 trade wars was of much reduced trade, leaving both sides worse off. The outcome is suboptimal because gains from trade are foregone and a cooperative outcome, even in a tariff-ridden world, is likely to be superior to a trade war. Many commentators see the postwar trading system, which has been free of major trade wars, as a cooperative system enforced by the threat of retaliation, with the GATT playing the key role of spelling out which trade barriers will trigger retaliation.

Just as there is an optimal tariff, a large country can also impose an optimal export tax, the magnitude of which depends primarily upon the elasticity of demand for exports. For domestic reasons barriers to exports are far less common than barriers to imports (see chapter 14). Moreover, by working on the terms of trade an optimal export tax is confrontational and invites retaliation. Nevertheless, countries often have more readily identifiable market power in their export markets and have been tempted to exploit this. The long-run success of such measures depended critically on the availability (or development) of substitute products and alternative sources of supply.

In the first half of the twentieth century attempts by the rubber producers to raise world prices encouraged the development of artificial rubber, and Brazilian restriction of coffee exports led to loss of market share as other suppliers entered the world coffee market. During the 1960s and 1970s several developing countries tried to use their monopoly power in international commodity markets to raise prices, but instead they lost market share to other countries able to produce the same crop (for example, Sri Lankan tea, Egyptian cotton, and Ghanaian cocoa; see box 12.1). Whatever a country's current market share, an optimal export tax (or quantity restriction) can succeed only if there are no actual or potential alternative significant sources of supply. The world diamond market, centered in London but with a single dominant supplier of uncut diamonds (South Africa), is one of the rare cases of successful, long-term use of monopoly power in world markets.

The most publicized recent example of exporter market power is in the world oil market. The Organization of Petroleum Exporting Countries

BOX 12.1   Ghanaian Cocoa Pricing Policies

Since 1950 the Cocoa Marketing Board has had a monopoly on buying cocoa in Ghana, and this has been the source of significant tax revenue by paying farmers less than the world price. Besides being a redistribution mechanism, the Board's pricing policy could also be seen as an attempt to improve the terms of trade given Ghana's dominant share of world markets (40 percent in the early 1960s). From the mid-1960s to the end of the 1970s the effective export duty increased from 54 percent to 89 percent.

The effects of the increased export tax can be seen by comparing Ghanaian experience with that of two neighboring cocoa producers. Producer prices in Ghana fell drastically relative to producer prices in the Ivory Coast and Togo; from being approximately equal in the three countries in 1965, the Ghanaian price fell to 23 percent of that in Togo and 18 percent of the producer price in the Ivory Coast by 1980. The reduced incentive to producers was accompanied by a fall in Ghana's cocoa output from 566,000 metric tons in 1965 to 249,000 in 1979. Ghana's share of the world market fell to 18 percent in the early 1980s and she dropped from first to third biggest cocoa exporter. Meanwhile, Togo's share rose slightly and the Ivory Coast's increased from 9 percent to 29 percent. Part of the latter increase was due to extensive smuggling across the Ivory Coast/Ghana border to avoid the export tax.

Source: *The World Bank* World Development Report 1986, *p. 76*

(OPEC) involved several producers, and hence the free-rider problem of a cartel; individual OPEC members had an incentive to sell more than their agreed quota, benefiting from the higher price resulting from other OPEC members' restricted supply but also increasing their own revenue over what it would be if they observed their own agreed quota. The free-rider phenomenon did happen, but given the dominant position of one country (Saudi Arabia) in OPEC supplies it was not a serious problem for the cartel. In the longer term OPEC's ability to increase oil prices was undermined by reductions in demand due to oil-saving measures and by the emergence of new oil producers outside the cartel (see table 12.1). Thus, OPEC lost influence for the same reasons that other attempts to exercise market power failed, but the adjustment mechanisms operated more slowly in the case of

Table 12.1　Crude oil production of selected countries, 1973 and 1986 (million barrels)

	1973		1986	
OPEC	11,316	(53 percent)	6,692	(31 percent)
Saudi Arabia	2,773		1,840	
Iran	2,139		683	
Venezuela	1,229		632	
Iraq	737		616	
Nigeria	750		534	
Kuwait	1,102		517	
Libya	794		377	
Indonesia	489		492	
NonOPEC	9,893	(47 percent)	15,171	(69 percent)
USSR	3,140		4,520	
US	3,995		3,760	
Mexico	192		1,004	
China	391		960	
UK	3		950	
Canada	772		656	
Norway	12		331	
World total	21,209	(100 percent)	21,863	(100 percent)

Source: GATT: *International Trade 1986–87*, p. 196

oil because of time lags in designing and introducing energy-saving equipment and in finding and bringing into production alternative sources of supply. Ultimate loss of monopoly power does not necessarily mean that it is not worth exercising in the short term; by 1981, with an oil glut, OPEC members' current revenues were declining, but with their cartel profits of the previous eight years they could afford to laugh all the way to the bank.

12.2　Imperfect Competition

The optimal tariff argument invokes a form of imperfect competition, insofar as it relies upon use of market power by national governments. It does not, however, question the assumption of perfectly competitive firms, which is why the global optimum in the previous section was considered to result from free trade. If firms have market power then this conclusion is no longer guaranteed, and active trade policies may increase both national and global welfare.

The problem in determining the best policy for dealing with imperfectly competitive world markets is the absence of any global regulator who could plausibly enforce an antitrust policy. Successful international agreements have been reached where worldwide natural monopolies exist (for example, the Universal Postal Union), but these are tightly circumscribed by considerations of national sovereignty. More typically, the policy responses are at the national level, presumably with due regard for other nations' reactions.

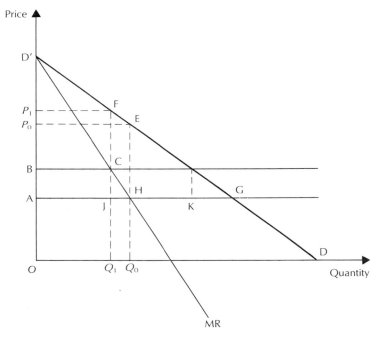

Figure 12.3 An import duty on a good supplied by a single foreign firm. The tariff shown here is levied on the cost price, and an *ad valorem* tariff of AB/AO would have the same effect as the specific duty AB. If the tariff were related to the selling price, then an *ad valorem* duty of AB/AO percent would be preferred to the specific duty AB, because it would yield more tariff revenue on the same imported quantity. This could be shown by representing the specific duty as a parallel downward shift in D'D so that it passes through K and the monopolist's profit-maximizing supply is $\frac{1}{2}$AK ($=$BC$=OQ_1$), and the *ad valorem* tariff as a counterclockwise pivot of D'D from the D origin passing through K so that the profit-maximizing supply is still $\frac{1}{2}$AK but the tariff component of the price, OP_1, is bigger.

In the simplest case of a single world producer, importing countries can use an import tariff to appropriate part of the monopoly rent. In figure 12.3 the monopolist supplies this particular market at constant cost, OA, maximizing profits under free trade by selling OQ_0 at price OP_0. By introducing a specific duty, AB, the importing country induces the foreign supplier to raise the price to OP_1 and reduce sales to OQ_1; the importing country gains $ABCJ$ in tariff revenue and loses P_1P_0EF in consumer surplus, and as long as the former exceeds the latter national welfare is increased (although global welfare is reduced). Total monopoly profit in this market is reduced by the tariff ($AP_1FJ < AP_0EH$), and consumer surplus is reduced by a greater amount, but because part of the rent is snatched by the government a tariff can increase the importing country's net national welfare.

In the presence of a foreign monopoly a tariff may be better than doing nothing, but it is not the best policy. Price controls set just above the exporter's average cost would be superior; for example, in figure 12.3 the welfare gain to the importing country from a price limit OA would be the area $AGEP_0$, which is greater than any possible benefit from a rent-shifting tariff (because the maximum monopoly rent $AHEP_0 < AGEP_0$). The price ceiling also leads to a global welfare gain because, although $AHEP_0$ represents a welfare transfer, the part of the importing country's gain measured by HEG is not offset by any losses to others.

The above analysis is rather simple, perhaps most appropriate to a monopoly based on possession of a unique natural resource. If the monopoly is based on possession of a patent, trademark, or secret formula, the firm may react to a tariff by opening up a branch plant in the importing country and thus avoiding customs duties. If it is based on scale economies, then sufficiently high trade barriers may stimulate local production, introducing new complications. The initial tariff is unlikely to be a first-best policy (the argument for supporting infant industries by trade barriers is considered in section 12.3 below), but once the domestic firm is in place and earning its own monopoly rents tariff increases can raise national welfare by redistributing rents from the foreign to the domestic supplier. Again the rent-switching rationale for a tariff is global-welfare-reducing. Moreover, the original monopolist's home government has an incentive to deter the new entrant, although such a one-shot negative-sum game does not have a clear outcome. Much-quoted cases of this type of "strategic" trade policy are the Boeing–Airbus duopoly in the civil aircraft industry and various branches of the informaties industry (box 12.2 will provide an example), but it is unclear what practical conclusions emerge and whether there are any other cases to which they could be applied.

More complex imperfectly competitive markets would have to be analyzed on a case-by-case basis. The analysis of chapter 8 indicates that theoretical examples of welfare-improving tariffs should be easy to construct;

BOX 12.2   Trade Policy when the Chips are Down

The US dominated semiconductor technology until the late 1970s, when Japanese firms entered the market and rapidly became important suppliers of random access memory chips (RAMs). An important issue was whether this shift in comparative advantage was due to natural causes, or whether it had been induced by restrictions on foreign firms' access to Japanese markets.

Chip manufacture is characterized by economies of long production runs; the learning process during the production of any particular chip reduces unit costs as more are produced. A protected home market allows producers to cover their high initial costs and then supply foreign markets at the much lower marginal costs. These firms gain a competitive edge in third markets over firms without a protected home market, who are forced to price at average costs in all markets.

Baldwin and Krugman (1988) have incorporated the above features into a model of the market for RAMs. They model the behavior of oligopolistic firms via the assumption of constant conjectural variations (that is, managers believe that the response of total supply to a one-unit change in their firm's supply is always the same). This is a rather mechanical assumption and rules out subtle "strategic" behavior by market participants, but it does allow numerical results to be calculated.

Baldwin and Krugman compare the actual early-1980s situation with the hypothetical situations of unrestricted US access to the Japanese market and of a trade war in which both markets would be reserved for domestic suppliers. With free trade there would be seven US suppliers and no Japanese suppliers (compared to the actual six US and three Japanese firms), implying that Japanese commercial policy did account for their industry's existence and export success. Without a protected home market Japanese firms' output would be lower, their marginal cost higher, and they would make losses and therefore exit from all markets.

This study illustrates the possible links between protection and export promotion in an imperfectly competitive industry. The welfare effects of encouraging Japanese production are, however, negative, not only for the US whose firms lose sales but also for Japan whose consumers lose more than her producers gain, and for the world which has

> *higher total costs of chip production, with nine producers than with seven. US policy-makers face a dilemma because retaliating against the Japanese policy would reduce US welfare still further, as the protected domestic firms would operate with smaller production runs and higher unit costs. This study is based on simplistic behavioral assumptions, and possible externalities from having a domestically based chip industry are omitted from the welfare effects, so the specific conclusions should not be considered too reliable; but the general points may be valid in this or other imperfectly competitive industries.*

in a second-best situation a deviation from the first-best optimal conditions, for example by introduction of a trade barrier, may or may not increase national or global welfare – the only generalization is that generalizations are theoretically impossible. The growth in interest in imperfect competition models of international trade since the mid-1970s has thus opened up a limitless range of possible situations in which trade barriers may be in the national interest.

There are, however, two reasons for thinking that in practice the validity of an uncompetitive-markets argument for trade barriers is limited. Firstly, international markets are much more competitive than smaller national markets, and with fewer insurmountable barriers to entry; here it is relevant to recall from chapter 8 that the phenomenon of intra-industry trade which stimulated interest in imperfect competition turns out to be explicable without having to resort to uncompetitive market structures as an explanation. Secondly, even when perfect competition is absent, a trade barrier is unlikely to be the first-best policy; the simple monopoly case (figure 12.3 and the associated discussion) provides one example in support of the general microeconomic proposition that a sales tax is not the best public policy response to uncompetitive markets, and a sales tax falling only on imports is also unlikely to be a first-best measure.

Anti-dumping duties can also best be discussed in the context of imperfectly competitive markets. Such duties, the use of which is triggered by foreign suppliers selling imports at less than their home market price or at less than average cost, have been legislated by the US, the European Community, and other major trading nations, and have been frequently implemented (or else threat of implementation has induced voluntary export restraint) in recent years.[1] At first sight, the popularity of anti-dumping

---

[1]Countervailing duties triggered by export subsidies are closely related, because "dumping" is often associated with some form of export subsidy which allows the export price to be below

duties is surprising. If a firm charges less in its export market than in its home market (for example, because its own government enforces import barriers to the detriment of consumers) or charges below average cost (as firms with declining costs often do in recessions when it is rational to take any price which covers variable costs), then why should the importing country be dissatisfied? A foreign firm using its monopoly power to increase prices is obviously harmful, but if goods are being offered at sales prices why not accept the bargain? Of course, import-competing firms suffer from the low prices, but their losses are more than offset by consumers' gains. The exception to this is in a dynamic setting where the foreign suppliers use low prices to drive domestic firms out of business and then use their monopoly position to increase prices later; such predatory dumping may lead to net welfare loss for the importing country (and for the world). This scenario is possible but not very common, because not only must the predatory pricing succeed in driving out domestic firms but also the threat of a price war must be sufficient to forestall any new entry when the price rises again.

Despite the weak theoretical support for anti-dumping duties, there was a rapid increase in the number of anti-dumping proceedings initiated during the 1980s. Since the proceedings are typically set in motion by a complaint from domestic producers, there is a strong suspicion that they are being used simply as a protectionist measure to benefit these producers (that is, they belong in the next section of this chapter). The foreign suppliers are requested to give price and cost information, and simply to comply with these demands and to monitor the importing country's calculations and legislative proceedings can be costly for a small exporting firm; thus there is a bureaucratic NTB even if no duty is levied. Moreover, there is considerable latitude in calculating anti-dumping margins (see box 12.3), which is sometimes blatantly biased in favor of a positive finding; for example, US calculations assume an 8 percent return on capital in constructing "fair" prices, although many industries seeking anti-dumping duties have much lower rates of return. The EC calculation methods are less publicized, but a December 1988 decision to levy provisional anti-dumping duties of 8–59 percent on Hong Kong VCRs was clearly not based upon comparison with Hong Kong domestic prices which, given Hong Kong's free trade policy, could not be maintained above world prices or the VCRs would be re-imported into Hong Kong.

---

the home-market price. In practice, up until the late 1980s countervailing duty actions were limited to the US. They often involve difficulties in defining an export subsidy and the same problems in calculating subsidy margins as are discussed below for anti-dumping margins (see also box 14.1).

BOX 12.3   Measuring "Fair Value" for Anti-dumping Cases Against Imports from Nonmarket Economies

When a product is exported from a nonmarket economy it is difficult for the importing country to determine whether dumping is taking place. Because exchange rates, domestic prices, and production processes may differ greatly from market-determined ones, it may be inappropriate to compare the export price with the domestic price or even with costs valued at domestic input prices. Some of these problems were illustrated by a famous case involving Polish golf carts.

Polish golf carts, exported to the US since 1971, were the subject of an anti-dumping (AD) case in 1975. Because the golf carts were sold only in the US, their "fair value" could not be assessed by reference to their price in the home market or in any other export market. The US constructed a value based upon the costs of a Canadian golf cart manufacturer and reached a positive AD finding. In 1976 the Canadian producer went out of business, and no other foreign supplier produced similar golf carts. To get around the absence of market-determined prices in Poland, the US subsequently constructed values based upon what the golf carts would have cost to produce in a market economy at Poland's level of economic development (Spain was the selected economy). Based on this calculation the US determined that the golf carts were not being sold below fair value, and the earlier AD finding was revoked in 1980.

The use of surrogate countries to assess "fair value" is a dubious process, because countries at similar levels of economic development have differing relative prices and comparative advantage. In an AD case against potassium chloride imports from East Germany, the US Department of Commerce made a preliminary assessment, based on West German prices, of a 112 percent duty, but in the final assessment, based on Canadian prices, a zero margin was calculated and the case dismissed. In the Polish golf cart case the two surrogates led to opposite findings, illustrating the potentially arbitrary outcome of AD cases using this approach.

With the re-entry of China into the world economy and the rapid growth of its exports during the 1980s, China became a major target for AD actions (among developing countries second only to South Korea in the number of AD proceedings instituted against its exports during the

BOX 12.3—*cont'd*

1980s). The US has used Paraguay, Indonesia, Sri Lanka, Malaysia, Pakistan, and other developing countries as surrogates in calculating "fair value" in AD cases against Chinese exports. The Chinese have complained not only that the process is inappropriate, but also that the surrogate is chosen only after the particular case is opened and thus may be biased toward reaching a positive finding.

12.3   Protecting Specific Producers

Trade barriers are microeconomic measures, and their most common motivation is to maintain specific domestic production activities above their free trade level. Although such arguments may be supported by national interest or cultural or other noneconomic reasons (to be discussed in section 12.7 below), they are inherently distributional. In terms of figure 10.3 greater weight is being explicitly given to a unit of producer surplus gained than to a unit of consumer surplus lost. Thus it would be inappropriate to dismiss such arguments on the chapter 10 grounds that with equal weights a trade barrier (in the absence of terms of trade effects) must incur a net welfare loss.

A common setting for this argument is when a surge of imports threatens to reduce domestic output levels and increase unemployment; an especially potent setting if the declining industry is located in a region where unemployment is already high. A trade barrier can forestall the adjustment necessary to compete with ever cheaper imports; for example, if the price of the imported good falls by one dollar then a customs duty of a dollar will maintain the *status quo*. In principle a trade barrier can maintain domestic production at any level up to that supported by a prohibitive tariff, although higher trade barriers may be undermined by substitution effects and by evasion (see the last paragraph of section 10.2).

There are costs to shoring up domestic activities with trade barriers, but because they do not involve direct payments to the protected industry they are often overlooked. The payments to the protected industry take the form of higher prices, covering transfers from consumer to producer surplus. Consumers also pay a higher price for the remaining imports, with the mark-up going to the government as tariff revenue. The net loss to society arises from foregone opportunities to gain from trade (see the two triangles in figure 10.3), but because they are hidden in a much larger loss of consumer surplus the costs of protection may pass unnoticed. However, if the social costs and benefits are carefully assessed, it is possible that the benefits from protecting domestic production may be considered to exceed the costs, in which case the trade barrier is a superior policy to doing nothing.

The primary case against using trade barriers to protect domestic producers is that they are not the best way to achieve the goal. Supposing the government desires a domestic output level higher than the free trade level, then this could also be achieved by a production subsidy. In figure 10.3 a desired output level OQ_2 can be obtained either through imposing a tariff $(P_d - P_w)/OP_w$ or by offering to domestic suppliers a subsidy of $P_d - P_w$ per unit produced. In both cases the gain in producer surplus is area a. The subsidy costs the taxpayer $P_d - P_w$ multiplied by OQ_2, involving a net welfare loss to society equal to the area b. This is less than the welfare loss from the tariff by the amount of the second triangle, d. Supporting the additional output over the free trade level must involve a cost (the foregone gains from specialization), but a subsidy limits these costs to their absolute minimum while a tariff imposes the additional consumption-side loss arising from consumers not facing world prices. In terms of figure 10.1 the subsidy shifts the domestic output mix from its free trade point (involving a loss in national income), but then permits utility to be maximized by consumption taking place on the highest possible community indifference curve (to the right of C_1 along P_1W'); a trade barrier cannot do this because it distorts prices for both producers and consumers.

The above argument is a very potent one. The trouble with trade barriers is usually not that they cannot achieve their aim, but rather that they achieve too many things. They are a clumsy and inappropriate instrument for attaining policy objectives which are essentially domestic. The problem addressed in this section is of an industry whose output is considered to be undervalued at market prices because there are some additional social benefits; the solution to such a problem is to provide additional incentives for producers with as few harmful side-effects as possible. The general rule is to tackle any domestic distortion at its root; a trade barrier, by definition, does not do this.

An important variant among arguments for protecting specific producers is the infant industry argument. Its distinguishing feature is a dynamic element, most plausibly represented by incorporating learning effects into firms' production functions. In this case a domestic firm may have a long-term comparative advantage in a product, but be discouraged from starting production by the set-up costs and initial losses before the learning effects have been absorbed. Trade barriers can shelter the infant industry from foreign competition during the initial period, and then be removed when the domestic industry is competitive. If the flow of net benefits, suitably discounted, is positive then the country is better off as a result of the infant's establishment. Again, however, a subsidy would be a superior method of supporting the infant industry, because it would eliminate the negative consumption-side effect of separating domestic from world prices. A subsidy paid continually out of the public budget also has the advantage of focusing policy-makers' minds on the need for the industry to grow up; infant tariffs have a tendency to persist because their budgetary effects are positive rather than negative and consumers may exert insufficient political pressure for their removal. Incidentally, even better than a subsidy may be capital market reform, because if a project has a positive net present value some capital market imperfection is presumably responsible for the absence of unsubsidized private investment. The central point, however, is that whether a trade barrier is the second-, third-, or fourth-best method of promoting an infant industry, it is never the first-best approach.

In decreasing cost activities the infant industry argument can be combined with market structure considerations. Thus a prohibitive tariff may initiate domestic production and, by allowing the domestic firm to recoup its fixed costs by exploitation of domestic market power, it may also promote exports if marginal costs are below the world price. Domestic consumers lose, but the new firm obtains not only monopoly profits from its home market but also the difference between average costs and average revenue from exports. Even if such a policy succeeds in establishing a domestic industry which exports, the welfare effects are ambiguous, and a trade barrier is not the first-best policy (see box 12.2). Moreover, it is likely to generate resistance from importing countries, who can legally initiate anti-dumping suits. Nevertheless, this class of argument holds a strong appeal for policy-makers, and is often illustrated by the success of Japan and the newly industrializing countries in collapsing import substitution and export production into a single step of an industry's development. An inferior outcome may, however, arise if the prospect of supernormal profits induces several new entrants who then collude to share the market and make monopoly profits even though operating at a suboptimal scale (and hence not exporting); Eastman and Stykolt (1967) have observed this outcome in several Canadian industries.

There is also a more limited infant exporter argument for export subsidies. If there is a marketing technology specific to exporting which must be learned, then there is a case for subsidizing exports during the learning period (Mayer, 1984), although a superior policy may be for the government to set up institutions which can advise on export marketing and provide export promotion services. Export subsidies are controversial because many importing countries view them as "unfair" pricing practices, similar to dumping, and levy countervailing duties to offset the subsidy. The economic argument for such duties is no stronger than that for anti-dumping duties but, as with any tariff, levying a countervailing duty benefits import-competing producers and their use has increased during the 1980s in response to protectionist pressure. As a digression, it may be mentioned that the sufferers from an export subsidy include not only taxpayers in the exporting country but also third-country suppliers of the good. Thus, subsidized food exports from the European Community have been welcomed by Poland, Egypt, and other countries receiving the cheap butter and flour, but have been a source of friction with food exporters such as the US, Australia, and Argentina, whose terms of trade suffer.

12.4   Changing Consumption Patterns

A tariff increases the domestic price and reduces domestic consumption of a good. If a government wishes to reduce consumption of a luxury or of a sinful good which is imported, then a trade barrier can achieve the goal. Thus developing countries may impose high tariffs on automobiles to deter conspicuous consumption, and developed countries place trade barriers on alcoholic beverages and pornographic literature to reduce drunkenness and debauchery.

The argument is a valid one, but again trade barriers are not the first-best policy measures to achieve the goal. A sales tax would reduce consumption to the desired level, incurring the net cost to consumers of the triangle d in figure 10.3, but avoiding the distortion of production patterns resulting from a tariff (that is, the welfare loss measured by triangle b). Figure 12.4 uses the two-good general equilibrium diagram to illustrate how a desired consumption level of the imported good (OX^*, which is less than the free trade consumption level) can be better achieved by a sales tax affecting consumer but not producer prices than by a tariff. With the former instrument consumption of the export good it is Y_s, while with the tariff it is at the lower level of Y_t; that is, the country is on a lower community indifference curve. The general rule of tackling a domestic distortion at its root is confirmed once more.

Trade barriers may also be used to change the savings ratio. By making traded goods more expensive, trade barriers will affect consumption patterns and savings decisions, although such macrolevel effects are difficult for policy-makers to fine tune. Sometimes the relationship to savings ratios may appear more direct and hence manipulable by trade barriers; for example, some developing countries levy export taxes because plantation-owners are perceived to have low savings propensities, and higher savings and investment ratios are socially desirable. There is, however, a negative side-effect insofar as the export tax reduces the quantity exported, and hence the national gains from trade are less than they would be if more direct policies to encourage saving were adopted.

Thus, trade barriers can affect consumption (and savings) patterns but

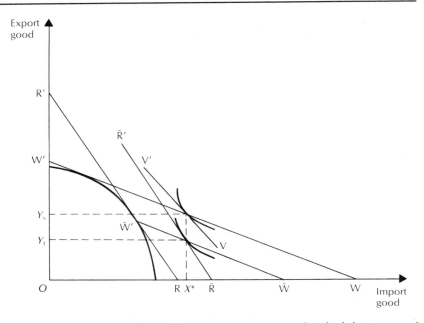

Figure 12.4 Achieving a desired domestic consumption level of the imported good using an import restriction or a sales tax. The world price ratio is the slope of W'W. In order to reduce domestic consumption of the imported good to OX^* a trade barrier increasing the relative price of that good to the slope of R'R is necessary. The same consumption level would result from a sales tax which changes the domestic price ratio to the slope of V'V.

are usually an inferior policy instrument to achieve the goal. It is sometimes argued that the production side-effect may be a benefit if, for example, the government wants both to discourage wine consumption and to encourage the domestic wine industry; a trade barrier can achieve both qualitative targets at the same time, but it would be a coincidence if it achieved the desired levels of both domestic output and consumption. A production subsidy plus a consumption tax would be a better way to meet the two goals – in other words, tackle each distortion at its root. The only valid case for using a trade barrier to achieve a consumption target is if there is no actual or potential domestic production, in which case a tariff and a sales tax are equivalent, and collection at the frontier may be the least costly method.

12.5   Revenue Considerations

Before the present century the most common reason for tariffs was to raise government revenue. Trade taxes levied at border crossings were a relatively easy method of raising finance for governments without large bureaucracies.

BOX 12.4   *The Relationship between the Optimal Tariff, the Revenue-maximizing Tariff, and the Protection-maximizing Tariff*

The optimal tariff is obviously lower than the protection-maximizing tariff, which prohibits any imports, but is it also lower than the revenue-maximizing tariff?

The optimal tariff sets the cost to society of imports equal to their value to society at the margin. Since the demand for imports curve (D_m in the diagram) values the marginal benefit of each unit imported, the optimal tariff is that which sets the marginal cost of imports equal to their price; that is, it is the tariff associated with point A.

The government's tariff revenue can be seen as its profit from operating as a monopolist in buying goods from foreign suppliers and then selling them at the tariff-inclusive price to the domestic buyers. The profit-maximizing behavior is to buy the quantity at which marginal revenue equals marginal cost; that is, the quantity associated with point B.

Point B involves a higher domestic price and a lower price paid to the foreign suppliers than does point A. Thus, the revenue-maximizing tariff must be higher than the optimal tariff and must be associated with a smaller amount of international trade.

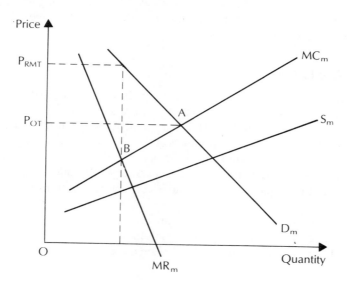

As governments became capable of assessing and collecting income and sales taxes of varying degrees of sophistication, reliance on trade taxes for governments' financial needs became minor; thus 150 years ago European and North American governments raised well over half their revenue from trade taxes, but today these account for less than 5 percent of total revenue.

The reason for the declining reliance on trade taxes to finance government expenditure is that the resource misallocation costs of trade barriers are well-recognized. All taxes have distortionary side-effects, but those due to trade taxes are seen as worse than those due to income taxes or to expenditure taxes which do not distinguish between domestic and foreign products. In practice the government revenue from trade measures is today a negligible consideration in the more developed countries, which helps to explain the apparent disregard for what happens to the tariff revenue/quota rent in much public discussion of alternative trade barriers. Even in the comparison between tariffs and subsidies, the fact that the former involves an inflow and the latter an outflow from the public purse is no justification for giving special weight to the government component of the welfare effects; even in the nineteenth century Canada was able to establish a major infant industry (steel) with the aid of subsidies without budgetary strain.

Trade taxes retain some fiscal importance in less-developed countries where other revenue sources are constrained by the preponderance of non-marketed output, the lack of an efficient bureaucracy, and so forth. Under such conditions, the social return from government expenditure may be sufficiently high to justify the resource misallocation costs of tariff. Over the postwar period this argument has been losing force, and this is reflected in a strong negative correlation between *per capita* income and the share of government revenue raised by trade taxes; as developing countries' incomes have risen this share has rapidly approached the low percentages obtaining in the more developed countries.

12.6 Employment

The most common, fallacious argument in favor of trade barriers is the pauper labor argument. In its crudest form, the argument is that if country A's wages are lower than country B's in all activities then the latter's producers will be undersold in all products and trade will bring unemployment. The fallacy is based on failure to recognize that the gains from trade arise from comparative rather than absolute advantage. As long as opportunity costs differ, some trade cannot be inferior to no trade from the national perspective.

The pauper labor argument does, however, point to the presence of distributional effects. The Stolper–Samuelson theorem indicates that one factor will lose from the introduction of or increase in a trade barrier. If a trade barrier increases the imported good's relative price, the scarce factor will be the gainer and the abundant factor the loser. This will not be true if the terms of trade effect is sufficiently large to reduce even the tariff-inclusive price of the imported good, but this outcome (known as the Metzler Paradox) is highly unlikely. Under normal conditions, unskilled labor in the high-wage countries and physical capital in the low-wage countries will benefit from trade barriers. This prediction matches closely the observed pattern of lobbying for trade barriers analyzed in chapter 14, reflecting also the typically far larger magnitude of the distributional consequences than of the net welfare effects of a trade barrier.

Apart from private interests, there could be a public interest justification for a trade barrier if the resulting change in income distribution is desirable. Such arguments are often used to support protection of an industry employing low-wage workers. For by now familiar reasons, this is a poor argument; income redistribution could be achieved more efficiently by other means (for example, through the tax and social security system), which avoid the resource misallocation associated with trade barriers. The country does best to realize the gains from trade by specializing according to its comparative advantage, and then implementing by other means any desired income redistribution.

Finally, trade barriers are often proposed as a means of reducing unemployment. Analytically, this is a distinct argument from the use of trade barriers to promote employment in specific activities (section 12.3 above). In a simple Keynesian framework imports are a withdrawal from and exports an injection into the circular flow of income, and an increase in net exports will work via a multiplier effect to increase the equilibrium income and employment level. Since this argument features changes in the trade balance it cannot be analyzed with the tools so far developed; it will be revisited in part IV. The obvious drawback of such an approach to unemployment reduction is, however, its shifting of unemployment from one country to another (increasing net exports must reduce the rest of the world's net exports because imports and exports must match globally), which invites retaliation with likely adverse consequences for all countries (a situation which arose during the 1930s). Moreover, the second-best argument remains valid; trade does not cause unemployment at the macroeconomic level, so the first-best policy is to realize the gains from trade and use other (domestic) instruments to achieve full employment.

12.7 Noneconomic Arguments

All of the above arguments in favor of trade barriers can be analyzed in economic terms. Explicitly noneconomic arguments, of which the most potent emphasize the link between international trade and national culture or national security, are more difficult to deal with.

The opening up of an autarchic country to international trade inevitably involves a degree of culture shock. New goods, new ideas, and new ways of doing things will all undermine the traditional life-style and values. In the face of major changes in tastes and in the availability of new goods and loss of cultural identity, the welfare analysis of previous chapters loses relevance. Were the indigenous peoples of the Americas, subSaharan Africa, and Australasia made better off by their contacts with European traders? Perhaps not, although in these cases the local people could not refuse to deal with the foreigners.

The above, possibly valid, argument for avoiding international trade is sometimes extended to specific industries in countries already heavily involved in the world economy. The so-called culture industries, such as publishing, broadcasting, and film-making are protected from foreign competition in order to protect the national identity. Since many governments strictly control these activities (for example, by limiting licenses to broadcast TV or radio programs) such restrictions may be a part of national "culture" policy rather than of trade policy. In some cases, however, the benefits appear slight, and the restrictions on foreign competitors support a welfare transfer from domestic consumers to producers and a net welfare loss as with any trade barrier. Domestic content rules requiring a minimum percentage of records played on Canadian radio stations to feature Canadian performers, for example, benefit domestic singers and producers at the expense of listeners, with dubious contributions to Canadian cultural identity. Protecting domestic markets has become more difficult in some culture industries as a result of technical progress. Satellite dishes for receiving TV images and VCRs for home-viewing of movies have eroded governments' ability to reduce viewers' choice – and in many cases the viewers have clearly indicated that they were suffering substantial consumer surplus loss as a result of previous policies.

The national security argument for trade barriers is likewise potentially valid, but may be used to cover distributional benefits for domestic producers at the nation's expense. A country crucially dependent on imports for a vital strategic product will be disadvantaged if it enters a war in which the suppliers are enemies, or supplies can be disrupted by the enemy. The threat of disruption may itself be sufficient to make import dependence undesirable. Imposing a trade barrier will encourage domestic production or search for a substitute which can be produced domestically.

However, for many countries there are few goods which fit the foregoing description. Even where the national security argument is valid there may be better policies than imposing trade barriers; for example, maintaining stock-

BOX 12.5   Who R "Us"?

The discussion of international subcontracting in chapter 7 and of imperfectly competitive industries and transnational corporations in chapter 8 raised the question of a product's nationality. Economists tend to finesse the question by distinguishing between where a particular activity takes place (the value-added is counted in the gross domestic product of the country of location) and the residence of the owners of factor inputs (their income is included in the national income or gross national product of their country of residence). In popular discussion, however, names have national identities. Chevrolet is the heartbeat of America even if the cars are imported from Taiwan, and the McDonald's restaurant in Moscow is seen as an American transplant even though it is a Canadian–USSR joint venture. Ownership issues are especially evocative when national champions are taken over by foreigners, although the reaction is not always consistent. Thus, when Sony of Japan purchased Columbia Pictures there was a xenophobic outcry in the US, but little attention was paid to the purchase of Smith & Wesson (producers of another archetypical American product) by the British firm Tompkins Plc or of Burger King by Grand Metropolitan Plc.

The nationality issue is relevant for trade policy in determining which goods are to be considered imports and in determining where they come from. Customs officials have to decide whether a finished good is domestic or whether it has been imported as a semi-finished product (perhaps subject to a lower tariff) and then had a domestic label slapped on it: or when a country has discriminatory import barriers it is necessary to check whether a good really comes from a favored trading partner or whether it was simply routed through that country in order to gain easier access to the eventual market. Policy-makers can provide guidelines by establishing domestic content rules (see section 11.3) or rules of origin (see section 15.1), but these are both difficult to specify and subject to abuse.

There is also a problem for governments trying to pursue strategic trade policies or market-opening policies. Should they be helping domestically located production or domestic companies? The US, for example, has warned the European Community against taking measures to include shipments of Toyotas, Hondas, and so on from US factories in

BOX 12.5—cont'd

any voluntary export restraint agreement with Japan; a Toyota made in Kentucky or a Honda made in Tennessee creates American jobs. At the same time the US government is pressing Japan to remove restrictions on the US corporation Toys R Us setting up marketing outlets in Japan for its toys, which are mostly manufactured in Asia. All of this raises the question: Who are us?

(For a discussion of this topic with a different grammatical view, see Reich, 1990.)

piles of strategic minerals. In other cases the argument may not be valid, but is used by domestic producers of the good to hide the fact that the trade barrier is in their interests, although the nation is being forced to pay more for its national defense by foregoing the gains from specialization and trade.

With respect to both cultural and national security considerations there are counterarguments in favor of freer trade. International trade helps the interchange of ideas, promoting cultural development and possible enrichment. The net impact of trade is difficult to evaluate and any conclusion is necessarily subjective, but the high points of Western culture have historically occurred in open mercantile economies rather than in economically inward-looking states. On balance, and despite the publicity given to trade disputes, international trade also promotes international understanding, and by integrating national economies into a world economy helps reduce the possibility of more lethal disputes.

12.8   Conclusions

The arguments in this chapter can be divided into four groups. The first group consists of cases in which trade barriers can increase national welfare and this cannot be achieved by alternative domestic policies. These cases, the optimal tariff and some imperfect competition arguments, are valid arguments in favor of trade barriers from the importing nation's perspective, assuming no foreign reaction. In general, however, foreign countries will suffer from the trade barrier and will retaliate, with negative consequences for the first country which are likely to turn the net national gains into losses.

The second group consists of cases in which a trade barrier can achieve the desired goal of raising domestic output or reducing consumption of a good, increasing government revenue or combating a market imperfection. Here an active trade policy is better than doing nothing, but it is not the first-best policy. A more direct method of achieving the goal always exists, which will avoid the negative side-effects of a trade barrier. It should be noted here that advocating a free trade policy does not necessarily mean endorsing a *laissez-faire* economic policy of leaving the market system to itself; there may be good reasons for the government to correct or influence the market outcome, but *trade* policy is the appropriate instrument only if the source of market failure is not domestic.

Arguments emphasizing noneconomic benefits from restricting international trade are difficult to evaluate, and by their nature often involve value judgments. They may be valid, but this is not always true.

The fourth group consists of invalid arguments, such as the pauper labor argument and simple anti-dumping arguments based on a comparison of price and costs, which reflect misunderstanding of the concept of comparative advantage as the basis for gains from trade. All of these arguments may, however, be used for public relations purposes by the domestic producers who benefit from a trade barrier, since national security, cultural identity, or xenophobia are more likely to gain policy-makers' support than blatant reference to the producer's economic self-interest.

Upon close scrutiny, the generalization made in chapter 9 that there is a strong presumption in favor of free trade policies still holds. Valid arguments in favor of trade barriers being in the national or even in the global interest can be put forward, but their practical applicability is limited. The most common arguments in favor of trade barriers are second-best, and thus not valid guides to optimal public policy; superior policy instruments exist. Thus, the challenge to be faced in the next two chapters is to explain the prevalence of barriers to international trade in view of their weak theoretical support.

Further Reading

Johnson (1954) analyzes the optimum tariff in the presence of retaliation. The theory of domestic distortions originated in Meade (1955), and was developed in many articles, principally by Corden, Johnson, Bhagwati, and Ramaswami. The most thorough treatment is by Corden (1974), who also emphasizes that this approach breaks the link between the case for free trade and the more general argument for *laissez-faire* economic policies. The argument underlying figure 12.3 was developed by Katrak (1977) and Svedberg (1979). The share of trade taxes in government revenue is analyzed by Greenaway (1984).

13

Measuring the Effects of Trade Barriers

The analysis in the last three chapters identified the consequences of various trade barriers, and enabled us to evaluate arguments used in support of trade barriers. The present chapter summarizes the large body of empirical research which has attempted to quantify the consequences of trade barriers. Measurement is useful for several reasons. The presumption from the qualitative analysis is that most trade barriers reduce national welfare, but it is useful to know whether this is a large or a small loss. Moreover, measurement can point to which trade barriers are the most costly and which are the least costly to the nation, indicating where policy change would be most beneficial. Finally, given the multiplicity of consequences of any trade barrier, measurement can identify which consequences are more or less significant, and since there will be both gainers and losers from any trade policy change it can identify which groups will be most affected in either direction. These last findings provide the basic material for the next chapter, which seeks to explain why actual trade barriers exist.

Measuring the consequences of trade barriers requires accessible data on trade flows and domestic output, as well as on the size of the barriers themselves. During the 1920s and 1930s empirical work focused on calculating average tariff rates for various countries and products, in itself a major undertaking. Only since the 1940s, with better and more internationally consistent data, has this become a straightforward exercise, allowing economists to progress to measuring the consequences of the tariffs. The major conceptual advance was the development by Corden and Johnson in the 1950s of the partial equilibrium model described earlier (see figure 10.3) as an operational framework. Since then, numerous studies have measured the consequences of various countries' trade barriers within this framework, with consistent findings across the major trading nations.

Section 13.1 discusses the strengths and weaknesses of the Corden–Johnson "welfare triangles" approach. The second section summarizes estimates of the national costs of trade barriers based upon the partial equilibrium framework, and considers whether the conclusions need to be modified to take account of general equilibrium effects. In some product groups, involving large international trade flows, trade barriers have been especially restrictive in several major trading nations (for example, textiles and clothing, agriculture, automobiles, and steel); section 13.3 reports on microeconomic studies of the effects of trade barriers in these heavily protected sectors. Finally, a series of less studied empirical topics (for example, trade taxes as a source of government revenue, smuggling, and rent-seeking behavior) are briefly covered in section 13.4.

13.1   The Partial Equilibrium Approach to Measurement

The great strength of the partial equilibrium framework is that it can be made operational with a limited amount of readily available data. In figure 13.1, which reproduces the essentials of figure 10.3, the quantities S and $S+M$ are actual volumes of domestic supply and consumption. To measure the

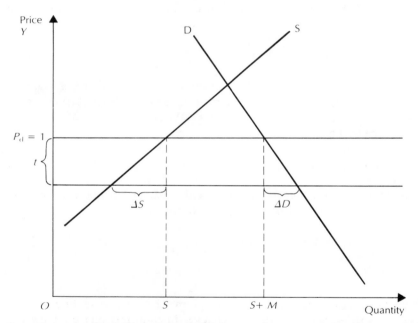

Figure 13.1   Measuring the effects of a tariff. By selecting units such that $P_d = 1$ the "quantity" data can be the values of S and M. The tariff rate, t, is measured as a proportion, for example 0.05 for a tariff the removal of which would reduce P_d by 5 percent. The change in domestic supply (ΔS) and in domestic demand (ΔD) resulting from removal of the tariff add up to the change in imports (ΔM).

effects of a trade policy change all that is needed is an estimate of the percentage change in the domestic price, P_d, and knowledge of the price elasticities of demand and supply, e_d and e_s. Defining one unit of the good as the amount purchased by one currency unit (a dollar's worth or one mark's worth, and so on) then values of S and $S + M$ can be obtained from the national trade and production statistics, while P_d is equal to unity and the percentage change in price due to removal of a trade barrier follows from the tariff rate or the *ad valorem* equivalent to an NTB. Thus, the only data posing serious difficulties are the elasticities, and for all commodities there is a bank of existing estimates of domestic elasticities to which the trade economist can turn.

Calculation of the various effects of trade barriers follows directly from the definition of elasticities as change in quantity divided by change in price. Using the symbol Δ for "change in," e_s is $(\Delta S/S)/(\Delta P/P)$, and the change in domestic supply due to removal of a trade barrier which raised domestic price by a percentage t is equal to $e_s\, tS$. Similarly, the change in domestic demand due to removal of this trade barrier is $-e_d t(S + M)$; the minus sign occurs because, strictly speaking, e_d is negative, but it is sometimes omitted and the absolute value of e_d used. The total change in imports is therefore:

$$\Delta M = -e_d t(S + M) + e_s tS. \tag{13.1}$$

Expression 13.1 measures the base of the two "welfare triangles" (areas b and d in figure 10.3), the area of which captures the deadweight loss from the trade barrier. Thus, the deadweight loss (DWL) is equal to ΔM multiplied by half the triangles' height (t):

$$DWL = \tfrac{1}{2} t\Delta M = -\tfrac{1}{2} e_d t^2(S + M) + \tfrac{1}{2} e_s t^2 S. \tag{13.2}$$

The other welfare changes (in producer and consumer surplus tariff revenue) can be easily computed from the same information:

$$\Delta CS = t(S + M) - \tfrac{1}{2} e_d t^2(S + M). \tag{13.3}$$
$$\Delta PS = tS - \tfrac{1}{2} e_s t^2 S. \tag{13.4}$$
$$\text{tariff revenue} = tM. \tag{13.5}$$

It can be seen that while estimates of DWL may be sensitive to the elasticities used, this is less true of estimated changes in consumer and producer surplus, and not at all true for the lost tariff revenue.

Before considering estimates based on the above expressions, let us first discuss the robustness and biases of the method. Its major advantage is that trade and output data are both readily available and among the most reliable economic data. Tariff rates are also easy to obtain, although aggregating the thousands of individual tariff lines into a manageable number of categories involves problems discussed earlier (section 10.3) and introduces a downward bias into the welfare calculations because the t term is squared (averaging the tariff lines then squaring the average tariff must yield a smaller number than if the individual tariffs were squared and then their average taken).

The most imprecise data inputs are the elasticities. There is also imprecision because the demand and supply curves may not be linear (so that the "welfare triangles" are not triangles), and because the appropriate demand curve is one compensated for income changes, whereas empirical estimates focus on the uncompensated relationship between price and quantity demanded. The elasticity problems may, however, be minor insofar as for most commodities the range of plausible elasticities is fairly narrow, and some of the welfare effects (those other than the deadweight loss triangles) tend to be fairly insensitive to changes in the elasticities used. There is a downward bias in studies which aggregate commodities, because elasticities are lower for broader than for narrower categories of goods (for example, demand for food is less elastic than demand for meat, which is in turn less elastic than demand for beef); aggregation is usually necessary not only for the manageability mentioned above in the context of tariff data, but also because elasticities may not be available at very fine aggregation levels. In sum, although the estimated consequences of trade barriers will not be precise because the elasticities will be approximate, the range of error due to data limitations is unlikely to be great.

More important weaknesses in the partial equilibrium approach to measuring the consequences of trade barriers involve things omitted from the figure 13.1 framework. The elasticities used in applications of this approach are short-run; that is, they reflect the quantity response within at most a year of a price change. Long-run elasticities are larger because they permit adjustments in productive capacity and in tastes, so that measured losses from trade barriers may understate the long-term benefits from their removal. More generally, all dynamic effects are ignored by the static framework of figure 13.1. Trade barriers may discourage innovation or even efficient use of existing technology because they remove competitive pressures and may reduce the flow of technical ideas, or trade barriers may allow new firms to survive their infancy and establish new technologies in the national industry when under free trade they would be driven out of business. In sum, if long-term or dynamic effects matter, the estimates will be inaccurate but the direction of bias is uncertain.

Another important omission is terms of trade or exchange rate effects.

Figure 13.1 invokes the small-country assumption by drawing an infinitely elastic import supply curve. For many individual import items this is a reasonable assumption for most countries. However, if the aim is to measure the consequences of all one country's trade barriers by estimating each barrier's effect and then adding together the estimates, then there will be an impact on the overall terms of trade, or in a monetary setting on the exchange rate. An increase in all imports will increase the trade deficit and, in the absence of other adjustment mechanisms (see chapter 18), will lead to a fall in the price of the domestic currency. In an early attempt to capture this effect, Basevi, assuming an average US tariff equivalent of 15 percent in 1958–62, found that the terms of trade losses from reducing America's trade barriers exceeded all other benefits (implying that the optimal tariff was higher than the actual tariff), although the magnitudes involved were "very small, representing at most 0.11 percent of national income" (Basevi, 1968, p. 851). Basevi's study faced criticism for its aggregation level and for ignoring the behavior of America's trading partners, but it did highlight the potential significance of this omission from the partial equilibrium approach to measurement.

Other omissions are less significant. The estimated costs of trade barriers will not be fully captured by their removal because there are adjustment costs of moving labor, capital, and so on from protected industries to their best use in a free trade setting. Such adjustment costs are well-publicized because they are unevenly distributed, often falling on relatively poor workers in depressed regions, and they appear to arouse common feelings of "unfairness." Given the latter aspect the policy implication is to use public funds to compensate or retrain or help relocate the workers who suffer from the trade policy change. As a measurement issue the adjustment costs are likely to be minor because they are once-and-for-all, whereas the allocative efficiency benefits from removing trade barriers accrue in perpetuity; only if society has a very high discount rate, giving present costs and benefits much greater weight than future ones, are adjustment costs likely to be very significant. ("Society" probably does not have such a discount rate, but politicians looking to the next election might well have!)

Finally, all estimates leave out the administration costs of trade barriers. These are discontinuous; that is, low trade barriers may require as much administration as high trade barriers and only total elimination of trade barriers allows the customs service to be disbanded. Even with total free trade the reduction in administrative costs would be small relative to the other magnitudes involved. There would, however, be unmeasured benefits to travellers, as well as traders, freed from the threat of summary search by omnipotent customs officials at every national border.

13.2 Estimates of the Costs of National Trade Barriers

Application of the previous section's methods has focused on the trade barriers of the more developed countries. Most work has involved the US, and specific studies referred to will mostly concern the US, but the American results are similar to the empirical findings for other countries' trade barriers. Although little work of this nature has been carried out for less-developed countries, it seems likely that the results would be qualitatively similar but quantitatively larger, because effective rates of protection tend to be higher in those countries.

The study by Magee (1972) of the costs of US trade barriers is representative of empirical work using the partial equilibrium framework. As a careful study with a reasonable degree of disaggregation in sectors where quotas are important, Magee's work can be taken as a good example of the results which this framework yields. The findings are clear:

- the deadweight loss from US tariffs circa 1970 was a small fraction of GNP
- the total cost of US trade barriers is dominated by the cost of NTBs
- with both tariffs and NTBs the redistribution effects are large

These results are confirmed by other studies of the US and by similar findings for other countries' trade barriers.

Magee divides total US imports in 1971 ($45.6 billion) into three groups: those competing directly with US production and subject to tariffs (27 percent), those competing only partially (53 percent), and those subject to quotas (20 percent). Removal of the 7.9 percent import-weighted average tariff on the first group is estimated to have the following welfare effects (in million dollars):

	Short run	Long run
increased consumer surplus	4,275	4,350
reduced producer surplus	− 3,215	− 3,096
loss of tariff revenue	− 963	− 963
deadweight loss	97	291

The deadweight loss is larger in the long run because Magee assumed long-run demand and supply elasticities to be three times the short-run elasticities, but the other magnitudes are fairly insensitive to the elasticities used. The lower tariffs on the larger second group of imports have a slightly smaller deadweight loss, but still incur a large loss in consumer surplus (about $3.8 billion). By far the biggest net national welfare loss arises from quantitative restrictions; on six products (petroleum, steel, textiles, sugar, meat, and dairy products) Magee estimates a net national welfare loss of $3.6 billion, of which $2.4 billion are deadweight losses and $1.2 billion transfer of quota rent to foreigners.

More ambitious studies in the late 1970s went into greater detail than Magee, but came up with essentially similar results. Baldwin, Mutti, and Richardson (1980) distinguished 367 sectors of the US economy, while a Brookings study (Cline et al., 1978) considered 12 countries or country groups with a less-detailed industry breakdown (about 21 sectors). These, and other studies stimulated by the Tokyo Round of multilateral trade negotiations, all estimated net welfare gains to the major trading nations resulting from substantial multilateral tariff reductions to be a small fraction of 1 percent of GNP. Cline, for example, estimated the net welfare gain from a 50 percent cut in tariffs to be less than half a billion dollars for the US and EC and about a quarter of a billion dollars for Japan. Baldwin's work came up with even smaller gains for the US, equal to about one-tenth of 1 percent of American GNP.

Cline's study also indicates the sectoral concentration of international trade barriers. Reducing NTBs on agricultural products by 60 percent would yield larger benefits than reducing tariffs on all goods by 60 percent. Globally, the main effect of agricultural trade liberalization would be to increase EC imports and North American exports, with large welfare gains to the EC and smaller benefits to the US and Canada, and with quite a large impact on farm employment in Europe and small employment effects in North America. This finding indicates the economic consequences of the EC's Common Agricultural Policy, which imposes a large cost on EC consumers and a high net welfare loss to the Community in order to protect European farmers who are, at the margin, far less efficient than North American farmers. Cline also indicates the crucial importance for developing countries' exports of industrialized countries' barriers to trade in textiles and clothing; a 60 percent reduction in tariffs on these goods is estimated to be more beneficial to the developing countries than a 60 percent cut in all other tariffs.

Since the mid-1970s empirical work on across-the-board trade liberalization has increasingly been based on general equilibrium models. These have obvious advantages in tackling effects omitted from the partial equilibrium framework. General equilibrium models become very complex, however, with much disaggregation, so that existing empirical work must be considered indicative rather than precise measurement. Numerical results vary from study to study because of differing specifications of utility and production functions (because the number of unknowns exceeds the number of equations some variables, the sectoral capital stock or wage rates for example, must be taken as given). Some studies (such as Boadway and Treddenick (1978) on Canada, or Dixon et al. (1977) on Australia) focus on a single economy assuming exogenously given world prices, while other studies (such as Deardorff and Stern, 1979; Whalley, 1985) use multi-country models to determine world prices endogenously, although at the cost of having a more aggregated structure for the national economies. Despite this variety, the empirical results from the general equilibrium literature do follow some general patterns.

The general equilibrium literature confirms the main findings of Magee and Basevi described above. The net welfare cost of industrialized country tariffs by the 1970s was a very small proportion of GNP, nontariff measures are more substantial and more costly trade barriers, and the distributive effects of trade barriers are large relative to the net welfare effects. This last result applies to both internal distributive effects (involving producers and consumers) and international effects (involving terms of trade). Whalley in particular has estimated large terms of trade effects from unilateral tariff reductions by the US and EC, implying even larger "optimal tariff" rates than Basevi found and providing a strong justification for multilateral tariff reduction. These results may, however, be upward-biased due to the small number of countries in Whalley's world trade model, which consequently understates the competitiveness of international markets.

The main distinctive feature of general equilibrium results has been with respect to the distribution of gains and losses from trade liberalization across sectors and among factors. In a partial equilibrium setting the costs from trade liberalization inevitably fall on the producers in protected sectors. This result carries over to general equilibrium analysis, but is supplemented by evidence of the gains to export sectors. Moreover, general equilibrium models also indicate that sectors producing nontradables suffer from trade barriers, which increase the price of traded goods relative to that of non-traded goods; the biggest gainers from trade liberalization in the US, Japan, and the EC tend to be the retail trade, restaurants and hotels, and personal services. The impact of trade liberalization on factors of production is also much clearer in a general equilibrium framework, although the results are not surprising; for example, trade liberalization has been found to increase the demand for professional and farm workers and reduce demand for unskilled labor in the US and in Australia.

Overall, the practical benefits from using more sophisticated general equilibrium models of international trade have been slight insofar as the results do not differ greatly from those of Basevi's early study and of partial equilibrium studies such as Magee's. The main results are fourfold. Firstly, the largest trading nations are not "small" and their optimal tariffs are higher than their current average tariffs. This finding indicates why unilateral trade liberalization by large nations is uncommon, and why a cooperative approach to multilateral trade negotiations is desirable to attain the global optimum of free trade. Secondly, the deadweight loss from trade barriers in the more developed countries is a small fraction of GNP. This finding aroused great debate and suggestions that the methods were faulty but, as discussed in section 13.1, even though there are some biases in the partial equilibrium method, these work both ways and the net bias is unlikely to be large enough to alter the assessment. A more tenable position is to emphasize that few economic policies yield benefits which are large relative to GNP, and the absolute value of the benefits from trade liberalization are not insignificant. In sum, the empirical studies consistently find evidence of nontrivial positive benefits from trade liberalization, even if these are modest relative to GNP. Thirdly, the most important trade barriers are NTBs. This points to sectors where more detailed studies would be most useful, and some of these studies are reported in the next section. Fourthly, the distributive consequences of trade barriers are quantitatively far greater than the net welfare effects. This provides the basis for discussion in the next chapter of why trade barriers exist and what form they take.

13.3   Sectoral Studies

One feature of estimates of the national welfare losses from trade barriers in the major trading nations is the recurrence of few sectors as the location of a large part of the total costs. In Magee's study of US trade barriers he found especially high costs from quotas on textiles and clothing, agricultural goods, steel, and petroleum. Cline's study of trade liberalization in the Tokyo Round pointed to the overriding importance for developing countries of industrialized countries' restrictions on textile and clothing and agricultural imports. The most publicized new trade barrier of the 1980s was the VER on Japanese automobile sales to the US. Given the significance of these barriers, it is worth examining their effects in more detail.

Practically all of the heavy protection cases involve nontariff barriers. They are therefore difficult to quantify, and in some cases it is not easy even to observe the full nature of the trade barrier. Thus, for some agricultural products part of the full protective effect is hidden in unjustified health standards, which are difficult to distinguish from justifiable health standards. Imports of automobiles into Japan are hampered by detailed requirements for obtaining type approval of the model to be imported – requirements which the Japanese deny using as import barriers and the impact of which is difficult to measure (other countries do this too – see box 11.2). Even when the NTB is a simple quantitative restriction, the equivalent tariff needed to estimate the welfare effects as in section 13.1 will vary from year to year; for example, booming demand for imports in the US between 1983 and 1985 greatly increased the tariff equivalent on anything from Hong Kong shirts to Japanese automobiles. In sum, measuring the effects of NTBs is subject to even more caution than the measures of the welfare costs of tariffs reported in the previous sections; all that follows is to be treated as approximate, but the magnitudes involved do offer some fairly unambiguous conclusions.

Table 13.1 brings together some of the best estimates of the welfare losses to the US from its major NTBs in the mid-1980s. Because the individual NTBs take different forms, their effects are measured differently and may not be strictly comparable. Nevertheless, the magnitudes are striking. The Multifiber Arrangement is by far the most costly trade barrier, both in terms of deadweight loss to global efficiency and in terms of national welfare cost to the US. Also costly were the steel and automobile VERs, although the cost to the US mainly took the form of transfers to foreigners. A third group (dairy products, meat, sugar, and fish) indicates that agricultural protection is also costly (in total more so than steel or automobiles), and it involves substantial efficiency costs. The final industry group – shipbuilding and other maritime industries – has received less attention because it has been protected ever since American independence. The trade barriers listed in table 13.1 (which includes all industries for which the estimated net national welfare cost of the NTBs exceeded $100 million) impose a national welfare loss on the US of over $15 billion or roughly 0.4 percent of 1984 GNP, well above the loss from all US tariffs.

The US is, of course, not alone in relying on NTBs for heavy protection. The list of most costly NTBs is surprisingly similar across the major trading

Table 13.1   Costs to the US of its major NTBs (in US$ million)

	Transfer to foreigners	Deadweight loss	Total cost to US
Textiles, 1984	300	350	650
Clothing, 1984	1,500	4,500	6,000
Automobiles, 1984	2,200	200	2,400
Steel, 1984	2,000	330	2,330
Dairy products, 1983	250	1,370	1,620
Maritime industries, 1983	0	1,000	1,000
Sugar, 1977–84 average	410	130	540
Meat, 1983	135	145	280
Fish, 1983	170	15	185

Source: Hufbauer, Berliner, and Elliott (1986)

nations. The World Bank has assembled roughly comparable figures for the domestic costs and benefits of agricultural protection in the European Community, Japan, and the US (table 13.2). The EC's Common Agricultural Policy imposes huge costs on domestic consumers and taxpayers, and the deadweight loss of over 15 billion dollars makes it the most costly trade restriction of all. The domestic costs of Japanese agricultural protection fall entirely on consumers (because import duties are more important relative to price support or subsidies than in the other nations), and in absolute amounts they are less than the costs of EC or US agricultural policies, but the Japanese policies are very inefficient in that it costs consumers and taxpayers $2.58 for every dollar transferred to producers (compared to $1.50 in the EC which relies mainly on price supports, and $1.38 in the US which relies more on subsidies). The most costly parts of the EC's Common Agricultural Policy involve similar items to those most protected by US agricultural policies (dairy products, meat, and sugar) together with grains. Several of the western European countries outside the EC also have high trade barriers on these items.

The high protection and long life of these agricultural policies have generated responses which have distorted world trade patterns considerably. The Common Agricultural Policy has changed the EC from an importer to an exporter of many agricultural products, with important consequences for other trading nations. Thus, the shrinking EC demand for butter hurt the most efficient exporter, New Zealand, which also was under threat of increased competition in third markets as the EC accumulated surpluses (the famous butter mountain). In 1979 the EC and New Zealand signed an agreement respecting a minimum butter price in world markets, with implicit support from the US which could undercut the minimum price by releasing its butter stocks. The International Dairy Agreement is a new NTB, the existence of which stems from a distorted international market,

Table 13.2 Domestic costs and benefits of agricultural protection in the EC, Japan, and the US (in US$ billion)

	Consumer surplus	Net tax revenue	Producer surplus	Deadweight loss
EC, 1980	− 34.6	− 11.5	+ 30.7	− 15.4
Japan, 1976[a]	− 7.1	+ 0.4	+ 2.6	− 4.1
US, 1985	− 5.7	− 10.3	+ 11.6	− 4.4

[a] Japanese agricultural policies have a positive effect on tax revenue because the tariff is a major instrument; the EC and the US rely more on price supports and subsidies which have a negative impact on net tax revenue.

Source: World Bank *World Development Report 1986*, p. 121

and it has itself led to new distortions. For example, in 1984 the EC found that some of its butter mountain had spoiled and it was sold as "butter oil" to the USSR for $450 per ton – 14 percent of the price originally paid to EC farmers and well below the agreed minimum price for butter of $1,200 per ton. Similarly, the VER on Thai cassava sales to the EC (box 13.1) is difficult to assess because it is hard to know with what it should be compared; in a free trade situation the exports would be minimal!

The MFA has become so complex and has governed world textiles and clothing trade for so long (see box 11.1) that it is too difficult to compare with a free trade alternative. The best measures of the MFA's costs are based on Hong Kong exports because in Hong Kong export licenses are transferable, and the active market permits calculation on the tariff equivalent of the quota on any item to any market. The quota rents are substantial, estimated

---

BOX 13.1   *The Cassava Caper*

A consequence of the European Community's Common Agricultural Policy was to increase the price of grain, not just for human consumption but also for animals. Thus livestock farmers in the EC began to search for nongrain feed ingredients for their animals. The most popular mix was cassava (also known as tapioca or manioc) and soybean meal, which has the same nutrients as a feed grain and the big advantage that cassava was imported and its EC tariff rate had been bound in GATT negotiations.

The EC's imports of dried cassava increased from half a million metric tons in 1965 to 1.5 million tons in 1973 and peaked at eight million tons in 1980. At this point the EC negotiated a "voluntary" export restraint agreement with Thailand, the principal supplier, and imposed quotas on imports from Indonesia and other suppliers so that total imports would be held below six million tons.

The limitation of cassava imports may have had the intended effect of encouraging sales of EC grain to the livestock farmers. It also had effects on other countries. Brazilian and US sellers of soybeans, used as a complement to cassava in feed mixes, lost export sales. On the other hand, corn exporters benefited because this had now become a price-competitive feedstuff.

Source: *McCalla and Josling (1985), p. 81*

by Hamilton (1986) to have been worth US$507 million, or 1.7 percent of the colony's GNP in 1983. They also vary greatly by destination and by year. The tariff equivalent of quotas on Hong Kong clothing exports to the US rose from 56 percent in 1982 to 140 percent in 1983. Nobody has attempted to put together the cost of all MFA quotas, but judged by the US estimates given in table 13.1 and by the magnitude of the Hong Kong quota rents there are substantial transfers involved (which is one reason for developing countries' ambivalence toward the MFA) and large losses in global efficiency.

The 1981 VER limited US imports of automobiles from Japan to 1.68 million per year. Crandall (1984) has estimated that the price of Japanese cars in the US was about $1,000 higher in 1983 than it would have been in the VER's absence, and 26,000 American jobs were saved by the import restriction. Thus, some $1.68 billion in quota rent was transferred to Japanese suppliers. In addition to the quota rent, Crandall estimated that the VER cost US consumers $2.56 billion in higher prices for domestic cars, so that the cost to domestic consumers of saving a job in the automobile industry was $160,000. This recurring annual cost was far higher than the annual wage rate, so it would have been more effective to have paid 26,000 autoworkers their annual salaries plus a bonus to do nothing rather than to have artificially saved their jobs by the VER. The healthy profits earned by US car makers and the high costs to consumers persuaded President Reagan not to request renewal of the VER in 1985, but the Japanese kindly agreed to continue restricting automobile exports on a truly voluntary basis, and continued to earn quota rents until their comparative advantage was wiped out by the rising yen in 1988–9.

Some European countries, notably Italy and France, have even more restrictive limits on Japanese automobile imports. The costs of these VERs appear, however, to be less than those of the American VER. The reason for this is the competition within western Europe among makers of smaller cars so that, even if Toyota or Nissan are excluded from the Italian market, Fiat's ability to raise prices is limited by competition from Volkswagen, Renault, and so on. Thus, the quota rent and total cost to consumers are less than in the US case, although they are still present together with the deadweight losses. In Canada too the effectiveness of automobile VERs in supporting higher domestic prices was undermined by competition from a third country when Hyundai from South Korea entered the market in 1984 and became the best-selling imported car by 1986. Finally, it should be mentioned that the long-term ability of VERs to protect domestic car producers is doubtful, because they provide an incentive for the foreign firm to build a factory in the protected market, avoiding the trade barrier, but from a global perspective probably creating an inefficient location of production (this issue is taken up in chapter 17).

13.4   *Other Measurement Topics*

In addition to studies measuring the national costs of trade barriers and the costs of individual trade barriers, there has been empirical work on other topics. Some results will be reviewed at appropriate points in later chapters (for example, in chapter 14, section 15.4, and chapters 16 and 19), but a few topics do not fit anywhere neatly and will be summarized here.

One of the strongest empirical regularities is the tendency of governments' reliance on trade taxes as a source of revenue to fall as national income increases. Thus, over the past two centuries, governments of the more economically developed nations have shifted from raising most of their revenue through trade taxes to being almost oblivious to the revenue implications of trade policies. In Canada, for example, tariff revenues accounted for 75 percent of the federal government's income in the 1870s, but this percentage had fallen to 40 percent by 1929, 10 percent by 1949, and close to zero by the 1990s. In the US 84 percent of federal revenues came from tariffs in 1800; by 1900 this had dropped to 41 percent, and it will be insignificant by 2000.

Cross-country comparisons reveal a strong correlation between income level and trade taxes' share of government revenue (Greenaway, 1984). The differences between high- and low-income countries in this respect do, however, appear to have been shrinking in recent years, as more and more governments reduce their reliance on trade taxes for revenue.

The reason for these patterns is the relatively low administrative costs of collecting trade taxes and the relatively high resource misallocation costs of trade barriers (see section 12.5). Taxing imports or exports at a country's entry points is much easier than trying to tax all sales transactions or income within a country. This is especially true in less-developed economies where most activities are not marketed (for example, subsistence farmers growing only to meet their own needs) and where the skilled labor needed to run an efficient tax collection service is the country's scarcest resource. Establishment of a bureaucracy which can administer income and sales taxes without widespread evasion typically occurs with economic development, but the process can be accelerated with international help (such as the World Bank has been giving to some developing countries in recent years). Once such a bureaucracy is established, economically less injurious sources of government revenue can be tapped.

A related issue is smuggling. Whenever a tax is imposed some people will try to avoid paying it, but under what conditions is smuggling to avoid trade barriers most likely and how much smuggling actually takes place? Note first that smuggling can take two forms; either the traded items may be misrepresented in order to circumvent a trade barrier or pay less duty (for example, by underinvoicing when there are *ad valorem* duties), or they may be physically smuggled into the country avoiding any customs check. Both forms are more likely if trade barriers are more restrictive and if boundaries are poorly policed, but physical smuggling can also be facilitated by geography. It used to be said that England with its many small harbours in easy reach of other countries was made by heaven for free trade, and today smuggling enterprises in the islands of the Philippines and Indonesia are notably successful.

Measuring the extent of smuggling is by its nature difficult. A simple approach to checking for false invoicing is to compare the value of country A's exports to B with the declared value of B's imports from A. Even allowing for transport costs, differences in recording definitions, and so on, such discrepancies can be large; some of this is due to underinvoicing of imports, and there is anecdotal evidence from an unnamed southeast Asian country of a large export being underinvoiced by 90 percent (Bhagwati, 1974, pp. 123–47). The difficulty here, however, is to determine how much of this is deliberate falsification and how much is due to recording errors (see box 1.1).

Physical smuggling is even more difficult to track. Simkin (1970) estimated that Indonesia's unrecorded exports in the early 1960s were at least $140 million a year and possibly over $200 million, of which physical smuggling accounted for two-thirds and underinvoicing the remainder (the goal was to avoid paying the required export taxes); these numbers can be compared to total recorded exports of $800 million. Indonesia was a tractable case study both because smuggling was known to be extensive and because of the large export share of a few smugglable goods (rubber, copra, coffee, tobacco, tea, and pepper), where the official output data could be cross-checked on a product-by-product basis (in these six commodities alone estimated unrecorded exports were $127 million a year). Today, Indonesia remains a base for smuggling, although the government has taken the unprecedented step of hiring a Swiss firm to run its customs service in an attempt to improve efficiency. By the 1980s much of intra-African trade was also conducted outside of legal channels, primarily to avoid extensive regulation; Deardorff and Stolper (1990) conclude that smuggling accounts for at least a third of exportable production. The value of smuggled goods is probably dwarfed by that of drugs illegally imported into North America and western Europe, the value of which can only be guessed.

Smuggling is one example of a directly unproductive economic activity; it adds to the smugglers' welfare – as long as they are not caught – but not to national welfare.[1] Other DUP activities associated with trade barriers are

---

[1] Smuggling occurs in a setting of distorted prices, and therefore is a second-best phenomenon, the welfare implications of which are ambiguous. The added real costs of smuggling may lower national welfare (Bhagwati and Hansen, 1973), but if smuggling circumvents highly distortionary trade barriers it can be welfare-improving (Deardorff and Stolper, 1990).

legal, but costly to the nation because they waste resources which could be used productively (Bhagwati, 1982). Resources put into obtaining import licenses, for example, can lead to private gain but do nothing for national welfare (section 11.1). The maximum possible costs of such rent-seeking could be measured by the techniques discussed in this chapter; that is, area tM in figure 13.1, where the trade barrier is an import quota of M units and t is the equivalent tariff. There may, however, be additional DUP activities, such as lobbying to obtain new trade barriers which will generate future rents, the costs of which are difficult to measure even in principle (if the lobbying succeeds the value to the lobbiers is all the future additions to producer surplus, appropriately discounted, but the lobbying may fail, so that there are never any actual rents).

Studies measuring the costs of rent-seeking activities have consistently found these to be much larger than the conventional costs of trade barriers reported in the previous two sections. Anne Krueger (1974) estimated the rents on import licenses to be 15 percent of Turkey's GNP in 1968, and the World Bank's 1987 *World Development Report* (pp. 75–6) quotes estimates of 7 percent for India and 24 percent for Kenya. These estimates are rough guides and may be upper bounds (because some import licenses are routinely administered and do not generate rent-seeking), but they are well above the costs of trade barriers reported in section 13.2.

The measurement of DUP activities has had limited success, but the topic has been of theoretical interest. Many economists have seized upon the large income distribution consequences of trade barriers and the potential for rent-seeking in order to explain the existence of trade barriers the national welfare effects of which are negative and rather small. This is the subject of the next chapter.

Further Reading

The most recent development in measuring the costs of trade barriers is to drop the assumption of perfect competition. Applying imperfect competition models to international trade is still in its infancy and the numerical results are not robust, so they are not reported here. For surveys of this literature see Richardson (1988) or Helpman and Krugman (1989, chapter 8).

14

The Political Economy of Trade Barriers

The analysis of arguments in favor of trade barriers (chapter 12) concluded that the case for using such policies is a weak one. Logically valid arguments for trade barriers to improve national welfare are either at the expense of other countries' welfare (hence inviting retaliation) or are second-best arguments (other policies could achieve the goal more efficiently). Only arguments based on imperfectly competitive markets or noneconomic goals may avoid these shortcomings, but so rarely as to be risky guides to public policy. Nevertheless, trade barriers are common, and do not seem to be most prevalent in areas coming closest to the valid theoretical arguments. The empirical findings described in the previous chapter confirm that trade barriers consistently involve net national welfare loss. Why then are trade barriers such a common feature of the international economy?

The previous chapter provides a key to answering this question. Net welfare losses from trade barriers exist but they are small relative to the impact on gainers and losers. In chapter 10 the conclusion that trade barriers reduce a small country's national welfare rests on the possibility of constructing a social welfare function. Arrow (1951) has shown that a mapping from individual to social ordering of economic states is impossible without imposing severe restrictions on preferences or without a dictator. If the social welfare function is determined by a grand ranker with its own preferences, the nature of political institutions assumes a critical role; for example, in a representative democracy where "Parliament" is the grand ranker, trade barriers will be determined in a political marketplace where interest groups whose income will be increased by a trade barrier are the demanders and elected representative seeking to maximize the probability of re-election are the suppliers of protection. This simple formulation of a "pressure group" theory has dominated economists' attempts to explain why trade barriers exist.

14.1 An Historical Example

An example of how economic impact and political institutions can be combined to explain the imposition of trade barriers is provided by Europe in the last quarter of the nineteenth century (Kindleberger, 1951). Up until the 1870s the European nations had been reducing their trade barriers. An important turning point occurred in the 1870s when world wheat prices fell rapidly. Shifts in the world supply curve due to falling transport costs, agricultural mechanization, and the end of the Crimean and US Civil Wars led to a surge in North American and Russian grain exports to western Europe. With free trade the presumption would be a net welfare gain to western Europe with benefits to food consumers and nongrain producers and costs to wheat producers. Yet, in practice, some countries retained free trade policies, while others introduced barriers against grain imports.

Great Britain stuck to her free trade policy; farmers demanded tariff protection, but Parliament was dominated by industrial interests. In Denmark the farmers' influence was stronger, but a shift toward livestock farming had already begun, and farmers used the falling grain prices to accelerate this structural change; thus demands for protection were not strong enough to produce trade barriers. France provides the opposite extreme; the revolutionary settlement, which had created an agriculture based on small-scale grain farmers, plus universal male suffrage combined to make for a large politically powerful grain-farming sector which was able to obtain high protective tariffs as soon as world prices fell. In newly united Germany the situation was more complex, but the end result was the same as in France; the eastern German landowners were politically powerful but so were nonagricultural producers in western Germany, so that a political alliance between the landowners and heavy industry (that is, where there was less concern about increased food prices pushing up wage rates) was formed in order to introduce trade barriers on imports of grain and of some capital-intensive industrial goods. In Italy and Austria the agricultural sector was large but political institutions were less responsive to its demands for protection; falling wheat prices led to emigration rather than structural change, because impoverished grain farmers did not have the alternative employment opportunities which their British and Danish counterparts had, and only later were trade barriers introduced.

The actual policy decisions in the above cases depended upon the intensity of farmers' costs and on their ability to obtain a policy which would reduce these costs. These cases were important, because the trade barriers were high and, at least in France and Germany, fundamental to future economic and social development. They are also relatively easy to analyze because the interest groups are clearly defined and so is their input in the political system. There is, however, a logical problem insofar as where the grain farmers could obtain tariff protection, they should have had sufficient political power to ensure the first-best policy of free trade plus redistribution of income to compensate them for their losses. To make sense of the pressure group explanation of trade barriers it must be assumed that redistribution schemes are not feasible alternatives.

14.2 The Role of Institutions

Most trade barriers involve much smaller sectors of the economy than the European grain tariffs of the 1870s and 1880s. Several asymmetries arise. Consumers of a good accounting for a small part of their total budget or which they purchase infrequently may be unaware of a price increase or fail to relate the price increase to a trade barrier. Even if the consumer realizes that he or she will be a loser from the trade barrier the magnitudes involved may be too small to justify letting this issue influence the consumer's vote. Producers, on the other hand, may well give their vote and campaign contributions to politicians who will vote in favor of the trade barrier. Moreover, producers of a good tend to be more geographically concentrated than consumers, so that in an electoral system based on representatives for geographic areas the producers are likely to gain voices in Parliament, whereas nobody will speak up for the more diffused consumer interest.

An extreme case of producer-biased trade policy-making was the US Congress in 1929–30. In a situation in which each congressman supported protection for some import-competing activity, each was prepared to vote for others' proposals in return for their vote on his own proposals, and nobody stood for the general interest, the special interests carried all before them. The Smoot–Hawley tariff of 1930 took US tariff barriers to record heights, as almost every group that requested protection was granted it. Over a thousand economists signed a letter requesting Congress to think twice before passing the tariff bill, but their advice was ignored.

Because it was so extreme, the 1930 US tariff carried the seeds of its own destruction. Very quickly America's trading partners retaliated by raising their own trade barriers, or taking specific measures against US exports (for example, through public procurement decisions). It was soon recognized that the Smoot–Hawley tariff exacerbated rather than eased the economic depression. To counter these adverse effects the President was authorized in 1934 to make trade agreements aimed at bilateral tariff reductions. The Reciprocal Trade Agreements Act was the first step in a major shift in the institutional framework for determining US policy. After World War II Congress repeatedly granted the President authority to make substantial reductions in US tariffs during successive rounds of multilateral trade negotiations under GATT auspices. Because the President is elected on a national basis, this shift in trade policy-making power reduced the influence of special interest groups and increased the priority given to consideration of the

BOX 14.1   Tales from the Washington Woods

Between 1979 and 1982 the US lumber industry fell on hard times, as lumber prices fell from $344 to $204 per thousand board feet. The prime cause was the depressed housing market during the most severe postwar depression, but another identified cause was competition from Canadian lumber companies, whose share of the US market had increased from 19 percent in 1975 to 29 percent in 1982.

In 1982 US lumber producers petitioned for protection against unfair competition from Canadian imports. The main complaint was that provincial governments levied stumpage fees (that is, the price loggers paid to cut timber on public lands) which were below the market price (in the US logging rights were auctioned off and therefore market-determined), and hence constituted a subsidy for log users. The petition was rejected on the grounds that other Canadian buyers purchased logs (for example, the furniture industry), so the stumpage fees were a general subsidy rather than an export subsidy to the lumber industry and were not subject to countervailing duties.

In 1986 the US lumber industry renewed its plea, and this time was successful – a countervailing duty of 15 percent was imposed in October. There had been no change in Canadian practices since 1982 and, if anything, the plight of the US industry was less severe as the Canadian imports' market share stabilized around 30 percent. The crucial difference was that in 1986 the US lumber industry obtained the active support of politicians from lumber-manufacturing states in the Northwest and Southeast, some of whom were facing close electoral battles in November.

Two economic issues stand out in the softwood lumber case. Firstly, export subsidies are often difficult to identify, and in this case the identification was false – but not for the legalistic reason advanced in 1982. The number of logging licenses issued by the Canadian provinces was limited, and if they were sold below their (unknown) market value then the loggers receiving the licenses gained rent, not profits. This would be reflected in the price charged to the Canadian log users (unprocessed logs cannot be exported from Canada), which would be market-determined; the lumber industry gained no benefits from low stumpage fees.

Secondly, this case shows the power of producers to obtain protection via the political process. Kalt (1988) estimates the gain in US producer

BOX 14.1—*cont'd*

surplus from the 15 percent countervailing duty to be $417 million, while the US government would receive $340 million from the duties and US consumer surplus would fall by $557 million. There is a net US gain because the US is the only serious foreign market for Canadian lumber, whose supply is inelastic; that is, the optimal tariff is likely to be well above zero. The Canadians were, of course, unhappy with the outcome, as they suffered a welfare loss (estimated by Kalt at US$223 million per year) due to the lower price received for their lumber, and they began to retaliate. The Americans had no desire for a trade war and once their elections were safely over they reached a negotiated settlement whereby the Canadian provinces levied a 15 percent export tax on lumber in return for the dropping of the US countervailing duty. Because demand is also inelastic and Canada is the sole serious foreign supplier to the US, the export tax improves Canada's terms of trade. Kalt's estimates of the effects on US consumers and producers turn out to be the same as with the import duty, but the US government now receives nothing and Canada enjoys a net national gain of US$118 million. Both of the measures are global-welfare-reducing (by about $23 million), but the distributional effects are crucially different.

In political economy terms the above calculations suggest that the US government's goal was to satisfy their lumber industry's demands for protection while not alienating their country's major trading part-

national interest. During the 1970s and 1980s, however, Congress has tried to reassert its control over US trade policy both directly and indirectly (for example, by increasing its authority over bodies such as the International Trade Commission). This institutional change may help to account for increased US protectionism since the mid-1970s – or increased demand for protection may have encouraged members of Congress to seek greater control over the supply.

The American political system, with fairly independent elected representatives for specific geographic constituencies, is an especially fertile institutional set-up for interest groups to influence trade policy. In a Westminster system with strong political parties and no separation between executive and legislative branches of government, import-competing industries may influence members of Parliament in whose constituencies the industry is concen-

BOX 14.1—*cont'd*

ner. *The losers from all this were of course the US consumers, but they may not have been aware of how much the softwood lumber settlement added to, say, new house prices (an estimated $1,000!) and even if they did they were too dispersed to organize opposition in Congress against the powerful senators and representatives from Washington, Oregon, Idaho, Georgia, and Alabama, who considered this issue vital to their states' economic interests (and to their own re-election prospects).*

Box table 14.1: *The annual welfare effects of the two trade barriers (in US$ millions)*

	US producers	US consumers	US government	Net US	Net Canada
CVD	+ 417	− 557	+ 340	+ 200	− 223
Export tax	+ 417	− 557	0	− 140	+ 118

Note that these estimates are calculated as large-country conterparts of figure 13.1; they do not include the lobbying costs of US producers or Canadian legal costs in fighting the CVD action (which are deadweight losses).

Source: *Kalt (1988)*

trated, but they will then have to convince the party leadership of their case. Thus, trade barriers for individual products may be harder to obtain. On the other hand, if the party leadership is committed to free trade or to protection, dramatic changes in trade policy can follow after a change in government. Thus, Britain moved quickly from more or less free trade to across-the-board tariffs in 1931. Australia and New Zealand, which had on average the highest tariffs among more developed countries at the start of the 1980s, both moved quickly towards less restrictive trade policies after Labour governments came to power.

The European Community is a case of unchanging institutions providing over time a different framework for trade policy formation. With the establishment of a supranational tariff-setting body, trade policy appeared to be moved further away from the grasp of special interests. Studies of EC tariff changes under the Kennedy Round found them to be more general-interest-based than the corresponding US tariff changes; that is, the biggest EC tariff cuts were on those items with the highest tariffs. Meanwhile, the EC was shifting from the use of tariffs to subsidies in order to maintain specific activities. More recently, however, EC trade policy has shown itself more open to pressure group influence as industries have learned how to coordinate their lobbying in Brussels to win support within the EC Commission for trade barriers. European consumers, on the other hand, have little influence on EC trade policy because their natural advocates in the European Parliament sit on the sidelines as trade policy is made.

The EC also illustrates the possibility of offsetting action when several levels of government implement trade policy. Although, in theory, the EC has a common commercial policy, until the 1980s this only applied to agriculture and to tariffs on nonagricultural imports. National governments still negotiated voluntary export restraints to protect industries for which the common external tariff was considered insufficient. Subsidies were granted by national governments to "underprotected" industries. Public procurement policies and other NTBs still favored national producers. Thus, even if gainers from trade barriers were unable to affect tariff policy, they had other routes to follow. This may have pushed EC policy in a "first-best" direction by promoting the use of subsidies rather than trade barriers, but multilevel policy-making may also be harmful in making restrictions less transparent, adding to the costs and uncertainty of doing business internationally. Similar phenomena occur in federal states; for example, in Canada the British Columbia liquor board, which had a monopoly on wine sales in the province, protected local wine by imposing high mark-ups on foreign wines for many years until the practice was condemned by GATT in 1987.

The argument so far has been conducted within the realm of representative democracies, since this political system characterizes the major trading nations. In a dictatorship the role of pressure groups should be smaller, unless the dictator's policy is based upon maximizing income from bribes. In practice, undemocratic societies often seem to pursue restrictive trade policies. This may be because their leaders are poor economists, or because they are pursuing an inward-looking development strategy (see chapter 16), or it may be because dictators fear the interchange of ideas and economic dynamism which accompany freedom of international trade.

14.3   The Inter-industry Structure of Protection

The market for trade barriers is characterized by imperfect competition. The asymmetries analyzed in the previous section explain why producer interests receive greater weight than consumer interests in the policy-making process (and, incidentally, help to explain why trade barriers tend to be higher on goods for final consumption than on intermediate goods, the purchasers of which are fewer and well-informed, and tend to be rare on exports). Another imperfection in this market is the free-rider problem, which prevents some industries from effectively obtaining protection from imports.

A trade barrier can be viewed as a "public good" in the sense that any domestic producer of the good shares in the benefit, whether or not he or she has contributed to the costs of lobbying for the trade barrier. Thus any individual firm has an incentive to under-contribute to lobbying costs in the hope that the efforts of its fellow-producers will be sufficient to obtain the trade barrier; that is, there is an incentive to be a free-rider. Olson (1965) has developed this idea to hypothesize that trade barriers are more likely if the affected producers are few or if the benefits of protection are unequally distributed so that the lion's share goes to a small number of firms.

Pincus (1975) has tested Olson's hypothesis, in conjunction with some institutional points, against the Tariff Act of 1824. The 1824 tariff was the first seriously protectionist US tariff, so its structure was not greatly affected by previous legislation. Pincus expected that the tariff would be highest for goods where the anticipated gain in producer surplus was largest, where producers could lobby effectively for protection, and Congress would respond positively. The second-stage hypotheses invoked the free-rider problem by predicting more effective lobbying by industries concentrated in a few firms or a small geographic area. Success in Congress, however, also depended upon being spread across a sufficient number of states to mobilize sufficient support in the Senate. In regression analysis the variables measuring within-state geographic concentration (the number of counties in which production took place) had the expected signs and appeared to be substitutes for one another; "concentrated industries or those in geographically concentrated counties obtain higher tariffs" (Pincus, 1975, pp. 773–4). The statistical evidence that production in a larger number of states increased the probability of a positive Senate response to demands for protection was rather weak, although Pincus claimed to have indirect evidence that such geographic dispersion helped an industry to obtain higher tariffs *ceteris paribus*.

Attempts to test Olson's hypothesis against more recent tariff schedules have been less successful. Despite its obvious theoretic attraction, industrial concentration does not appear to explain much of the inter-industry variation in tariffs when cross-sectional regression analysis is applied to current tariff schedules of the US, Canada, and other trading nations. Even on a casual empirical level, it is apparent that the heavily protected sectors dealt with in section 13.3 involve both concentrated (for example, automobiles) and highly atomistic (for example, agriculture and clothing) industries.

A more simple explanation of inter-industry variations in tariffs is to invoke the Stolper–Samuelson theorem. Reductions in domestic price harm the relatively scarce factor of production, so in high-income countries one would expect unskilled labor to be most adversely affected by reducing trade barriers. Moreover, in democracies labor has the votes, which it can use to influence policy-makers. Alternatively, referring back to an idea mentioned in the previous chapter, producers may be considered to have some kind of property rights to rents due to existing trade barriers, and the sudden imposition of adjustment costs by removing the trade barrier may be considered "unfair." Variants on this theme such as Corden's "conservative social welfare function" suggest that a policy change harming a significant group in society is undesired, or that trade barriers can be viewed as a form of insurance to which any group faced by loss of income due to import competition is entitled. All of these arguments can be formulated to yield hypotheses linking the inter-industry tariff structure to the size of the labor-adjustment costs which would arise from removing trade barriers.

Cheh (1974) found precisely such a negative relationship between variables proxying labor-adjustment costs and the cuts in nominal tariff and nontariff rates agreed to by the US in the Kennedy Round. He found that almost 50 percent of the inter-industry variation in the trade barrier reductions may be accounted for by labor-adjustment variables. The significance of Cheh's finding has, however, been a matter of debate. Critics point out that over 50 percent of the inter-industry variation is not picked up by Cheh's six labor-adjustment variables. In western Europe tariffs appear to offer greatest protection to more unskilled-labor-intensive activities (Constantopoulos, 1974), but Kennedy Round reductions in nominal protection were not related to labor adjustment costs (Riedel, 1977). This last point does not reflect a disregard for such costs, but rather a shift from assistance by trade barriers to the superior policy of assistance by domestic subsidies and tax allowances. Helleiner (1977) has argued that even for the US trade policy formation is more complicated than Cheh implies, because large firms are often multinational enterprises for whom trade barriers are a nuisance since they inhibit global planning. Thus, protection is observed in labor-intensive industries where multinational firms are few (such as textiles) but less often where they are many (such as electrical assembly). The matter may, however, be even more complex if multinational enterprises can benefit from trade barriers through their use of intra-firm pricing or by specific advantages (for example, the US oil companies' control over import licenses before 1973).

The overall impression is that labor-intensity affects the inter-industry tariff structure, and that concern for labor-adjustment costs may influence changes in trade policy, but it appears to be a rather weak influence because other (superior) measures can soften adjustment costs and because other influences are at work. Evidence against the Stolper–Samuelson theorem's usefulness in explaining trade policy changes is the frequently observed phenomenon of all factors of production in an industry taking a common position towards trade policy; for example, in 19 out of 21 industries lobbying on the US President's trade bill in 1973, labor and capital took the same position (Magee, 1980). This may reflect the fact that the rents accruing to a protected industry are shared between owners and workers, or that adjustment costs are dominant considerations for all factors of production whose attributes have become to some extent specifically valuable in the protected industry.

A common pattern of the industries seeking protection in the more industrialized countries is that they tend to be declining industries; high-growth sectors are often less active in this context despite the (second-best) respectability of the infant industry argument and politicians' expressed concern for promoting "sunrise" industries. This phenomenon can be explained in terms of the theory of public goods. A true public good has two features; anybody can benefit from its provision, whether they pay for it or not, and increased benefits to one person do not reduce benefits to another. Trade barriers possess the first feature (hence the free-rider problem), but not the second: a tariff-induced increase in producer surplus will attract entrants to a newly protected industry, reducing the benefits to existing domestic producers. Thus, the demand for protection may be less than the potential gain in producer surplus suggests because of under-contribution to lobbying costs due to the free-rider problem, and because of fear that the rents generated will not be appropriated by existing firms. The latter force is, however, weaker in a declining industry because existing producers know that outside capitalists will be unwilling to invest and outside workers unlikely to seek employment in an industry known to be in long-term decline. If existing producers can successfully combine to lobby for a trade barrier, the gains will accrue to them and will be unlikely to attract new entrants, whereas in a growing industry the existence of tariff-generated supernormal profits and wages will attract new investment and workers to the industry.

The appropriability argument is not only applicable to declining industries; it applies to any industry with high barriers to entry. Thus, heavily protected industries such as steel and automobiles in the US and some EC countries may be thought of as declining, but a more general point is that barriers to new entrants are high. In the automobile industry absolute costs, reputation, dealer, and after-sales networks act as entry barriers. In both industries in the US strong labor unions have been successful in maintaining substantial wage differentials by preventing free movement of labor into the industry. Moreover, in the presence of entry barriers monopoly power is likely and the benefits from quantitative import restrictions may be greater, which helps to explain North American and western European demands for such restrictions on automobile imports.

The many empirical studies on inter-industry variations in trade barriers have not come up with simple conclusions. In part this is because national trade policies evolve gradually, and at any moment contain many historical artefacts reflecting past rather than present conditions. The mixed results are also due to the complexity of the issue. Nevertheless, some generalizations are possible.

Pressure group theory helps to explain why, despite the net national welfare losses incurred, trade barriers are so prevalent. The redistribution effects are by far the largest domestic consequences of trade barriers, and the gainers are typically better informed and better organized than the losers – especially in the case of final consumption goods, where the losses per individual consumer are small. The gainers will put more effort into lobbying for protection if the gains are higher, organization costs are lower, and potential new entrants and free-riders are few. The success of their lobbying will depend upon the nature of the political system. In practice there are further complications, such as the ease with which redundant factors can exit from an industry (or are they specific to that industry?) or the multinationality of firms. Thus, individual variables are not strong enough determinants to stand out in cross-sectional analysis of trade barriers, but the arguments summarized in this paragraph work well in explaining individual cases (see box 14.1).

14.4   The Role of the Bureaucracy

The pressure group theory explains trade barriers in terms of the interaction between interest groups demanding protection and a government which can supply protection. The government process is often left as a black box; it is sufficient to locate the source of trade policy-making power, without inquiring too closely into policy-makers' own motives. Even in detailed discussions of institutions, such as the analysis of shifts in US trade policy-making power between Congress and the President by Baldwin (1985), the government actors are portrayed as intermediaries (that is, the President for national interests and Congressmen for their constituents' interests), with the simple objective function of maximizing their probability of re-election. The bureaucracy plays a neutral role, simply implementing the trade legislation which the politicians have passed.

Recently, and especially with the post-1974 rise of the "new protectionism" based on NTBs rather than tariffs, trade policies have become more discretionary and the discretionary power has been exercised by nonelected bureaucrats as well as by elected representatives. Resort to NTBs was in part due to international constraints, such as commitments within GATT not to increase tariff rates, but it also reflected a preference by the administrative or executive branch of government for discretion rather than rules, because discretionary policies maximize the policy-makers' influence and power. The increased use of voluntary export restraint agreements has been an important example of the trend toward flexible NTBs. Since the VER is a result of bilateral negotiation, it is difficult for the legislative body to tie the negotiator's hands in advance. The VER is flexible because it can be publicized to head off further domestic demands for protection or it can be kept secret to forestall opposition from opponents of protection. In the US the government switched emphasis from orderly marketing arrangements in the mid-1970s to VERs by the early 1980s because the former had to be published in the "Federal Register" while the latter, being imposed by the foreign government, did not. At the same time President Reagan used highly publicized VERs on automobiles and steel to stop the progress of protectionist measures through Congress or the legal process.

The role of the bureaucracy in trade policy-making varies from country to country. Within the EC the Commission increasingly determines nontariff as well as tariff barriers to imports from outside the Community. In some countries, such as Australia, a quasi-judicial board reviews trade policy. Everywhere the more detailed implementation of trade law is carried out by the customs service. Issues such as the interpretation of conformity to technical standards, the time taken to clear customs, the exact description of a product (for example, a recent dispute arose over whether exports of British telephone booths to the US were to be included in the steel quota) are all regularly taken by government officials, usually in good faith but potentially with a bias toward more or less restrictiveness.

The goals of nonelected officials are likely to differ from the objectives of politicians. Their jobs are usually secure, although they are unlikely to support policies which would make them redundant. Customs departments seldom favor free trade, but even in their role as agents of the law the zeal of customs officials in tracking down smugglers may spill over into unnecessary checks and delays for legal imports. More importantly, where bureaucrats' offices are industry-specific, they will favor measures to increase their industry's size in order to increase their own prestige; the most universal example of this phenomenon is agriculture, which invariably has its own government department, and that department tends to favor protection for any importcompeting branches of agriculture. Even if this is not done consciously, the bureaucrats, by constant association with and exposure to the ideas of producers in their industry, are likely to identify the industry's interests with the national interest; the argument is similar to the "capture" theory, according to which regulatory boards tend to be captured by the industry which they are supposed to be regulating. For all of these reasons the goals of nonelected officials tend to be biased in favor of protecting domestic producers.

Just how important the bureaucracy as an independent influence is in determining trade policy in the market economies is an open question. Even within the EC, where the power of the Commission to determine trade policy by its administration of such complex schemes as the Common Agricultural Policy or the thousands of bilateral agreements under the Multifiber Agreement is substantial, political approval for protectionist trade policies toward agricultural and textiles and clothing imports has been given by the elected national governments. Thus, the bureaucrats do operate within constraints. It is, however, important to bear in mind that any future shift from rules to discretion in trade policy is likely to have a bias in favor of protection.

As a digression from the topic of this chapter, it is an appropriate point to note that advocates of discretionary policies assume efficient implementation. In chapter 10 we saw some reasons why trade barriers may be less efficacious than expected; a further reason is inadequately qualified administrators. For example, arguments based on imperfect competition assume that administrators can identify monopolists' costs curves with some accuracy and then determine the optimum tariff level. In practice the strongest argument against authorizing such actions, even if in principle trade barriers could improve social welfare, is that:

. . . policy is generally formulated by fourth-best economists and administered by third-best economists; it is therefore very unlikely that a second-best welfare optimum will result from policies based on second-best arguments. (Johnson, 1970, p. 101)

This is, of course, no ground for ruling out any interventionist trade policy, but it reinforces the point made in chapter 12 that trade policies are a blunt instrument unsuited to fine tuning. Modern bureaucracies can undoubtedly administer complex trade policy regimes, but their ability to achieve sophisticated goals (as opposed to simply increasing domestic output, reducing consumption, and so on) is questionable.

14.5 International Considerations

Preoccupation with the pressure group approach to trade policy determination has led to a relative disregard for international considerations. Indeed, some economists explicitly state that only domestic variables are significant determinants of tariff structure (see Finger, Hall, and Nelson, 1982, on the US – but see box 14.1). There is, however, some evidence that goods of interest to trading partners with a longer record of bilateral bargaining or participation in multilateral trade negotiations have lower tariffs. This is often claimed to explain the higher tariffs on goods of interest to developing countries, who have largely abstained from GATT negotiations, although this impact is mitigated by the generalized system of tariff preferences (see chapter 15). In the US tariff schedule, tariffs do tend to be higher on goods of greater weight in imports from Japan and lower on goods of greater weight in imports from Canada (Lavergne, 1983).

International considerations are more obviously important in explaining the average level of trade barriers. Domestic variables cannot explain global events such as the move to free trade which culminated in the 1860s or the swing back to protectionism which ended in the 1930s. By far the most important postwar development in trade policies has been the decimation of tariff barriers. The US average (import-weighted) tariff fell from over 50 percent in the early 1930s to less than 5 percent after the Tokyo Round reductions were implemented in the 1980s. The EC's common external tariff is at a similar level, compared to 1931 average levels as high as 69 percent in Spain, 48 percent in Italy, 41 percent in France, and 38 percent in Germany.

There is no generally accepted explanation of the dramatic postwar trade liberalization. The unfavorable experience with protectionism during the 1930s, and the expansive economic conditions of the 1950s and 1960s contributed. So too did the commitment of the US as the leading economic power to a postwar system based on liberal nondiscriminatory trade policies. The institutional arrangements established under the GATT also proved highly successful (see box 14.2). The GATT establishes acceptable trade policies and procedures, and the situations in which retaliatory measures are permissible; thus, despite weak enforcement, there is a credible legal framework. The GATT does not ban trade restrictions but favors tariffs as the least harmful trade barriers, and by binding their tariff rates GATT signatories guarantee one another against increases in tariffs on their exports. In various rounds of multilateral trade negotiations, countries have agreed on reductions in their bound tariffs. The procedure whereby countries negotiated with the leading supplier of a product and then passed on to other countries the tariff reduction granted to the most favored nation ensured substantial tariff-cutting progress in the early rounds. In the Kennedy and Tokyo Rounds, the more drastic approach of establishing formulae for across-the-board tariff reductions, from which countries negotiated mutually acceptable exceptions, was adopted. The GATT provided the framework for multilateral tariff reductions whereby participants shared the gains from trade, while large countries were deterred from trying to use tariffs to improve their terms of trade by the threat of internationally sanctioned and coordinated retaliation.

BOX 14.2   The General Agreement on Tariffs and Trade

In the spring and summer of 1947 the Western allies and some neutral countries met in Geneva to draft the charter for the International Trade Organization (ITO) and simultaneously they negotiated tariff reductions (a pressing need after the protectionism of the 1930s). The agreements were embodied in the General Agreement on Tariffs and Trade (GATT), which was a provisional statement of the principles of the ITO. The ITO Charter agreed upon in Havana in 1948 was never approved by the US Congress, and the idea of an international organization to oversee world trade fell into abeyance, but the provisional GATT was extended as a framework for trade liberalization.

Meanwhile, the 23 GATT signatories and ten other countries met in Annecy in 1949, and further rounds of trade liberalization talks were held in Torquay (1950-1) and Geneva (1956). Other negotiations accompanied the accession of new members (notably Japan in 1955). The last of these bilateral negotiations was the Dillon Round (1960-2). Diminishing returns were being encountered because product-by-product negotiations gave domestic interest groups too much scope for blocking the reduction of trade barriers, so that tariff cuts were only successful when there was no serious harm to import-competing firms (US law forebade American negotiators from cutting tariffs below the "peril point" at which domestic producers would suffer material injury).

The US's 1962 Trade Expansion Act, which abolished the "peril point" principle and authorized sweeping tariff cuts, provided the impetus for the Kennedy Round of multilateral trade negotiations (1964-7). As a result of this round, tariffs on GATT signatories' imports of industrial goods were cut by over a third between 1967 and 1972. The Tokyo Round (1973-9) continued the process of across-the-board tariff reductions on industrial goods, and reached agreement on some nontariff barriers. The Uruguay Round (1986-90) aims to bring neglected areas such as agricultural products, textiles and clothing, and services into (or back into) the GATT and to cover trade-related issues such as intellectual property rights and investment.

The GATT has always had a small staff. As the GATT is extended into more opaque areas of trade policy there is growing pressure for its secretariat to be expanded and for it to be given greater enforcement powers. Stricter surveillance by GATT may reduce trade barriers, but it could also harm GATT's credibility, as national policy-makers have been unwilling to be seen to be granting a supranational body control over their commercial policy (which is why the ITO did not fly). Some commentators believe that part of GATT's success stems from the absence of a large bureaucracy which might become tempted to meddle with the international economic order, and contrast it favorably with the United Nations' economic agencies.

The postwar trade liberalization has, however, been incomplete. Agricultural trade has been largely excluded from GATT negotiations and remains blocked by substantial tariff and nontariff barriers. More recently there has been concern about the failure to extend GATT rules to newly important sectors, notably services. The developing countries have for the most part remained outside GATT negotiations and retain higher rates of protection than the more developed countries, although this has been changing, and by the late 1980s most developing countries had become GATT signatories (see chapter 16). Textile and clothing imports by the more developed countries from "low-wage" countries is covered by the Multifiber Arrangement, which is negotiated under the GATT aegis but contravenes GATT principles by permitting discriminatory quantitative restrictions. Other voluntary export restraint agreements have flourished, especially since the mid-1970s, totally outside GATT. The arguments in the previous sections of this chapter help us to understand why and where these exceptions occur.

Further Reading

Hillman (1989) and Magee, Brock, and Young (1989) are important recent books, which also include surveys of other contributions to the literature on the political economy of trade barriers. On a less technical level, see Bhagwati (1988) and Tumlir (1985).

15

Discriminatory Trade Policies

The analysis so far has concerned policies which affect international trade without distinction among trading partners. Tariffs or quotas have been assumed to apply to all imports regardless of origin, and other nontariff barriers are defined simply as measures which fall unequally on domestic and foreign goods. Yet in practice most nontariff barriers do fall more heavily on some trading partners' goods than on others', and the tariff schedules of all of the major trading nations offer some countries preferential (that is, lower) tariffs.

Nondiscrimination is the fundamental principle underlying the postwar international trading system. Article I of the GATT requires each signatory to treat all other GATT signatories' products as favorably as the most favored nation's products are treated; in other words, if all GATT signatories are given most favored nation (MFN) status then their goods will receive equal treatment. The GATT permits some exceptions to MFN treatment, but these are limited and the overall intent is to create a nondiscriminatory trading system. Contrary to popular opinion, although GATT stands for equal and liberal trade, the former element is foremost in the actual agreement.

The conflict between an international trade agreement based on nondiscrimination and the prevalence of discriminatory trade policies by the signatories of that agreement is at first sight paradoxical, but it can be explained using ideas developed earlier in this book. After a survey of actual discriminatory trade policies, section 15.2 analyzes the consequences of discrimination, concluding that there is a strong case in favor of the MFN principle. The third section then discusses why discriminatory trade policies are so common, offering explanations in terms familiar from chapter 14. The final section summarizes empirical studies on some of the more important discriminatory trading arrangements.

15.1 A Checklist of Discriminatory Trade Policies

Some trade policies mentioned earlier have been explicitly discriminatory.

Voluntary export restraint agreements, for example, apply to goods coming from the specific trading partners with whom agreements are reached. Some VERs may appear in effect to be nondiscriminatory because they cover all suppliers but this is hardly ever the case, not least because the higher prices may encourage new entrants into the international market. Thus the 1981 VERs on Japanese automobile exports to the US and Canada effectively covered all low-priced imports at the time, but within a few years the Japanese suppliers were complaining about discriminatory treatment *vis-à-vis* South Korean automobile exports to Canada. The Multifiber Arrangement aims to cover all low-wage suppliers of textile and clothing items, but it too inevitably discriminates in favor of excluded competitors such as Italy.

Moreover, even when they are not explicitly discriminatory, NTBs tend to be discriminatory in practice. Thus, quantitative restrictions on imports which are not allocated by country tend to favor neighboring countries who can get their goods to the customs-post first and who can react most rapidly to changing quotas. If the so-called "greyhound" system of first come, first allowed in is replaced by a system of national quotas, then these again are likely to be discriminatory. For example, allocating quotas on the basis of existing market shares discriminates in favor of established suppliers and against dynamic new entrants; for example, US steel quotas between 1984 and 1989 protected the US market share of Japanese and EC suppliers, and blocked further increases in market share by South Korea, Brazil, and other newly industrializing countries. Other NTBs may favor culturally and linguistically similar countries at the expense of more exotic trading partners. Thus, even when a government introduces an NTB without intending any discrimination, it is unlikely that incidental discrimination will not occur. This is an additional reason, as well as those already listed in chapter 11, why GATT tries to promote tariffs as the least harmful barriers to imports.

Governments also use tariffs (or NTBs) for the primary purpose of discriminating among trading partners. The distinction between positive and negative discrimination, with MFN treatment as the criterion for non-discrimination, is useful for classifying such policies, although analytically it makes little difference. Negative discrimination usually takes the form of economic sanctions against a country whose policies are considered undesirable. The League of Nations sanctions against Italy after the invasion of Abyssinia, United Nations sanctions against Rhodesia, Arab oil exporters' sanctions against the Netherlands in 1973–4 and the US embargo on grain sales to the USSR after the invasion of Afghanistan are some of the many examples. Other cases of negative discrimination have been longer lasting; for example, the American refusal to grant MFN treatment to most Communist countries so that they continue to face the 1930 Smoot–Hawley tariff. During the 1980s the use of discriminatory trade policies to punish trading partners who were not playing fair was frequently discussed in the US Congress, and occasionally retaliatory measures were actually introduced by the US and other countries in response to unfair trade practices by specific trading partners, although none of these actions degenerated into major trade wars such as had been frequent before 1939.

In the postwar era most deviations from MFN treatment having the primary purpose of discrimination have involved positive discrimination. The simplest form has involved charging less than MFN tariffs on imports from specified sources. For example, all the more developed countries have schemes under the generalized system of preferences (GSP) for offering favored access to developing country exports, and some offer more far-reaching tariff preferences to subgroups of developing countries (such as the EC to African, Caribbean, and Pacific countries under the Lomé Convention and to Mediterranean countries, the US to Caribbean Basin countries under the CBERA, and Australia and New Zealand to certain Pacific islands under SPARTECA). Preferential trading arrangements may also be bilateral; for example, members of the Association of Southeast Asian Nations (ASEAN) offer preferential tariff treatment to one another's exports.

A more far-reaching bilateral arrangement is a free trade area, in which each member's goods enter other members' markets duty-free while each country maintains its own trade policy toward nonmembers: the European Free Trade Association (EFTA) is an example. The problem with a simple free trade area is that it encourages *trade deflection*: imports from nonmembers will be routed via the member with the lowest tariff and then transshipped to the eventual destination. Especially where the members are contiguous and hence the extra transport costs of such indirect routing are minor, the member states cease to have independent trade policies because the low-tariff country determines the height of trade barriers and receives all the tariff revenue. The trade deflection problem can be solved by establishing rules of origin; that is, formal criteria for determining the nationality of a good (typically, a minimum proportion of the good's value must have been added in a country). Similar rules are also required for simple preferential trading schemes to stop, say, a European exporter shipping goods to the US via Mexico in order to claim GSP treatment. In these cases discriminatory policies involve higher administration costs because customs officials need to control not only whether a good is imported but also where it is imported from. There is also the possibility that rules of origin may become a trade barrier as well as a means of defining a good's nationality (the discussions of local content laws in chapter 11 and of the globalization of production in chapter 7 are relevant here).

Other forms of positive discrimination involve some loss of national sovereignty. A customs union is a free trade area in which the members have a common trade policy towards nonmembers; this avoids trade deflection, but requires agreement on the common policy and on the use of tariff revenues, since some countries (for example, those with ports, such as Belgium or the Netherlands in the EC) would receive a disproportionate share. If the customs union is accompanied by free movement of factors of production between member countries, then it is known as a common market. An economic union exists if a common market is characterized also by union-wide economic policies. The taxonomy customs union/common market/economic union can be viewed as steps toward or degrees of economic integration, although in practice the steps need not follow sequentially. Moreover, the categories are indicative rather than clear-cut; the EC is an incomplete common market with some common economic policies (such as toward agriculture), whereas federal nations such as Australia, Canada, or the US have most features of an economic union but still have some barriers to interstate or interprovincial movement of goods or factors (for example, state public procurement policies or incomplete recognition of professional qualifications from other states). The taxonomy does, however, remind us of the point made in chapter 1 about the analytic distinction between international and domestic trade not being completely clear-cut. In today's world it is, for example, becoming increasingly difficult to decide whether Franco-German trade within the EC needs to be treated more like Ontario–Quebec trade within Canada, or trade between two nations with independent trade policies.

The discriminatory trade policies described in this section cover a large part of international trade. The EC is especially important in this context because roughly a quarter of international trade is intra-EC trade, and a quarter is EC members' external trade. The external trade policy is characterized by a network of preferential trading arrangements: a free trade area in manufactured goods with EFTA, the Lomé Convention, preferential agreements with all Mediterranean nonmember countries except Libya and Albania, GSP treatment for other developing countries, and special arrangements for goods from other Communist countries. In sum, the EC's common external tariff only applies to seven countries: Australia, Canada, Japan, New Zealand, South Africa, Taiwan, and the US! Other countries have maintained a stronger commitment to the MFN principle, but they too have geographically discriminatory policies. Even the US, the main postwar defender of the nondiscrimination principle, has special treatment for Communist countries, a sectoral free trade agreement with Canada for automobiles, a GSP scheme, the Caribbean Basin preferences, a free trade area with Israel, and the various VERs, as well as being in the process of implementing a free trade agreement with Canada and negotiating new arrangements with Mexico. All told, over half of world trade today is carried out under other than MFN treatment – and in this situation MFN treatment itself ceases to be nondiscriminatory.

BOX 15.1   Key Steps on the Road to Western European Economic Integration

In 1950 the French government made the momentous decision to work for a rapprochement with Germany. The first step was the signing of the European Coal and Steel Community Treaty in April 1951, which placed coal and steel production under a supranational High Authority. Italy and the Benelux countries also signed the Treaty, but other European countries refused to accept any supranational authority over these industries.

In 1955 the foreign ministers of the six ECSC countries met in Messina and set up a committee to report on the possibility of a common market and sectoral integration in transport and energy. The committee's work culminated in the Rome Treaties establishing the European Economic Community and Euratom. Seven other European countries, opposed to the common commercial and agricultural policies in the Rome Treaty, responded with the 1959 Stockholm Treaty establishing the European Free Trade Association.

During the 1960s the EEC successfully completed the dismantling of tariffs on trade among its members, established a Common Agricultural Policy, and participated actively and with a single voice in the Kennedy Round. It became increasingly obvious that the mainstream of western European integration was centered in the EEC's working capital, Brussels. In 1961 Britain, Denmark, and Norway applied for EEC membership, but Britain's application was vetoed by France and the other applications lapsed. A second British application was successful and in 1973 Britain, Denmark, and Ireland became EEC members (Norway's membership was rejected by her voters).

The Nine member countries gradually became more economically integrated and increased their political coordination. In 1979 eight of the members (the UK was the exception) formed the European Monetary System to reduce fluctuations in their bilateral exchange rates. In recognition that the Nine members were moving beyond a simple customs union the word "economic" was increasingly omitted from the Community's title.

After the ending of dictatorships in Greece, Portugal, and Spain, these countries applied for EC membership. Greece became a member in

1981, and Spain and Portugal in 1986. The EC of 12 now includes all of western Europe apart from the "neutrals" (the remaining EFTA members: Austria, Switzerland, Sweden, Finland, and Norway) and the island economies (Iceland, Cyprus, and Malta), which are linked to the EC by free trade agreements.

For trade policy purposes the economic integration of western Europe is essentially complete. Many NTBs are still administered at the national level and impede internal trade, but the EC is actively working to reduce these – arousing some fear among nonmembers of trade diversion effects, and perhaps even surreptitious increases in the NTBs facing outsiders. Nevertheless, the trade policy independence of the EC's member states is now severely limited, and the coverage of the EC's common commercial policy is similar to that of federal states.

15.2 Economic Analysis of Discriminatory Trade Policies

The simplest framework in which to analyze a discriminatory trade policy is to assume that one country, A, offers another country, B, duty-free access while maintaining its existing tariff on imports from other sources. Assume that A is a small country and imports from both B and the rest of the world have perfectly elastic supply curves over the relevant range. Figure 15.1 illustrates the case where the price of B's good, P_b, lies between the world price, P_w, and the tariff-inclusive price in country A, P_d; if P_b were greater than P_d the preferential tariff would have no impact, and if B were the least-cost supplier (that is, $P_b = P_w$) then the impact would be the same as that of removing all tariffs analyzed in chapter 10.

The effect of A's discriminatory trade policy is to bring the domestic price down to P_b and to increase A's imports from Q_2Q_3 to Q_1Q_4. All of these imports now come from B, whose exports to A have increased for three reasons:

- B's goods displace some domestically produced goods Q_1Q_2
- lower prices have stimulated increased consumption Q_3Q_4
- B's goods displace imports from other sources Q_2Q_3

The first two components are the familiar production and consumption effects of reducing trade barriers, and yield the usual gains from trade, but the third component is the distinctive feature of a discriminatory trade policy

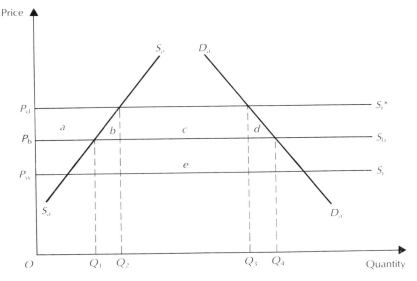

Figure 15.1 Partial equilibrium analysis of discrimination with a perfectly elastic supply of imports. S_a and D_a are domestic demand and supply curves in A. S_b is the supply of imports from the preferred source, B, which is perfectly elastic at a price P_b. S_r is the supply of imports from the rest of the world, and P_w is the world price; S_r^* is the tariff-inclusive supply curve, and P_d is the pre-preference domestic price in A.

and its welfare consequences are negative because B is not the least-cost supplier of the good. Thus, the crucial distinction in analyzing discriminatory trade policies is between their trade-creating consequences and their trade-diverting consequences.

The net welfare effect on the importing country of giving preferential treatment to imports from certain trading partners is ambiguous. In figure 15.1 the gain in consumer surplus and loss in producer surplus are the familiar areas $(a + b + c + d)$ and a, but the foregone tariff revenue is $(c + e)$, so that the net welfare gain is $(b + d - e)$, the sign of which is ambiguous. Thus, the distribution of gains and losses appears similar to a nondiscriminatory tariff reduction, the welfare triangles representing the efficiency gains associated with the production and consumption effects remain, but the net welfare effects are uncertain because not all of the foregone tariff revenue accrues to domestic consumers. Measuring the welfare effects requires similar data to the measurement studies described in chapter 13, plus knowledge of the difference between the price of imports from B and the world price. The closer B's price is to the world price, the less likely the net welfare effects are to be negative.

In sum, a preferential tariff reduction increases international trade but may increase or reduce the importing country's net national welfare. The source of the welfare ambiguity is that, although trade is freed between B and A, allowing goods in A's market to be supplied by the cheapest supplier in either country, a new distortion is introduced. The new distortion arises because purchasers in A compare the tariff-free price of a good from B with the tariff-inclusive price of goods from other countries. Consequently, imports may not be purchased from the least-cost source worldwide. There are welfare gains to A from buying goods from B which were produced more expensively domestically or which were not demanded at A's old price, but there are welfare costs from buying imports from a higher-cost supplier; in this way of expressing it, the positive consequences of trade creation contrast clearly with the negative consequences of trade diversion.

The crucial distinction between trade creation and trade diversion was first made explicitly by Viner (1950). Before Viner both free traders and protectionists argued in favor of, for example, customs unions; the former seeing only the benefits of free intra-union trade, and the latter emphasizing the benefits of protection from nonmembers' goods. Viner clarified such debates by showing that no generalization about the net welfare effect of a discriminatory tariff reduction is possible; each case must be assessed individually.

The fundamental economic cost of discriminatory trade policies is the resource misallocation due to trade diversion. Any discriminatory increase in trade barriers, starting from a situation of nondiscrimination, must be harmful because it involves trade destruction as well as trade diversion. Discriminatory reductions in trade barriers may be welfare-improving because of the positive trade creation effects. In figure 15.1, however, even if the preferential treatment of B's goods is welfare-improving for A, it is clearly not the first-best trade policy. By reducing all tariffs on an MFN basis so that the domestic price fell to P_b, country A could have a net welfare gain equal to the two triangles, $b + d$, and retain area e as tariff revenue. Even better would be to unilaterally eliminate tariffs gaining the maximum benefits from trade creation without any trade diversion costs. The conclusion that unilateral tariff elimination must be at least as beneficial as a preferential tariff reduction (the Johnson–Cooper–Massell proposition; see Johnson, 1965) is rather paradoxical given the proliferation of preferential tariff reductions described in the previous section.

The small-country analysis in figure 15.1 is useful because it highlights the trade creation/trade diversion distinction, but it is an incomplete guide to why discriminatory trade policies exist. Indeed, the Johnson–Cooper–Massell proposition implies that A would do better not to pursue such policies and the horizontal import supply curves imply zero welfare effect on B or on other countries, so there is no advantage to anybody from instigating discriminatory trade policies. The main omission from figure 15.1 is the lack of any inter-country distributional effects, which surely lie behind most policies favoring some trading partners over others. This omission can be remedied most simply by introducing upward-sloping export supply curves for B and for the rest of the world.

The analysis of A granting duty-free access to B's goods while retaining its existing tariff on other imports is illustrated, for the upward-sloping exports supply curves case, in figure 15.2. To keep the diagram as uncluttered as possible, A's domestic demand and supply curves are combined in the import demand curve D_a, and B's export supply curve is not drawn separately (it is equal to the horizontal distance between A's total import supply curve, $S_r + S_b$, and the supply of imports from the rest of the world, S_r). The tariff is assumed to be a specific duty; in other words, tariff-inclusive import supply curves (marked with asterisks) are parallel to the correspond-

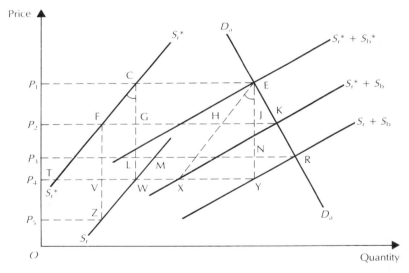

Figure 15.2 Partial equilibrium analysis of discrimination with upward-sloping supply curves. D_a is A's import demand. S_b is the supply of imports from preferred sources, and S_r is the supply of imports from the rest of the world; $S_b{}^*$ and $S_r{}^*$ are the same including A's tariff. Assuming no nontariff barriers or transport costs and no exchange rates changes, E, K, and R represent demand/supply equilibria with A's tariff, with free access for B's goods and without A's tariff, and P_1, P_2, and P_3 are the corresponding domestic prices. P_4 is the price received by exporters to A when A's tariff is in place, and P_5 is the price received by nonpreferred exporters to A when B receives preferential access.

ing tariff-exclusive import supply curves with the vertical distance between them equal to the duty; an *ad valorem* tariff would be represented by differing slopes for the tariff-inclusive and tariff-exclusive curves and the qualitative analysis would be similar to what follows.

With a uniform tariff P_1P_4 the domestic price in A is P_1 (equivalent to P_d in figure 15.1) and A imports CE units from B and P_1C units from the rest of the world. After granting duty-free access to B, A's imports increase by the amount JK, and A imports FK units from B and P_2F units from the rest of the world. The price effects are more complex than in figure 15.1, because A pays more for the goods now purchased from B (that is, P_2 instead of P_4), and less for goods still coming from other suppliers (P_5 instead of P_4). We can still refer to trade creation and trade diversion, which are equal to JK and FG respectively, but it is more difficult to refer in general to the least-cost supplier or to invoke the concept of a world price, since prices are not independent of A's policies.

The welfare analysis of the preferential tariff is also more complex in figure 15.2 because it is no longer only the importing country whose welfare is affected. The preferred trading partner, B, benefits unambiguously because it receives a higher price on its existing exports plus producer surplus on its additional exports (GJYW + HKX); both the trade creation and the trade diversion components of B's increased exports benefit that country, in addition to B receiving a partial transfer of A's tariff revenue on her existing exports. The rest of the world loses because it receives a lower price on its remaining exports plus losing producer surplus on exports diverted to B (that is, P_4VZP_5 + VWZ). The welfare effect for A consists of an increased surplus as importer, P_1EKP_2, offset by a reduction in tariff revenue from P_1EYP_4 to P_2FZP_5. Cancelling out overlapping areas in figure 15.2 the net welfare effect on A is as follows:

$$\text{net welfare effect on A} = \text{EJK} - \text{FGWV} - \text{GJYW} + P_4VZP_5, \qquad (15.1)$$

where EJK is the counterpart of the two triangles ($b + d$) and FGWV is the uncompensated tariff revenue loss in figure 15.1, but these are augmented by terms of trade losses (on imports from B) and gains (on imports from the rest of the world). The net welfare effect on A remains ambiguously signed, so the main conclusion from figure 15.1 remains valid.

The analysis with upward-sloping supply curves provides several important insights obscured by the small-country framework of figure 15.1. Because B definitely benefits from the discriminatory trade policy and A may benefit, there are stronger motives for such a policy to be adopted. A nondiscriminatory elimination of A's tariff would be less beneficial to B because her exports to A would sell at a lower price, P_3 instead of P_2. Even for

A, it is unclear whether the discriminatory trade policy is second-best because part of the benefits, the terms of trade gain at the rest of the world's expense (P_4VZP_5), could not be realized by nondiscriminatory tariff elimination; the Johnson–Cooper–Massell proposition no longer holds. The rest of the world, however, would prefer nondiscriminatory trade reductions or no change in A's trade policy rather than discrimination in favor of B. Thus, discriminatory trade policies almost always arouse discontent and bitterness among countries discriminated against.

Finally, the global welfare effects remain ambiguous. If all countries' welfare is equally weighted, then:

$$\text{net global welfare effect} = \text{EKY} - \text{GVZW}. \tag{15.2}$$

The first expression in (15.2) captures the resource allocation benefits from trade creation and the second expression the resource misallocation costs due to trade diversion. Nondiscriminatory elimination of A's tariff would be a superior policy from the global welfare perspective, since it would maximize the trade creation benefits (to ERY) while eliminating trade diversion, so that in a cosmopolitan sense the Johnson–Cooper–Massell proposition remains valid. In sum, nondiscrimination is a good guideline for international trade law but there will often be incentives for individual countries to make discriminatory trading arrangements. Some of these arrangements may be global-welfare-improving so it is difficult to castigate them, but they will be second-best ways to raise global welfare and they will be harmful to nonparticipating countries.

15.3   The Reasons for Discriminatory Trade Policies

Four sets of explanations lie behind the introduction of discriminatory trade policies. They are not equally important and any particular discriminatory arrangement may involve more than one category of explanation, but the fourfold classification helps to separate distinct motivations.

Firstly, any of the arguments in favor of trade barriers presented in chapter 12 can be adapted to discriminatory trade policies. In principle the optimal tariff, the size of which depends on the import supply elasticity, could be finely tuned by applying different tariff rates to imports from suppliers with different elasticities, just as a discriminating monopolist can earn higher profits than a nondiscriminating monopolist whenever markets can be segmented. The revenue motive may lie behind customs union formation if there are scale economies in tariff collection. For example, it has been argued that smaller German states joined the Zollverein in the 1830s because tariffs were the main source of government revenue, but administration costs were high relative to collected revenue where boundaries were long relative to the state's area and population. In today's world the only one of these arguments which is significant for explaining actual discriminatory trade policies is the argument for protecting specific activities. As seen in chapter 12 this is a second-best argument insofar as trade policy is not the best instrument, and as seen in this chapter discriminatory trade policies are second-best trade policies because they involve undesired trade diversion. Moreover, if the policy is very discriminatory it will fail to achieve the protectionist goal because the trade barrier will not exclude substitute suppliers of imports. This is well-recognized by participants, and the domestic industry would always prefer a general import quota to a system of voluntary export restraint agreements, although the latter is often adopted to avoid contravening the letter of GATT and to bribe exporting countries to accept the restriction. In practice, however, VERs are only stable if they cover all major actual and potential suppliers which ultimately requires their globalization into practically universal restrictions (as in the Multifiber Arrangement).

Secondly, discriminatory trade policies may be used as bargaining chips to obtain better market access for a country's exports. Because countries discriminated against unambiguously lose from discriminatory trade policies, this is at first sight an attractive approach. Historically, however, the bargaining approach has not enjoyed great success. After gaining independence, the US only granted MFN treatment to trading partners who in return offered at least as good treatment to American exports as the most favored nation granted. This so-called conditional MFN treatment was abandoned by the US after World War I as being ineffective and counterproductive; American exports received worse access to third markets than British exports did, despite the Britons making no bargaining use of discriminatory trade policies (all goods from all sources entered Britain duty-free apart from a few excise duties on liquors, and so on), and the conditional MFN treatment aroused frequent feelings of dissatisfaction among America's trading partners who felt unfairly discriminated against with respect to some export or another. A similar bargaining approach was adopted by France after 1918, but had been abandoned by 1927 in the face of retaliation. The postwar GATT system is based on unconditional MFN treatment and, although retaliation is permitted against countries adopting unfair trade policies, its use is strictly circumscribed.

During the 1980s there was growing sentiment in the US for going beyond these limits in applying discriminatory penalties to trading partners who did not play "fair" – the principal target being Japan – but so far such "reciprocity" legislation has failed to become law, although US (and other countries') anti-dumping and countervailing duties could be viewed as harking back to the conditional MFN view that only trading partners who play fair deserve fair treatment. Proponents of conditional MFN treatment or the use of discriminatory trade policies as bargaining chips usually claim that their ultimate goal is freer trade, and that any debate is about means rather than ends. The cooperative approach adopted since 1947 does, however, seem a superior means of achieving more liberal trade policies; unilateral interpretations of what constitute "fair" trade policies often diverge and are biased against foreigners, whose markets always seem harder to enter because of idiosyncratic business practices and so on, so that punitive measures breed resentment rather than leading to the desired change in the trading partner's policies.

Thirdly, since most of the arrangements described in section 15.1 involve positive discrimination, actual discriminatory trade policies appear to give greater weight to the benefits for the preferred exporter than to the global net welfare loss. The general acceptance of tariff preferences for developing countries can be viewed in this light. For a small developing country, receiving duty-free access to a developed country's market yields unambiguous welfare benefits. In figure 15.3 these benefits are divided into

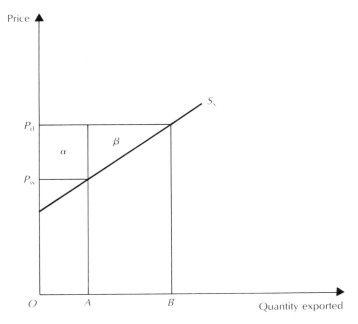

Figure 15.3 Trade preferences for a small country. S_x is the preference recipient's export supply curve, P_w is the export price received without the trade preferences, and P_d is the price received with the trade preference.

the transfer of tariff revenue, α, and the rent on additional exports, β. Even if the export supply is highly inelastic, the developing country receives α, which could be viewed as untied foreign aid, and by imposing an export tax equal to the developed country's tariff $(P_d - P_w)$ this could be turned into a simple government-to-government transfer. Thus, it is not surprising that developing countries lobbied hard for GSP during the 1960s, and continue to support GSP or other one-way preferential tariff schemes even when the coverage is made more and more restrictive by the importing country. If the main aim is to increase developing countries' welfare, the aspect of GSP which really matters is the degree to which these countries' exports are covered and stimulated by GSP, while the trade creation/trade diversion issue becomes relatively unimportant. These issues will be discussed in greater detail in the next section.

Once price changes are considered, it is possible that two-way discriminatory trading arrangements may be mutually beneficial for the participants, while the net costs are passed on to the rest of the world. In principle, formation of a customs union could shift the members' aggregate offer curve *vis-à-vis* the rest of the world in either direction. Under some not very restrictive assumptions, however, a customs union which does not change greatly members' terms of trade with one another can be shown to improve the union's terms of trade with the rest of the world (Mundell, 1964). This may be important in practice because successful customs unions are often based upon roughly reciprocal "concessions." Such a situation, in which a group of countries benefits at the expense of the rest of the world, again reveals why discriminatory trade policies breed political antagonism.

Fourthly, and finally, discriminatory trade policies may be adopted for noneconomic reasons. Such policies affect trade patterns and may be used to create or maintain spheres of influence; for example, Germany's policies toward southeast Europe in the 1930s or the EC's policies towards Africa and the Mediterranean region. Developed countries' acceptance of GSP was also political; whether or not acquiescing to developing countries' complaints about the inequalities of the international economic system, the donors accepted GSP as a policy involving minor costs to themselves in return for not stoking up developing country dissatisfaction. Economic sanctions aimed at achieving political change in the target country also fall under this category. In all of these cases it makes little sense to denigrate the policies on narrowly economic grounds, although since they all involve resource misallocation costs to at least one of the principals it is valid to calculate the economic costs of the policy, and hence question its cost-effectiveness in achieving the desired political goal. Some actions, of course, do not even achieve their goal, in which case they incur economic costs for no political benefit. Finally, some positive discrimination policies may be preludes to political integration, such as the German Zollverein or perhaps the EC, and as such have clearly to be judged on different criteria.

These four sets of arguments explain why discriminatory trade policies are so prevalent, but they do not justify such policies. Many of the arguments have serious logical or practical flaws. The strongest arguments are in terms of national benefits to participants at the expense of nonparticipants, and are thus confrontational. The basic difficulty is that most discriminatory trading arrangements involve some trade diversion, involving resource misallocation and reduction in global income. Even net global-welfare-increasing arrangements involve distributional effects which create in some countries real or perceived feelings of being disadvantaged. Thus the economic and political costs of discriminatory trade policies emphasized in this and the previous section are important, and provide support for a strong presumption that such policies are against the global interest, even when they are in some countries' perceived national interests.

15.4 Empirical Evidence

The basic problem in measuring the effects of discriminatory trade policies, as opposed to the nondiscriminatory policies dealt with in chapter 13, is the complexity of dealing with trade diversion as well as trade creation. Either separate export supply elasticities for preferred and nonpreferred suppliers (as in figure 15.2) or the elasticity of substitution between imports from different sources must be estimated. This is a significant added data requirement over the methods described in section 13.1.

By far the most studied discriminatory trading arrangement is the European Community's customs union in manufactured goods. Use of the partial equilibrium approach of figure 15.1 inevitably finds trade creation benefits close to the benefits from general tariff elimination by EC members, because for most goods at least one member is likely to be producing at near the world price. This is confirmed by many *ex post* studies, which compare actual trade flows with what they would have been in the absence of the EC. These studies vary in sophistication and their value depends upon how well the counterfactual no-EC situation is set up, but the recurring findings are of trade creation exceeding trade diversion and of the welfare effects being small relative to GNP.

The empirical results bring some comfort to European federalists (the common market did increase intra-EC tradeflows), but they are often disappointed with the magnitudes and argue that something has been omitted. Attempts to incorporate scale economies or dynamic changes in efficiency due to the EC's formation have, however, met with little success. It should not be surprising in light of section 13.2 that removing intra-EC tariffs did not have a large economic effect; MFN tariffs have become small, and reductions in nontariff barriers (as planned in the "1992" program) would have a greater impact.

Most empirical studies on the EC have focused on the original six members' customs union in manufactured goods. The EC's Common Agricultural Policy, put in place by the end of the 1960s, incorporated the principle of protecting the least-efficient EC producer; in other words, it was designed to exclude trade creation and may have led to considerable trade diversion. Subsequent nontariff barriers, in textiles and clothing and in automobiles for example, have also increased the trade diversion associated with the EC's common market by favoring the EC's least-cost supplier at the expense of lower-cost Asian suppliers.

There have been few attempts to measure the terms of trade effects of the EC. A study by Petith (1977), using a simplified version of Mundell's 1964 model, found terms of trade gains for the original six members worth between 0.3 percent and 1.0 percent of their GNP; that is, well above the welfare gains from trade creation. Sampson and Snape (1980) have estimated even more dramatic welfare transfers from nonmembers to EC members in agricultural trade. These measures are rough approximations, but they do suggest that while formation of the EC may have improved global welfare through trade creation, the customs union has also had substantial international welfare redistribution effects.

Other customs unions have been less durable than the EC. An important reason is that in these other cases significant trade diversion has not been offset by transfers from nonmembers. Members of the East African Community and of the Central American Common Market hoped to stimulate industrialization by forming a customs union which would allow greater realization of scale economies within the protected regional market. In both cases, less industrially developed members (for example, Tanzania and Honduras) grew dissatisfied with buying high-priced products from their partners, while their own industrial sectors did not seem to be growing. There were mechanisms for redistributing the gains, but the other member countries were reluctant to share their own slim benefits.

Economic considerations are not the only determinant of customs unions' success or failure. The UK joined the EC despite predictions of economic welfare loss which proved well-founded; the limited trade creation in manufactures was overshadowed by the huge economic costs of replacing the UK's relatively efficient system of national agricultural subsidies by the EC-wide support price system of the Common Agricultural Policy. Clearly, in the minds of most policy-makers and voters in the UK, the political desire to be part of the European Community outweighed the economic costs.

Empirical studies of other discriminatory trade policies have emphasized aspects other than the welfare effects. A recurring finding is that discriminatory trade barriers do affect trade flows. The magnitude of the impact depends upon the height of the trade barrier, the elasticity of substitution between favored and nonfavored trade partners' goods, and the export supply elasticities. This is apparent from the EC's trade preferences for imports from Mediterranean countries and from African, Caribbean, and Pacific signatories to the Lomé Convention; countries in the first group have responded more to trade preferences than have the Lomé countries, who tend to have very low supply elasticities, and preferential treatment has had the most significant impact in heavily protected areas such as textiles and clothing and automobiles.

The generalized system of preferences for developing countries has been particularly heavily studied. The declared goal of GSP schemes is to stimulate manufactured exports from developing countries. All studies conclude that such exports are higher than they would have been in the absence of GSP, but the amounts are rather small (in the order of a 2–3 percent increase). The reason for these meagre benefits is the schemes' many restrictions – in the definition of developing countries, in the products included, and in setting ceilings on the quantity which can be imported at the preferential rate – all of which are donor-determined. The ceilings are defended on the grounds that a country selling large amounts of a product no longer needs the help of lower tariffs, but this penalizes countries which do expand exports and discourages investment to expand exports on the basis of GSP tariff rates. Similar reasoning underlies the US decision to "graduate" Hong Kong, Singapore, South Korea, and Taiwan from its GSP scheme in 1989. The pattern behind the exclusions is that they cut out products and countries which provide serious competition for producers in the importing country (for example, textiles and clothing and leather goods are almost universally excluded from GSP schemes, but jet aircraft are not). Thus, we might expect most of the (rather limited) developing country exports induced by GSP to be trade diversion rather than trade creation. A study by Baldwin and Murray (1977) reached the opposite conclusion, but their results have been criticized because they assumed a low elasticity of substitution between GSP beneficiaries and nonbeneficiaries (and hence guaranteed low estimates of trade diversion). Later studies (for example, Karsenty and Laird, 1987) found more trade diversion, which implies that GSP schemes are globally-welfare-reducing but that beneficiaries would suffer if GSP were ended without compensation. A trade diversion bias in GSP schemes also explains the developing countries' suspicion of multilateral tariff reductions under GATT, which erode the GSP preference margins; however small the benefits from GSP, they are straightforward (see figure 15.3) and are at risk if the nonpreferential tariff rates are reduced. This suspicion does, however, appear to be diminishing as the Uruguay Round negotiations address areas of special interest to developing countries (for example, textiles and clothing and agriculture) and as the value of GSP schemes is reduced by a lengthening list of exclusions.

Further Reading

Important original contributions to the theory of discriminatory trade policies are those of Viner (1950, pp. 43–4), Mundell (1964), and Kemp and Wan (1976). For recent surveys of theoretical and empirical work, see Pomfret (1988) and Robson (1984).

16

International Trade and Economic Development

Before the 1940s little interest was shown in the economic problems of poorer countries. The classical economists such as Adam Smith, David Ricardo, J. S. Mill, and Karl Marx had been concerned with long-term economic growth, but almost exclusively in the context of the most developed countries. After the 1870s the neoclassical revolution in economic theory focused attention on resource allocation (and it was this approach which came to dominate international trade theory). The Keynesian revolution of the 1930s reawakened interest in macroeconomic matters, but in short-term disequilibrium rather than long-run structural change and economic growth.

Meanwhile, Asia, Africa, and Latin America had been drawn into the global trading network. The trade of these regions increased rapidly as transport costs fell with the spread of railways in the third quarter of the nineteenth century, and with falling long-distance shipping costs in the final quarter of the century. Such specialization by comparative advantage between regions of widely differing resource endowments permitted a higher level of global welfare.

In the early stages of this process there can be serious doubts about the universal desirability of international trade, especially when cultures were destroyed or in the extreme case of the slave trade when people became commodities whose welfare received no consideration. By the late nineteenth and early twentieth centuries the distributional inequities were less blatant and a more justified optimism about global progress was possible. The optimism was shattered after 1928 when primary product prices plummeted, and *per capita* income fell drastically in areas dependent on exporting such products.

Three forces contributed to the birth of "development economics" as a separate branch of economics in the 1940s. The adverse experience of the 1930s led many policy-makers, academics, and other commentators to reject the *laissez-faire* policies previously pursued and to seek justification for alternative non-market-dependent policies; this was especially visible in the already independent countries of Latin America. Secondly, the Anglo-

American architects of the postwar international economic order were concerned that economic forces had contributed to the outbreak of war and, as a small part of their efforts to create a better postwar world, a study group was set up to examine the economic problems facing the poorer countries of the world;[1] problems which would become more pressing as the colonial empires broke up. Thirdly, the emphasis of Keynesian economics on special cases (based on empirical observation) encouraged *ad hoc* reasoning and a questioning of the universality of neoclassical theory based on a few simple assumptions.

During the 1950s development economists challenged the applicability of neoclassical trade theory (that is, the theory set out in chapters 3–5 of this book) to developing countries. They questioned the benefits of international trade and recommended policies to limit exposure to world markets. The first three sections of this chapter examine these arguments and the consequences of inward-oriented development strategies. In the 1960s a few developing countries adopted strategies based on manufactured export expansion, and these countries' economic success encouraged wider reliance on more outward-oriented policies during the 1970s and 1980s. The consequences of such a development strategy are analyzed in section 16.4, and the risks posed by the trade barriers of industrialized countries are discussed in section 16.5.

16.1 Does Trade Theory Apply to Less-developed Countries?

The notion that neoclassical trade theory does not apply to less-developed countries (LDCs) was extremely popular during the 1950s. It had a major influence on LDCs' trade policies during that decade, and the influence has lasted until today in some countries. Although this view is now largely discredited, it is still useful to review the arguments and their shortcomings before examining the trade policies based upon it.

Neoclassical trade theory was criticized for being "static," dealing with resource allocation at a single point in time, whereas the concerns of the LDCs were "dynamic," having to do with economic growth and structural change. For the leading development economists of the 1950s the central problem for an LDC was to direct resources into capital formation in order to increase future output. The "static" nature of the trade theory set out in part I of this book does not, however, disqualify it from being useful in this

---

[1] A report by the head of this study group (Rosenstein-Rodan, 1943) was the first paper to use the term "underdeveloped" countries.

context. Specialization according to comparative advantage yields gains from trade which increase the resources available for investment. Moreover, as mentioned several times earlier in this book, international trade may have powerful indirect effects, exposing people to new ideas and technology which will shift out the production possibility frontier.

The main reason for rejecting the applicability of neoclassical trade theory to LDCs was widespread belief that LDCs' economies were structurally different from those of more developed countries. The belief was reflected in the rapid acceptance of terms such as LDCs or the Third World (after "underdeveloped" or "backward" countries had been discarded as too patronizing), and of the idea that a clear distinction could be drawn between this group of countries and the more developed countries, even though there were always some dubious borderline cases (such as Kuwait, some southern European countries, or even Japan during the 1950s). Third World countries were seen to be characterized by structural, institutional, or sociological rigidities which limited the flexibility of response to price changes. The neoclassical model, in which the price mechanism plays a central role, thus appeared of doubtful applicability to LDCs. These ideas have been generally abandoned, as historical experience has shown even the most traditional farmers to be price-responsive when it is rational to be so, and as it has become more obvious that not all LDCs have the same economic structure. Nevertheless, the popularity of these ideas during the 1950s had a major influence on policy-making in LDCs, as we shall see in the next two sections.

With respect to trade policy there was a continuing belief, born of the 1930s experience, that a liberal international trade system does not work in the LDCs' favor. There are intrinsic problems arising from the nature of LDCs' exports. Countries specializing in goods the demand and supply of which is price-inelastic will experience large fluctuations in their export prices, and if demand is income-inelastic the fluctuations will be around a long-run trend of deteriorating terms of trade. Whether or not this is true for an individual country or for LDCs as a whole is an empirical matter. In principle, arguments can be made either way about the long-run terms of trade; postwar development economists thought they moved against primary product exporters (which they identified with the LDCs), but earlier in this century British economists had worried that the long-run terms of trade would move in favor of primary product exporters because of the diminishing marginal productivity of land (an argument which reappeared in the 1970s after food and oil shortages occurred). In addition to problems associated with the commodity composition of LDCs' exports, these countries may also face difficulties in international markets due to the trade policies of the more developed countries. Such difficulties may arise from the general exercise of market power by the major trading nations or from specific features of their trade policies; for example, high effective rates of protection on processed raw materials or simple manufactures which discourage the type of export diversification most feasible for LDCs. Whether or not these difficulties are sufficient to invalidate outward-oriented trade policies by LDCs is again an empirical matter.

In sum, there is no justification for the view that trade theory does not apply to all countries. The method of analysis and general policy conclusions of part III are as applicable to poor countries as to rich countries, whether their government's goal is to maximize present or future welfare. Specific conclusions may of course vary from country to country, as the application of trade theory depends upon the conditions of the specific case (for example, for some LDCs, as for any country, trade barriers may be justified by the optimum tariff or export tax argument of section 12.1). Some arguments in support of trade barriers may be more applicable to poorer countries than to richer countries, especially if first-best policies are difficult to apply because of poorly developed administrative capabilities: for example, administering subsidies is more difficult than taxing imports if there are many domestic producers and few ports of entry; or raising revenue by income or sales taxes is more difficult than by trade taxes if a large part of output is nonmarketed as in subsistence-farming-based LDCs. On the other hand, most LDCs are "small" countries in the technical sense of being unable to influence world prices, particularly with respect to their imports, so there remains the presumption that free trade is likely to be the best trade policy. The political economy considerations analyzed in chapter 14 are also relevant to LDCs, and trade barriers may be cloaked in seemingly rational arguments to promote sectional interests while damaging the national interest.

16.2   Is International Trade an Engine of Growth?

Ragnar Nurkse, one of the most prominent development economists of the 1950s, popularized the view that international trade had been an engine of growth in the nineteenth century for countries such as Great Britain, the US, and Canada, but in the twentieth century conditions had changed so that the current LDCs could no longer rely on the trade engine. Meanwhile, Raul Prebisch and Hans Singer highlighted the declining terms of trade facing primary product exporters, a further reason for not relying on traditional exports as a source of economic growth. How valid was this pessimism about LDCs' participation in international trade?

The declining terms of trade hypothesis has fared poorly. Although it was plausible during the 1950s when primary product prices fell from the high levels of the Korean War boom, the trend was reversed by the commodity price boom and oil price increases of the early 1970s. Over the whole twentieth century there is no clear trend in the relative prices of primary and manufactured goods (Spraos, 1980), although primary product prices do fluctuate so that short-run trends can be identified in both directions. The implications of these terms of trade changes differ among LDCs depending upon exactly which commodities they export; the majority of LDCs suffered from the 1973–4 oil price increases, although for some of them the higher cost of imported oil was offset by increased prices for their own exports during the late 1970s (for example, coffee or phosphate exporters, but not copper exporters). By the late 1980s even the general characterization of the LDCs as primary product exporters and the more developed countries as exporters of manufactures had become misleading, because almost half of the exports of the nonOPEC LDCs were manufactured goods, and the major exporters of many primary products were more developed countries such as Australia, Canada, or the US. In sum, the validity of the Prebisch–Singer hypothesis depends upon the choice of the time period and the commodities studied, but over the long run it has no relevance to LDCs as a group.

Nurkse's hypothesized breakdown of the trade-fuelled engine of growth continues to be accepted by some people, despite the economic success of several export-oriented LDCs during the postwar era (see section 16.4). The Brandt Commission, reporting in 1980, believed that trade had continued to be an engine of growth during the 1950s and 1960s but that the engine broke down in the 1970s when the major markets were shielded by new trade barriers against imports from LDCs. Arthur Lewis (1980), in his speech accepting the Nobel Prize for economics, supported this argument with econometric estimates showing a fixed long-run relationship between LDC exports and industrialized countries' national income, implying that the slower post-1974 economic growth in the latter countries reduced the prospects for export-led growth in LDCs.

The Nurkse–Lewis engine of growth hypothesis is based upon a superficial reading of nineteenth-century economic history. Of the countries heavily engaged in international trade some had good economic growth records, but others (such as Ceylon) had poor records. The degree of participation in international trade does not distinguish the economic successes from the also-rans. Moreover, in the success stories economic historians give greater weight to domestic factors than to exports as the reason for success. Favorable external conditions helped in many cases but they were not the crucial element; in a phrase popularized by Kravis (1970), trade was a handmaiden of growth rather than the engine of growth.

In the twentieth century the explanation for LDC exports growing more slowly than industrialized countries' exports lies in supply constraints rather than unfavorable external demand conditions. Especially in the second half of the century these supply constraints have often been exacerbated by government policies inimical to exporters (see next section). In those LDCs where. the supply constraints were reduced export-led growth took place, largely on the basis of export diversification (section 16.4). By exporting labor-intensive manufactured goods these countries by-passed the elasticity pessimism of Nurkse, Prebisch, and Singer. Riedel (1984) has also shown that export diversification undercuts Lewis's empirical results, which are based on a definition of LDC exports in terms of primary product exports, which in fact applies only to a handful of LDCs whose exports are concentrated in tropical products.

The historical record provides no conclusive evidence of trade working as an engine of past economic growth or of a breakdown in the possibility of LDCs' increasing exports with beneficial consequences for economic growth. The role of international trade in economic development is less extreme; favorable world market conditions and appropriate trade policies can help, but are neither a necessary nor a sufficient condition for economic development to take place. The USSR built up a substantial industrial sector in the 1930s without international trade. Argentina failed to match the economic development of Australia or Canada despite their similar export bundles in the late nineteenth and early twentieth centuries. Unfavorable world market conditions can harm rich and poor countries, although the greater the dependence on goods produced only for export the more harmful the consequences. This was the experience of the 1930s which convinced many LDC governments of the dangers of international trade and of the market mechanism, and the politically independent LDCs moved quickly toward more autarchic and interventionist development strategies. The export pessimism discussed in this section, although weakly founded in fact, provided intellectual support for this position.

16.3   Import-substituting Industrialization Policies

The economic development strategies adopted by the LDCs during the 1950s were remarkably similar, despite the wide variety of historical, cultural, and resource endowment conditions in these countries. Some independent LDCs had moved toward autarchic policies as early as the 1920s (in the case of Turkey) or in the 1930s (many Latin American countries), but these countries adopted better-articulated economic development strategies after World War II. At that time newly independent nations or LDCs undergoing revolutionary political changes (such as India, Pakistan, The People's Republic of China, Egypt, and Israel) were also consciously adopting economic development as a major goal, and similarly aimed for industrialization based upon the domestic market. This development strategy became known as import-substituting industrialization (ISI).

Association of industrialization with economic development, emphasis on capital formation as the primary source of economic growth, and pessimism about export prospects and about the price mechanism determined the strategy of economic development. Governments raised capital by domestic fiscal and monetary policies, by taxing international trade, by borrowing, or by foreign aid, and then allocated the funds to industrial projects. The preferred industrial projects were those with a proven domestic market, which was indicated by the presence of imports. To assure the home market for the new domestic producers trade barriers were imposed – hence, the label ISI. Firms in the industrial sector might be given further encouragement via tax concessions, preferential allocation of import licenses, subsidized inputs, and so forth. The exact package varied from country to country, but the broad outlines were similar in almost all developing countries by 1960.

How successful were the ISI policies? During the 1950s and early 1960s much of the economic growth in LDCs was associated with ISI, and growth was at historically high rates. To what extent economic growth was due to government policies and whether it could have been more rapid with alternative trade policies are open questions which are difficult to answer. Nevertheless, the association was there, and newly independent LDCs in the late 1950s and early 1960s were eager to emulate the ISI development strategy.

The first problem with ISI strategies was that in the longer run industrial growth rates started to slow down; in medium-sized LDCs this typically became apparent after 15–20 years. There are some easy import-substitution opportunities for LDCs; for example, in industries with standardized technology, limited economies of scale, substantial demand at low income levels, low capital requirements, and high transport costs (such as textiles, shoes, cement, tires, and beer). In trade theory terminology, these are labor-intensive goods or mature goods in the product cycle, in which the LDCs, even if they had no comparative advantage, did not suffer a large comparative disadvantage (that is, the foregone gains from trade are small). Once imports of these goods have all been displaced by domestic products, however, it becomes increasingly difficult to pursue ISI. Moreover, as ISI begins to involve more complex goods, bottlenecks arise in the supply of inputs, some of which have to be imported. These constraints were first encountered by the Latin American countries which had embarked on ISI policies earlier than the other LDCs, and they were at the heart of the slowdown in industrial growth in those countries in the 1950s.

Economists oppose trade barriers because they distort price signals and hence lead to resource misallocation. Development planners ignored this warning because they considered trade theory "static" and they distrusted reliance on world markets (see sections 16.1 and 16.2). The resource misallocation induced by ISI policies was, however, substantial and its cumulative effect was to hamper the economic growth and structural change which policy-makers desired. Prohibitive import barriers sheltered inefficient domestic producers, which in turn harmed potentially efficient producers; for example, iron and steel was often a favored ISI sector, but by forcing domestic buyers to pay high prices for often substandard iron and steel the policy penalized iron-and-steel-using firms (in, for example, labor-intensive light manufacturing industries) which otherwise might have been competitive in world markets. More generally, ISI strategies discriminated against nontraded goods and export activities through three channels: (a) higher prices for inputs supplied by the protected industries; (b) distorted domestic prices such that the relative price of the nontraded or export good was well below its free trade price; and (c) an overvalued domestic currency due to artificially reduced import levels made it difficult for exporters to be price-competitive. A final source of resource misallocation was the skilled-labor requirements for administering complex interventionist policies in countries where skilled labor is often the scarcest resource. Also associated with the complexity of the ISI policies is the scope for corruption (in allocating import licenses, subsidized capital, and so on) which was stimulated by ISI controls and which involves real resource costs (such as energy spent in finding out whom to bribe) as well as incentives for socially incorrect decisions.

The magnitude of the resource misallocation permitted by the ISI policies and its long-term consequences were clarified in the late 1960s and the early 1970s by a series of case studies sponsored by the OECD (reported in Little, Scitovsky, and Scott, 1970) and other institutions. Estimates of effective rates of protection revealed some astronomical ERPs and considerable dispersion of rates across activities. The most favored industries were iron and steel, automobile assembly, pulp and paper, and other capital-intensive activities in which the comparative disadvantage of LDCs was pronounced, while the activities discriminated against were in the export sector and agriculture. As a consequence, export growth was sluggish in countries pursuing ISI policies, apart from exceptional cases such as oil-rich Iran. When import demand increased in the form of necessary inputs for ISI activities or in the form of food for a growing population whose needs were not being met by domestic agriculture, further economic growth was constrained by insufficient foreign exchange earnings. Some economists in the 1960s saw the foreign exchange constraint as a structural problem facing LDCs and even linked it to pessimism about export possibilities, but in fact it was a consequence of policies which encouraged resource misallocation and thus limited economic growth.

Import substitution policies also had adverse effects on employment creation and income distribution. Trade barriers in a labor-abundant economy encourage more capital-intensive activities than would exist under freer trade. In many LDCs this was exacerbated by subsidized interest rates on funds for ISI projects and by minimum wage laws, so that the managers would consider capital to be cheaper relative to labor than its real scarcity value and would adopt too-capital-intensive techniques. All of this would depress the amount of employment creation and would, according to the Stolper–Samuelson theorem, shift the income distribution in favor of the owners of capital; both of these effects were opposite to official policy aims in most LDCs. We should not forget, however, that in some countries the policy-makers may not have been adverse to the rich getting richer (since they themselves were among the gainers), and in all cases ISI created vested interests opposed to policy changes which would redistribute income away from them.

A final consequence of ISI provided the most ironic twist of all. Advocates of ISI were suspicious of international markets and often nationalistic, reserving their greatest distrust for transnational corporations. Yet one common result of ISI policies was increased direct foreign investment. If a foreign firm wished to supply a LDC market it could either export from its home country or open a subsidiary in the LDC. Highly protective trade policies by the LDC tipped the balance in favor of opening a subsidiary, because it could often supply at a price below the tariff-inclusive price of an import from the home country even if production costs in the LDC were higher. The LDC government could take a hard line against foreign investment (as in, for example, India or Turkey), but this might entail economic costs since capital was scarce and without the foreign firm's participation the product might have been unavailable. In other LDCs political considerations forestalled too negative a stance toward foreign investment, especially in Latin America, and the 1950s and 1960s saw a flourishing of direct foreign investment in manufacturing based upon supplying the LDC's domestic market.[2]

In sum, the protectionist trade policies of ISI development strategies were associated with accelerated economic growth for some time, but they induced resource misallocation which led to disillusionment with the policies when growth slowed down (see also box 16.1). What other development strategy was available? There was little faith in agricultural-led economic development. Attempts to stimulate domestic demand, for example by promoting construction as a leading sector in Columbia, had little success. The main alternative, by elimination, was industrial development led by manufactured exports; a strategy pursued by Hong Kong since the 1950s, essentially because the colony had no active trade policy, but looked down

[2]This consequence of high trade barriers is not limited to LDCs. Tariff-jumping foreign investment has been important in Australia and Canada. A similar phenomenon followed the formation of the EC and, more recently, the imposition of restrictions on Japanese automobile exports to North America and western Europe.

BOX 16.1   *Economic Sanctions and Import Substitution in Rhodesia*

The economic sanctions imposed against Rhodesia between the 1965 Unilateral Declaration of Independence and Zimbabwe's official independence in 1980 provide an interesting counterpart to the text discussion of import substitution policies, as well as an example of a discriminatory trade policy. Since sanctions can hurt producers in the sanctioning countries, there will be opposition to export embargoes (as after the US embargo on grain exports to the USSR following the latter's invasion of Afghanistan) or to restrictions on imports of intermediate goods (as in the US exemption of chrome imports from Rhodesia). Individual governments will worry that other countries' traders are free-riding, benefiting from the artificially high prices paid by the target country, and may take this as an excuse for turning a blind eye to their own traders' evasion of sanctions. Thus, effective sanctions need to be coordinated by all significant suppliers and buyers or they will be undermined by trade diversion. Even United Nations mandatory sanctions against Rhodesia proved to be porous because some countries did not comply (notably South Africa, and Mozambique before 1975), while others did not enforce compliance.

Despite being incomplete and evaded, economic sanctions against Rhodesia introduced significant trade barriers, reflected in discounts on Rhodesia's exports and premia on her imports. Initial expectations that the rebellion would last for weeks rather than months proved wide of the mark. Even for a rather open economy, the costs of trade barriers are not large relative to GNP. In fact, Rhodesia experienced an economic boom between 1969 and 1974; GNP grew by almost 9 percent a year, and the manufacturing sector in particular prospered. Estimates of the costs to Rhodesia of sanctions during these years are small, and the costs were more than offset by a mobilization of resources in response to the challenge (reminiscent of the initial rapid growth when nationalist governments in developing countries introduced import-substitution policies).

The situation changed after 1974 when Rhodesia's economy stagnated. How much of the decline was due to sanctions is debatable (higher oil prices, global recession, and the end of the Portuguese empire contributed too), but the lack of foreign exchange and access to

---

BOX 16.1—*cont'd*

international credit markets led to failure to renew the capital stock. A similar mechanism may underlie the recurring pattern in developing countries pursuing import-substitution strategies; that is, historically rapid economic growth for a decade or so followed by a slipping of the growth rate as the economy loses its dynamism. In the Rhodesian context the indirect impact via capital formation and the introduction of technical change embodied in new equipment helps to explain why sanctions did not quickly end the rebellion, although they may have contributed to the regime's long-term instability.

---

upon elsewhere because of the prevailing distrust of free trade policies. During the 1960s a handful of countries in East Asia and around the Mediterranean Basin plus Brazil (and to a limited extent Mexico) reacted to the limitations of their ISI strategies by encouraging manufactured exports. Their experience will be examined in the next section. Most LDCs, however, retained ISI policies through the 1970s, some – such as Morocco – even adopting an ISI policy at that late date (see box 16.2). Even in some countries ostensibly rejecting ISI (such as Egypt after 1974) trade policy remained restrictive because the political power of the owners and workers in the protected industries prevented removal of trade barriers. Thus protectionist trade policies remain the norm in LDCs, despite the overwhelming evidence of their shortcomings in terms of national economic well-being and despite the success of the export-oriented strategies to be described in the next section.

16.4   Manufactured Export Expansion as a Development Strategy

The 1950s characterization of LDCs as primary product exporters was largely correct. Total manufactured exports by developing countries was very small up until the early 1960s: $3 billion in 1963 compared to $66 billion by the more developed countries (table 16.1). India was the largest LDC exporter of manufactures, closely followed by Hong Kong; each of these two exported two-thirds of a billion dollars worth of manufactured goods, while no other LDC had manufactured exports worth a half a billion dollars.

BOX 16.2   *Trade Policies in North Africa*

The North African countries of Egypt, Morocco, and Tunisia provide contrasting experiences of trade policies and economic growth. Egypt became a republic in 1952 and under Nasser embarked on policies aimed at rapid economic development. Morocco and Tunisia gained their independence in 1956. Although there were differences in historical background and resource endowments, all three countries had roughly similar income levels and economies based primarily on agriculture. Their economic policies, and especially their trade policies, differed dramatically over the next quarter century.

	GNP per capita mid-1950s	($US) 1985	Exports/GDP 1965	1985
Egypt	133	610	0.18	0.14
Morocco	159	560	0.18	0.18
Tunisia	131	1,190	0.19	0.24

Egypt introduced licenses for imports and then established a government monopoly over foreign trade, using its ability to set prices for all transactions in order to obtain funds for investment in import substituting industries. The favored industries enjoyed high effective rates of protection (for example, 600 percent for iron and steel and 250 percent for tires) while the main export crops (cotton, rice, and onions) had negative ERPs; Hansen and Nashashibi (1973, p. 311) estimate that 16 times as many domestic resources were needed to produce a dollar's worth of steel as to produce a dollar's worth of cement. Establishment of the new industries was associated with accelerated economic growth from the mid-1950s to late 1960s but, especially during the 1960s, there was limited job creation, rising income inequality, and by the end of the decade a slowdown in economic growth. Faced with growing food imports and stagnant exports, trade policy was reversed by Sadat's opening to the West, although Egypt's attempt to adopt a MEE strategy was frustrated by vested interests opposed to reduced trade barriers and by red tape which remained difficult to cut through.

Tunisia adopted a milder ISI strategy during the 1960s, and by the

---

BOX 16.2—*cont'd*

decade's end encountered similar misallocation problems. In the early 1970s the ISI strategy was replaced by more open policies involving encouragement for direct foreign investment and reduced government intervention in the economy and in foreign trade. The result was a dramatic increase in manufactured exports during the 1970s; clothing led the way, followed by electronics and other labor-intensive manufactures. Political uncertainties and problems with primary product exports slowed Tunisian export growth in the 1980s, but a decade's rapid growth had already put Tunisian incomes well above their 1960s levels.

Morocco pursued more conservative trade policies aimed primarily at maintaining the interests of the landowning elite. Thus the emphasis continued to be on primary product exports, even though the markets in western Europe were being gradually closed off by the EC's Common Agricultural Policy. A mild ISI strategy was pursued with considerable bureaucratic control over imports. During the mid-1970s Morocco had a golden opportunity when a sudden increase in the price of phosphates (her major natural resource) provided a windfall gain, but the government chose to use the extra revenue plus foreign loans to strengthen the ISI policy by promoting capital-intensive industries. When phosphate prices collapsed Morocco was left to service her foreign debt from an economy with limited capacity to earn foreign currency. In the 1980s Morocco belatedly switched to more open trade policies in an attempt to emulate Tunisia's example.

The experience of these three countries reveals how sustained differences in growth rates can dramatically change relative incomes. From having roughly equal incomes in the mid-1950s, Tunisia enjoyed a per capita income about double that of the other two countries by the mid-1980s. Trade policy is not the only explanation of this difference, but it is the most obvious distinguishing feature among the three countries.

During the next two decades LDCs' manufactured exports grew at a phenomenal rate. By 1981 they were worth $116 billion, 12 percent of the world total – up from a mere 4 percent of the much smaller 1963 world total. By the 1980s LDCs' manufactured exports exceeded their nonoil primary

Table 16.1 Exports from industrial and developing countries (US$ billion)

Exports from	1963	1970	1975	1981
Industrial countries				
Primary Products	30	53	133	305
(Fuels)	(4)	(7)	(28)	(92)
Manufactures	66	158	415	873
Developing countries[a]				
Primary Products	28	45	178	422
(Fuels)	(9)	(18)	(125)	(323)
Manufactures	3	10	33	116
(Textiles)	(1)	(2)	(5)	(13)
(Clothing)	(0)	(1)	(5)	(17)

[a] The GATT definition of developing countries includes Latin America, Africa (except South Africa), and Asia (excluding centrally planned economies, Japan, New Zealand, and Australia).

Source: Moore (1985), Tables 8-3 and 8-4; summarizing data from GATT's annual *International Trade*

product exports. As we have already seen this changing commodity composition was ignored by Lewis in his analysis of trade as a broken-down engine of LDC growth, and more generally it reveals the irrelevance of the relative price of primary products and manufactured goods as a guide to the terms of trade of LDCs as a group.

What manufactured goods were involved in this phenomenal growth? Textiles, the only traditional manufactured export of LDCs apart from handicraft activities, was a leading product, but even more spectacular was the growth of clothing exports. Sewing has defied attempts to develop major new capital-intensive techniques since the invention of the sewing machine in the nineteenth century, and clothing is the archetypical labor-intensive industry. Other manufactured exports from LDCs often involved some type of sewing; for example, sporting goods (stitching baseball mitts), semi-conductors (sewing copper wire), or travel goods. In total, there was a wide range of labor-intensive manufactures, unpredicted by government planners, which LDC entrepreneurs found they could produce and sell competitively – from wigs to Christmas tree lights to artificial flowers to spectacle frames and so on, in an almost endless list.

A striking feature of the manufactured export expansion by LDCs during the 1960s and early 1970s was the small number of countries involved. In 1975 Hong Kong, Taiwan, and South Korea were each exporting over $4 billion worth of manufactures; Spain was in a similar range; and Yugoslavia, Singapore, India, and Brazil all exported around $2 billion, followed by Israel, Greece, Portugal, and Mexico. Together, these 12 countries accounted for over 80 percent of manufactured exports from LDCs. By the mid-1970s their economies were sufficiently different from those of other developing countries that the term "newly industrialized countries," or NICs, was coined to cover some of them (usually not India because she was too poor, and sometimes not all the southern European countries or Israel because they were considered to be more developed countries).

The emergence of the NICs cast doubt on the idea of LDCs as a separate group needing a different economic theory to that applied to more developed countries. Some people argued that NICs were never typical LDCs and are special cases, but with the possible exception of Mediterranean NICs they had featured on earlier lists of LDCs. In 1960 South Korea and Taiwan had *per capita* incomes similar to the Philippines or Thailand, and below Malaysia and all the large and medium-sized Latin American countries. None of the NICs, except Brazil, was well-endowed with natural resources, so they were rarely considered hopeful prospects among the LDCs of 1960. The metamorphosis of these countries from LDCs to NICs is much better explained by their development strategy than by special circumstances.

What sort of trade policies were pursued by the NICs? There is no simple answer: Hong Kong had more or less free trade policies, while South Korea, Israel, and other NICs had interventionist trade policies protecting import-competing producers, but also subsidizing exports. The general feature of all successful LDC exporters of manufactures was that the incentives to exporters relative to those for producers of import substitutes were no worse (or, at least, not that much worse) than they would have been under free trade; in other words, the domestic relative price line facing producers was not much different than the world price line. This was also achieved by reducing the red tape associated with international economic transactions under ISI regimes (in some cases by establishing free economic zones) or by devaluation. Whatever the method, the price incentives were significantly different from those prevailing under ISI policies. The NICs' experience indicates that with policies which do not discourage exports, as ISI policies do, the supply of manufactured exports from developing countries can be increased. How much of the NICs' rapid economic growth can be attributed to their export performance and hence to their trade policies? There is, of course, no clear-cut answer to such a question because we can never know what would have happened in each country with different policies. Nevertheless, there is a strong presumption of a close association between trade policies and growth, because in most NICs it is possible to date the policy change from ISI to more export-oriented policies, and export and output growth rates did in fact accelerate afterwards. This is not true of Hong Kong which had free trade policies in the 1950s and already had fast economic growth in that decade, but it is true of Taiwan (1960), Israel (1962), South

Korea (1964), Brazil (1964), Singapore (1965), and the southern European NICs. The annual growth rate of South Korean GDP, for example, doubled from about 5 percent in the 1950s to 10 percent in the 1960s and 1970s, with the dynamo after 1964 being a 30 percent per annum growth in exports. Further suggestive evidence of the significance of trade policies is the lackluster performance of the more industrialized LDCs who stuck with ISI policies, such as Argentina or India (table 16.2).

The NICs' policies removed the supply-side constraints on manufactured export expansion, but are there demand-side constraints to this strategy's success? Necessarily, the NICs have increased their dependence on foreign markets. The great majority of developing countries' manufactured exports go to the industrialized countries (about two-thirds of the total, and half of these to the US alone), and there is a fear that these markets could be closed. In fact, even at disaggregated commodity levels market penetration is small; imports from LDCs and NICs rarely account for over a fifth of total available supplies in a market. Nevertheless, competing imports are often a convenient scapegoat for an industry's troubles and protectionist measures against LDCs, who have less opportunity for retaliation than do the larger trading nations, may be a politically attractive solution (see chapter 14). There is a tendency for industrial countries' nominal tariffs to be highest on goods of special interest to LDCs, such as processed raw materials, textiles and clothing, footwear, and leather goods, which partly reflects domestic political considerations but is also a consequence of the LDCs' nonparticipation in the various GATT rounds of multilateral trade negotiations.

Two policy innovations have mitigated the negative effects of developed countries' tariff structures on LDC exports. The GSP schemes introduced

Table 16.2 Economic growth export performance and openness of the economy; selected countries, 1963–85

	Rate of growth of per capita GDP (percent)		Manufactured exports (US$ million, 1975 prices)			Exports/GDP (percentage)	
	1963–73	*1973–85*	*1963*	*1973*	*1984*	*1965*	*1985*
Hong Kong	6.0	6.3	1,333	4,592	11,938	71	106
South Korea	7.1	5.7	84	3,180	18,834	9	36
Singapore	9.5	6.5	73	1,176	5,205	123	n.a.
Taiwan	7.6	5.9	272	4,321	19,551	n.a.	n.a.
Argentina	3.2	− 1.4	169	860	1,002	8	15
India	1.1	2.1	1,445	1,838	2,952	4	6

Sources: Balassa and Williamson (1987), pp. 2–3, 8–9; World Bank *World Development Report* (1987), pp. 210–1

after 1971 fell short of expectations and have major gaps in coverage (see section 15.4), but they have been sufficient to leave the average tariff rates facing LDCs' exports the same as those facing industrial countries' exports (table 16.3). Most industrial countries have incorporated into their tariff schedules offshore assembly provisions permitting exemption from customs duties on that part of an import accounted for by inputs produced in the importing country; such provisions reduce the ERP as long as the exporting country purchases inputs from the country to which it will sell the export.

During the 1970s concern about access to the major markets shifted from tariffs to nontariff barriers. Many of the new NTBs introduced by the North American and western European countries fell disproportionately upon LDCs' exports – not surprisingly as the NTBs were usually intended to protect labor-intensive industries and the brunt of the new protectionist measures was borne by the NICs. The new NTBs were targeted at the NICs' most successful export lines and were often explicitly discriminatory (as in the Multifiber Arrangement and other "voluntary" export restraint agreements). The impressive point, however, is that the successful LDC exporters of the 1960s were also relatively successful in the less-favorable post-1973 economic environment (tables 16.2 and 16.4). Some NICs (such as South Korea) borrowed heavily in the mid- and late 1970s, when real interest rates were very low, to finance future growth. They continued to expand exports, which paid for more expensive oil imports and to service debts. In contrast, the LDCs still pursuing ISI strategies ran into serious trouble as they had insufficient foreign exchange earnings to cover their oil bill, and if they ran up foreign debts they could not earn the foreign exchange to service them. Thus, in adversity as in favorable world market conditions, there was among LDCs a continuing trend away from autarchic trade policies.

Other consequences of less restrictive trade policies can be analyzed under the same headings as those of ISI policies; resource allocation, employment creation and income distribution, and foreign investment. By pursuing comparative advantage a manufactured export expansion (MEE) develop-

Table 16.3 Tariffs (in percent)[a] applied to all imports and to imports from developing countries, 1983

Average tariff on	EC	Japan	US
-all imports	2.5	3.1	3.4
-imports from LDCs	2.1	2.3	3.6

[a] Figures are for trade-weighted average actual applied tariffs.

Source: UNCTAD, document TD/B/1126 (Part I), 23 January 1987, p. 19

Table 16.4 Developing areas' export of manufactures: the ten leading exporters, 1973 and 1985

	US$ billion		Percentage share	
	1973	1985	1973	1985
Developing areas' exports of manufactures[a] of which:	24	149	100	100
Taiwan	3.7	27.8	15.5	18.5
Korea, Republic of	2.7	27.7	11	18.5
Hong Kong	4.7	27.3	19.5	18.5
Brazil	1.2	15.5	5	10.5
Singapore	1.6	11.7	6.5	8
India	1.6	4.8	6.5	3
Malaysia[b]	0.3	3.9	1.5	2.5
Thailand[b]	0.2	2.4	1	1.5
Argentina[b]	0.7	1.4	3	1
Philippines[b]	0.2	1.2	1	1
Total of above	17	(124)	70.5	(83)

[a] The GATT definition of developing areas excludes the southern European NICs.
[b] Data for 1984.

Source: GATT *International Trade: 1987/8*, table 1.5

ment strategy promotes greater efficiency in resource allocation. It should be recalled, however, that trade policies which face producers with less distorted output prices do not necessarily exclude distorted domestic market prices. For example, all of the NICs' governments except Hong Kong intervene in directing investment to specific activities, sometimes with the effect of subsidizing firms the social value of which is small; even South Korea, often held up as the best "success story" of MEE, moved prematurely into heavy industry in the late 1970s as a result of misguided government policy. Nevertheless, in general the opportunities for resource misallocation are less than under a trade regime which shelters inefficient domestic producers at all costs. A sign of this greater efficiency is the flexibility of producers in NICs, who readily change their output mix in response to changing market conditions (usually moving to less labor-intensive items as their wage costs are undercut by follower NICs, but often moving sideways as fashions change or product-specific trade barriers are erected in their export markets). Another sign of efficiency in exploiting comparative advantage is the willingness of those same firms to use obsolete or second-hand equipment, or to find ways of demechanizing production stages which would be capital-intensive in high-wage countries, all in order to maximize their competitiveness in international markets and the gains from trade.

Specialization in labor-intensive activities and the innovative attempts to reduce capital-labor ratios of individual activities both contributed to job creation. Empirical studies have supported the unsurprising conclusion that in labor-abundant countries freer trade policies are more successful than ISI policies in creating jobs for low-skilled labor. In most NICs (and especially the most successful manufactured exporters) the price of labor to employers is close to the wage rate, maximizing the incentive to use labor rather than capital. The absence of social security benefits and workers' rights, restrictions on trade union activity, and lack of minimum wage legislation offer little security for those holding jobs, but they do create an environment in which rapid economic growth can lead eventually to a bidding up of real wages. For most NICs the process was definitely under way by the 1970s as labor-release from agriculture was exhausted, and in the 1980s workers experienced both higher incomes and increased social security; although, as South Korea illustrates, the transition toward this situation may be politically turbulent as the more articulate, better educated and wealthier labor force demands economic and political participation as well as improved material well-being.

Freer trade policies can be expected to promote a more egalitarian income distribution. The Stolper–Samuelson theorem applied to labor-rich economies provides theoretical support for this hypothesis, and the previous paragraph suggests that labor did in fact benefit from MEE strategies. It is, however, difficult to test the hypothesis, partly because some of the NICs (such as Taiwan, South Korea, and Israel) had relatively egalitarian income distributions even before embarking on MEE and, more important, because changes in income distribution are difficult to measure. A cautious assessment is that there is some evidence that the poorer people did benefit from MEE policies in the East Asian and Mediterranean NICs and in Brazil, and no evidence of these policies making the income distribution more unequal.

Marketing poses a problem for countries embarking on an MEE development strategy because it requires knowledge and skills which are likely to be scarce in LDCs. If there are externalities in developing export-marketing skills, there are grounds for interventionist trade policies; that is, export subsidies (section 12.3). A better solution, because it goes more directly to the market failure, is for the government to sponsor specialized advisory agencies and to act as intermediary putting potential exporters in contact with potential foreign buyers; such institutional arrangements have worked well (in Israel for example) but are less suited to LDCs with weak administrative capability due to lack of educated personnel. A third solution is to participate in subcontracting, as described in chapter 7 from the perspective of the more developed country's firms. Many producers in the NICs manufacture to order for retail chains in high-income countries: for example, Macy, J C Penny, Marks and Spencer, C & A Modes, and Karstadt all maintain permanent buyers in several NICs. Manufacturing firms in the labor-scarce countries subcontract out labor-intensive stages of production to NIC firms, a solution encouraged by the offshore assembly provisions described earlier in this section.

A variant on this solution is for the foreign firm to establish a subsidiary or a joint venture in the LDC, bringing in technical and managerial expertise as well as capital and marketing know-how. Starting in the late 1960s, export-oriented direct foreign investment in LDCs became increasingly important for manufacturing firms trying to cut costs in their high-wage home countries; such firms were lobbyists for and beneficiaries from the offshore assembly provisions, which reduced tariff barriers to such international division of labor. In some NICs foreign firms played a major role in their MEE strategies: for example, in Brazil and Singapore foreign-owned transnational firms accounted for over two-fifths of manufactured exports by the mid-1970s; while in Spain Ford Motors became in a single step the country's leading exporter when it opened a factory in Valencia. Direct foreign investment was less important in Hong Kong and Taiwan, perhaps because they had a pool of entrepreneurs from immigration and previous development. As a corollary to this last observation, direct foreign investment is likely to be more important for smaller second-generation NICs; a hypothesis supported by the experience of Tunisia, Malta, and Malaysia. Reliance on foreign-owned firms has led to fears of being locked into low-wage activities, because local managerial and technical skills are not being developed, or of vulnerability to being deserted by footloose firms when real wages increase (or even for more capricious reasons beyond the LDC's control). In practice, there is little evidence to support such fears; typically, some local skills are developed and transnational corporations have been reluctant to shift location at short notice.

In sum, MEE development strategies and the associated trade policy of not discriminating against exporters have worked well in promoting economic growth, efficiency, and employment. Fears of increased income inequality due to market forces, of vulnerability to protectionism in the more developed countries, and of being held hostage to transnational corporations' decisions have not been realized. This is, of course, not to advocate a high dependence on manufactured exports for all LDCs. For some LDCs comparative advantage lies elsewhere, such as in agriculture or other natural-resource-intensive goods, and the vulnerability of export-oriented development to external factors illustrated by the 1930s' experience is always a potential danger. Nevertheless, the success of the NICs proved the gross export pessimism of the late 1950s to have been unfounded; LDCs could increase their exports if they removed supply-side constraints and policy-induced disincentives, and they could benefit from MEE in terms of their economic goals of growth, structural change, employment creation, and equity.

16.5   Conclusions

Developing countries' trade policies are interesting to study, because the dramatic changes after the wave of independence and self-determination in the 1950s, and the policy reversals of later decades, offer many cases for assessing the effectiveness of different international trade policies. This is in contrast to the more developed countries, where a common experience of tariff reduction prevailed throughout the postwar period, accompanied by some increase in nontariff barriers to trade after the mid-1970s. Thus, differences in macroeconomic performance cannot easily be related to trade policy on the basis of developed countries' experience, but among the LDCs some strong conclusions can be derived from comparative studies.

During the 1950s, policy-makers in LDCs were almost universally attracted to restrictive trade policies. In part III, such policies creating a wedge between domestic and world prices were shown to incur national welfare losses. This analysis was ignored, on the grounds that LDCs were in some way different from the more developed countries, and that neoclassical trade theory applies to the latter rather than the former. In section 16.1 this view is examined and found unconvincing. There was also a widespread distrust of outward-oriented policies based on the belief that international trade was harmful (or, at least, no longer helpful) to economic growth, so that participation in the international economy was undesirable for LDCs. This hypothesis is examined in section 16.2 and also found wanting: a better characterization of the relationship between international trade and economic growth is that trade can assist growth, but is neither a necessary nor a sufficient condition for growth to take place.

Actual experience with trade policies in LDCs has been instructive. The almost universal pursuit of ISI, involving prohibitive or very high barriers to imports, was often associated with rapid growth as infant industries were established, but growth faded after one or two decades. The fundamental reason for the failure of restrictive trade policies to deliver self-sustaining long-term economic growth was precisely that predicted by trade theory: resource misallocation, which became more and more acute. Moreover, the side-effects on employment creation and income distribution, again predictable from trade theory, were generally undesired. In contrast, adoption of more open trade policies, which left domestic producers facing export/import price ratios similar to those in world markets, led to economic growth which was both more rapid and more sustainable. Again, the fundamental reason for success is obvious from part I of this book; specialization according to comparative advantage maximizes total output (valued at world prices), irrespective of whether this is distributed to favor present or future consumption. Moreover, the employment and income effects are likely to be beneficial in the long run, although there may be adjustment costs of moving from an ISI to an MEE strategy. More open trade policies have a cost in increased vulnerability to international market forces, but it has not seriously hampered the NICs, and is a cost more and more LDCs appear willing to risk as they seek to emulate the NICs.

The brightest feature of world trade policy during the 1970s and 1980s was the almost universal trend among LDCs to lower their trade barriers. Trade liberalization should increase both their own welfare and global welfare by permitting a fuller international division of labor according to comparative advantage. The institutional counterpart of this trend has been growing GATT membership as LDCs have seen the GATT responsibilities as less onerous when they are voluntarily pursuing liberal trade policies. This will lead to a shift of LDCs' political effort from UNCTAD, with its emphasis on satisfying the special interests of LDCs (for example, via GSP), to GATT with its emphasis on controlling trade policy malpractices for the benefit of all; a shift which could help to limit the threatened rise of protectionism in the more developed countries and the worldwide trend toward discriminatory trade policies described in chapter 15.

Further Reading

For recent developments in international trade and trade policy relevant to developing countries, see the *World Development Review*, published annually by the World Bank (the 1987 issue in particular focused on international trade issues).

Part IV

Beyond Pure Trade Theory

17

International Factor Movements, Trade in Services, and the Balance of Payments

The microeconomic–macroeconomic distinction made in chapter 1 is an artificial one insofar as real world policy issues often involve both aspects. The US trade deficit which emerged in the 1980s, for example, had macroeconomic origins, but policies advocated to deal with it included trade barriers. The exchange rate is a macroeconomic concept, but its level affects trade flows and attitudes toward trade policies. International flows of factors of production can be analyzed with microeconomic tools and they have resource allocation consequences, but they are mainly dealt with in terms of their impact on macroeconomic variables such as the interest rate, GNP, and so on. In part IV each of these topics will be considered from the perspective of its relevance to international trade and trade policy; macroeconomic implications will be mentioned, but not treated in depth.

This chapter deals with international movements of factors of production and international trade in services. At a general level these international flows can be analyzed similarly to the international flow of goods. The welfare assessments and policy conclusions are similar. If markets are perfectly competitive and factors can move freely across national boundaries in response to price differences, then capital or labor will move to countries poorly endowed with that factor, reducing factor price differentials and improving global resource allocation. Unrestricted trade in services would also maximize global welfare if markets were perfectly competitive, although familiar cases for protection arise, such as infant industry, national security, or culture-based arguments. Typically there are conflicts between sectional and national interests, which may explain the existence of barriers to international transactions, even though such barriers reduce consumer surplus or net factor rewards below what they would have been without the restrictions.

There are, however, special considerations surrounding international flows of capital and labor, of which the most fundamental and politically potent are fears of lost national identity if immigration is unrestricted or of reduced sovereignty over national economic policies if large segments of the economy are foreign-owned. Trade in services is dealt with at this point because delivery of services often requires a presence in the buyer's market, that is, labor movement or direct foreign investment (DFI), and most of the serious barriers to trade in services are restrictions on factor flows or on right of establishment.

17.1   *International Factor Movements*

So far, in the theoretical portions of this book, goods have been assumed to be internationally mobile, but factors of production have not. With some factors, such as land, this is a realistic assumption, but with labor it is less realistic and with capital rather unrealistic. Moreover, the restricted international mobility of labor and capital is a policy-determined rather than an inevitable phenomenon. What are the consequences of international factor movements, and why are some such movements stringently limited?

If factor flows respond only to relative prices, then the analysis is similar to that of goods insofar as international price differences will encourage movement from low to high price countries. The demand for a factor is given by the value of its marginal product, which will be negatively related to the quantity employed. Thus, in figure 17.1, the value of the marginal product of labor curve in country A determines the wage rate (w_A) if the quantity of labor is in fixed supply (OQ). A similar diagram could illustrate the determination of the wage rate in another country, B. Both of these diagrams can then be combined to show the effects of freedom of labor movement between A and B. The length of the base line in figure 17.2 is equal to the total labor force in the two countries; O_AQ in the first country and O_BQ in the second country. With no labor mobility there is a wage differential (w_B is higher than w_A), but with freedom of labor movement Q^*Q workers move from A to B, equalizing the wage rates at w^*.

In the initial situation country A's total output is measured by area O_ACDQ, of which O_Aw_ADQ goes to wage-earners and the remainder (CDw_A) to owners of other factors of production. Without any international labor mobility country B's total output is O_BGFQ, of which O_Bw_BFQ goes to labor and FGw_B to other factors. With the migration of Q^*Q workers from A to B, output in A falls to O_ACEQ^* and output in B increases to O_BGEQ^*. Thus, the combined output of the two countries increases by the shaded area DEF. The basis for these gains in global output is very simple; the labor moves to a location at which its contribution to output is higher than in its previous location. With competitive labor markets the wage rate signals where the value of marginal product is higher, and as long as wage differentials persist labor mobility can increase global output.

In the analysis of figure 17.2 nationals of both countries benefit from free

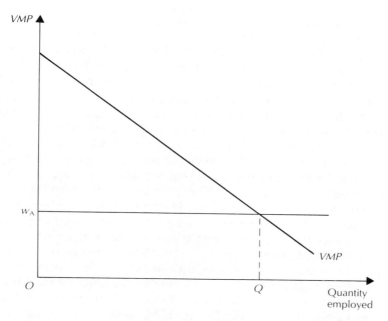

Figure 17.1 Wage rate determination. With competitive labor markets, the wage rate will be equal to the value of the marginal product of the last worker to be employed. Note the similarity to figure 3.12.

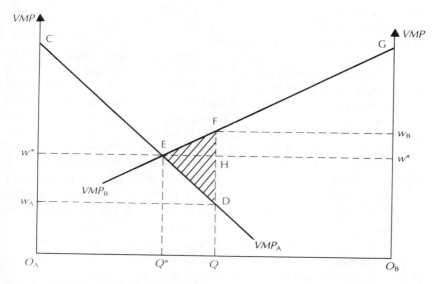

Figure 17.2 Wage rate determination in two countries. The horizontal axis measures the quantity of labor, with $O_A O_B$ being the total labor force in the two countries.

movement of labor: A by the area EHD and B by EFH. There are, however, internal income distribution effects. Workers from A (both those who stay at home and those who emigrate) enjoy higher wages, but the owners of other factors in country A see their income fall from CDw_A to CEw^*. Meanwhile, in country B, the workers see their wage rate bid down from w_B to w^*, but the owners of other factors enjoy an increase in income from GFw_B to GEw^*. The relatively scarce factor in each country is hurt by factor mobility (such as labor in B), while the relatively abundant factor benefits (such as labor in A).

Large international migrations in response to higher returns have characterized many historical periods. The emigration of labor from Europe and Asia to the lightly settled lands of the Americas and Australasia during the nineteenth century was a dramatic example. In that situation, where transport costs were high and there were strong complementarity relationships between labor and natural resources, factor flows were a more economical solution than goods flows (that is, export of land-intensive products from the lightly settled lands) to the problem of how to take advantage of the abundant land in some areas and abundant labor elsewhere. More recently, the labor migration from Mexico to the US, from the Mediterranean countries to northern Europe, or from poor Muslim countries to the Gulf states have all been primarily in response to wage differentials.

In the present world economy, however, international labor movements are severely restricted by immigration barriers in all high-wage countries and by emigration restrictions in some other countries. An economic reason for restrictive immigration policies emerges from the foregoing analysis and is similar to the political economy explanations of trade barriers; domestic labor loses as a result of immigration and in democracies labor has the votes to obtain restrictive immigration policies (of course the indigenous labor in pre-Columbian America, Australasia, or Africa was unable to enforce such policies). In principle, the sectional interests of labor could be bought off, if the gainers from free immigration were prepared to compensate domestic labor; for example, in figure 17.2 if area FHw^*w_B plus some part of EFH were redistributed to owners of labor in B then everybody in B would be better off. Such a compensation arrangement may have functioned in western Europe during the 1960s when large labor inflows added to, say, West Germany's GDP while domestic workers were rewarded with extensive social services from the public purse in addition to their wages. Opposition to immigration may, however, not be just a sectional interest if the incoming labor consumes more public services (for example, migrants are often young workers who may have children requiring education) than they pay for in taxes (because progressive tax systems demand little from low-wage workers), thus imposing a net cost on the host nation's citizens which may outweigh the immigrants' contribution to the host's GNP. Finally, immigrant labor may be perceived as a threat to a country's cultural identity, so that whatever the economic benefits it is excluded in the national interest; this explains (but does not condone) the racist aspects of many countries' immigration laws and the intensity of political debates about immigration.

The policy issues concerning labor migration become more complex when allowance is made for the heterogeneity of labor. Inflows of unskilled labor are more politically acceptable when there is a labor shortage and immigrants are seen as noncompeting, willing to do the "dirty work" which domestic labor is not prepared to do; in times of high unemployment, when any jobs are valued by the domestic labor force, competition from immigrants is less acceptable. On the other hand, skilled immigrant labor is welcomed in most countries most of the time; the exceptions tend to be when the competing domestic group can establish barriers to entry, by, for example, blocking recognition of foreign qualifications. Since skilled labor embodies past investment in human capital (usually financed at least in part by its home country taxpayers) and often yields externalities to the destination country (if the wage is less than the social value of its marginal product), international distribution issues arise. Thus, the brain drain from poorer to richer countries may thwart poorer countries' attempts to train their labor forces, although the emigrant and the country of destination both gain from the exodus; almost regardless of the magnitude of the gainers' benefits, many people regard this redistribution of income as undesirable. A similar issue arises for countries which try to reduce domestic income inequalities by public policy; potential high-income-earners will have an incentive to emigrate. In both of these cases there is a conflict between the economic rights of the group and of the individual; the Western democracies value freedom to emigrate (even though they restrict the freedom to immigrate into their countries), while some Third World and socialist states defend their right to try to retain their people, whose duty is to their own country.

The analysis of figure 17.2 can be applied to any mobile factor of production. Replacing labor by capital in the diagram permits analysis of the gains from allowing capital to move from capital-abundant to capital-scarce locations. Both countries' GNP would be increased, although the owners of capital would be worse off in the capital-scarce country and the owners of other factors would be worse off in the capital-abundant country as a result of the change. Capitalists in the richer countries can be expected to favor an international economic system in which international mobility of capital is permitted, while the domestic capitalists in poorer countries are likely to oppose such a regime unless they can be compensated for their losses.

The nineteenth-century flow of capital from England to the Americas illustrates responsiveness to differences in the return to capital. The adjustment process was a long one because the continuous expansion of the land frontier led to a continuous capital scarcity in the Americas. Interest rates. were far higher for frontier farmers seeking to borrow to establish their homestead than for English savers, so intermediaries in London and in eastern North American cities packaged farm mortgages which could be offered to English savers seeking a higher return with moderate risk. More recently, the surge in lending by rich country banks to LDC borrowers during the second half of the 1970s reflected the higher returns to be earned in the LDCs than in the recession-wracked industrial economies, although in retrospect the bankers' assessment of the riskiness of many of these loans was overoptimistic. The huge inflow of capital into the US during the 1980s was also in response to the interest rate differential between US-dollar bonds and assets denominated in other major currencies, although in this case the foreign capital was used to finance military and consumer spending rather than productive investment.

The last examples indicate that although factor flows can be analyzed within a microeconomic framework they also have macroeconomic implications. In all cases factor flows will shift the aggregate supply curve, and thus affect macroeconomic equilibrium. Macroeconomic concerns are, however, usually more related to capital flows and in particular short-term or easily reversible capital flows which may cause sudden movements in the exchange rate or in interest rates. These concerns will be addressed in the next chapter.

The analysis of capital flows becomes more complex when the foreign investor retains control over how the capital is used in the host country. The important distinction here is between portfolio investment, where the lender does not exercise control, and direct foreign investment (DFI), which does involve control. The nineteenth-century capital flows, bank lending to Latin America in the 1970s, or foreign investment in the US during the 1980s mainly took the form of portfolio investment, where the lender received a specified rate of interest over the term of the loan after which the principal was repaid. A less important component of the capital flows just described was the purchase of ownership shares in companies in which the foreign shareholders did not have the controlling interest; for example, railway shares were traded internationally in the nineteenth century. Such equity investment has remained relatively minor, although it is becoming more important as the global financial system has begun to absorb national stock-markets and as legal restrictions on foreign shareholding have been reduced in many countries. The foreign shareholder benefits from the flow of dividends and appreciation of the shares' value, but there is a serious problem of identifying and monitoring the performance of companies in distant lands. A more important source of long-term international capital transfer during the twentieth century, and especially since the 1950s, has been DFI, where the foreign lender retains a controlling interest.

Why does DFI exist? One enabling condition has been the improvement of communications, making long-distance control more feasible. Thus, the emergence of nationwide corporations in the US and the spread of their activities to Canada in the nineteenth century followed the development of railroads and the telegraph. The rapid expansion of DFI since the early 1950s likewise reflects improvements in international transportation and communications.

In practice most DFI has involved transnational corporations, and the question is why firms should establish affiliates in other countries. Clearly, the foreign firm must possess some ownership advantage over local firms, sufficient to offset the advantage of local knowledge possessed by the latter. Secondly, it must be more profitable to keep these advantages internal to the firm, rather than sell or lease them to local producers. Finally, the foreign firm's advantage can be better exploited by locating in the host country rather than by exporting from its other factories.

Together these three considerations make up Dunning's eclectic theory of DFI; it is called eclectic because it subsumes separate industrial organization, internalization, and trade theories of DFI. The first consideration suggests that DFI will primarily occur in oligopolistic industries, in which patents, secret formulae, trademarks, and other forms of product differentiation operate as significant barriers to entry. Thus DFI is better explained by industrial organization theory, applied to global markets, rather than by international trade theory, which for the most part avoids dealing with imperfect competition. The second consideration implies that DFI is likely to be most common in industries where the firm-specific advantages could be lost if tight control were not exercised; for example, high-technology industries or firms whose reputations depend upon high quality standards. The third consideration is where trade theory is most relevant. High import barriers encourage DFI in order to produce behind the tariff wall – especially if the protected market is large. Thus, the ISI policies described in the previous chapter encouraged DFI, and formation of the EC likewise encouraged US firms to open plant within the EC to supply the large internal market. Since the 1960s, with the growth of export-oriented DFI, the choice of location has increasingly been based upon production costs, reflecting Heckscher–Ohlin considerations.

For the host country, the major advantage of DFI over portfolio investment lies in the package of technical, marketing, and managerial skills which accompanies the capital flow. In the case of export-oriented DFI in LDCs, these accompanying skills can be more important than the capital flow, which may be small if arrangements are made to subcontract work to domestic suppliers. There is also the advantage that the financial outflows (that is, the repatriated profits) depend upon economic conditions, and unlike bank loans are not subject to a fixed schedule of repayments which must be met even if an unexpected recession strikes the borrowing country.

The costs of DFI arise from the noncompetitive industries in which it tends to occur and from the foreignness of the DFI owners. Repatriated profits have no social value to the country in which the profits are earned, and if they are the result of the exercise of monopoly power these profits may exceed the net benefits to the host country from the DFI. The simple solution is to tax excess profits, but this may be difficult to implement. The foreign investor will try to maximize profits and, if their repatriation is threatened by taxation, to disguise their magnitude. When the DFI is by a transnational corporation any international transaction internal to the firm can be priced so that profits are shifted from branches in high-tax countries to branches in low-tax countries; such transfer pricing is difficult to identify, especially when it involves proprietary knowledge or other inputs for which no world market price exists. During the 1980s several high-tax states in the US (for example, California and Montana), refusing to accept the TNCs' declaration of profits earned in these states, instituted "unitary taxation," which assumes that the share of a firm's profits earned in the state is equal to the share of the firm's global payroll or sales which is in that state. Such legislation was strongly opposed by TNCs and some foreign governments, and was eventually abandoned under pressure from the US federal government.

The most controversial aspect of DFI is the challenge which it poses to national sovereignty. If foreign firms control major segments of the economy, then their decisions may reduce the independence of national policy-making. In the past such issues have been most controversial in LDCs, where foreign firms have even appeared to be capable of changing the national government if it was unsatisfactory to them – regardless of the domestic population's wishes. One response was to expropriate the foreign-owned assets, as Cuba did after 1959, and as most of the oil-producing countries did in the 1950s and 1960s; if this was done without compensation, a cost to be weighed was the unlikelihood of foreign investors committing any future funds to the country. A more insidious threat to sovereignty has, however, also been seen by observers in developed countries experiencing an acceleration of incoming DFI, as in Europe in the 1960s and the US in the 1980s, where there is a fear of the national patrimony being sold off to foreigners, especially if the DFI consists of the purchase of existing domestically owned assets. Such fears have been strongest in Canada, the country where DFI is greatest; although examples of direct interference with Canadian sovereignty (for example, US bans on Canadian subsidiaries of US companies trading with Cuba) are few, there is a vaguer unease about lost economic independence and cultural assimilation into the US.

The recent history of DFI has reflected the love–hate relationship on the part of host countries. During the 1970s amidst considerable distrust of DFI, several countries drew up restrictive codes for DFI and pressed these at the United Nations. The counterpart of this distrust was the readiness of LDCs to turn to bank loans in the late 1970s when real interest rates fell, because bank loans were not associated with the bad aspects of DFI. Since 1982 attitudes have reversed as the disadvantages of fixed-term loans and the benefits of the DFI package became more apparent. Countries now vie with one another to woo foreign investors, although a sensible economic policy would require that foreign investors be subject to similar legislation (such as antitrust laws, health and safety regulations, and so forth) as domestic firms. Even old opponents of foreign investment such as China and the Soviet Union are now trying to attract DFI, although in the form of joint ventures in which domestic interests have an equity stake and can thus act as a regulator to prevent abuses by the foreign partner. Such a policy does, however, have its drawback insofar as any restriction on the foreign investor's flexibility will be an added disincentive to be weighed with the costs and benefits of DFI in a specific location.

In sum, international factor flows can be analyzed with the microeconomic tools used in the earlier parts of this book. There are, however, complications in making welfare assessments, because of the macroeconomic and noneconomic considerations involved. Moreover, in analyzing DFI there is the added problem that this is often an extension of oligopolistic competition, so that theories assuming perfect competition are inadequate. Nevertheless, the presumption of misallocation of economic resources if barriers are introduced holds for factor as well as goods flows.

17.2   Trade in Services

Trade in services became a major policy issue during the 1980s. A dispute arose between some developing countries, led by Brazil and India, and the industrial countries, led by the US, over the inclusion of services in the Uruguay Round of multilateral trade negotiations which began in 1986. Previously, the GATT had only dealt with trade in goods (see box 14.2). In the absence of international rules, service industries enjoyed high levels of protection, which involved similar costs and benefits to those analyzed in the previous section.

The service sector covers a wide range of activities: for example, construction, transport, insurance, banking and other financial services, advertising, education, health care, tourism, restaurants, and other personal services. Many of these are by their nature difficult to trade internationally, and most require some physical presence in the buyers' market so that service transactions are closely linked to the issues of factor mobility discussed in the previous section. Innovations in communications have reduced the need for physical presence in some activities (such as financial services), but trade in haircuts, for example, necessarily involves the barber going to the customer or the customer coming to the barber. Even if no international labor or capital movement is necessary, restrictions on the right of establishment may pose barriers to foreign firms wishing to enter new markets.

A second distinguishing feature of service industries is that trade barriers seldom take the form of tariffs or quotas. The NTBs are often highly protective, so that we would expect the costs of protection to be high, but the complexity of most NTBs has made it difficult to make comparative empirical studies. In the construction industry public procurement policies are more important than in other activities. Air passenger transport is regulated by bilateral agreements on international routes and total protection on most domestic routes. Within Europe the bilateral agreements often contain revenue-sharing arrangements, and hence no net trade or incentive to raise productivity; comparisons with similar US routes show European prices to be considerably higher and productivity levels lower. Since some services are inputs, high levels of protection can handicap traded goods; unreliable or expensive transport, and inadequate financial or legal advice can all hamper the ability of domestic products to compete with imports or in export markets. Lumber producers in Washington state, for example, are at a competitive disadvantage in the southwestern US because shipping rates from Seattle to the California ports, a domestic route on which only US lines can operate, are higher than those from Vancouver.

A third distinguishing feature of service industries is the degree of regulation, which is typically of a type and intensity unusual in goods industries. The difficulty arises of when legitimate regulation becomes discrimination against foreign suppliers, a problem already encountered in discussing health and safety standards as NTBs in goods markets. For service industries with less standardized products there is greater scope for administrative discretion, and as in other industries the likelihood that the regulators will be "captured" by the domestic industry. Different regulations, qualifications for doing business or accreditation procedures are themselves NTBs, and they can exist within federal countries (for example, in some professions within the US licenses or qualifications recognized in one state may not permit the holder to do business in other states).

The arguments used to justify protection are similar to those in goods industries, although as already hinted the explanation of trade barriers may owe more to the strength and political skill of the domestic producers. Infant industry, national security, and preservation of cultural identity arguments are all used. In view of the oligopolistic structure of some service industries (a structure nurtured by regulation and restriction on the right of establishment), rent-preserving and rent-snatching explanations of trade policy are often relevant. For example, in the dispute between the US and South Korea in 1985–6 over access to Korean insurance markets the issue was whether South Korea could preserve the rents for domestic companies or whether US companies could obtain a share of these rents; the US did not press for opening up of the market to all suppliers or for deregulation, and neither side showed any concern for the Korean consumers of insurance services. Externalities can also be reasons for restricting international trade in services; for example, Egypt tries to regulate the growth of the tourism trade to protect its cultural heritage (but could this also be to protect her poor residents from feelings of envy and deprivation in the presence of too many rich tourists, or are the restrictions like an optimal export tax, given the inelastic demand for seeing Egypt's unique monuments?).

In principle, the case for including services in the GATT as a means of liberalizing trade on a nondiscriminatory basis is strong. The motives of individual nations in proposing or opposing such a change tend to be responsive to national interest groups. The US is the main proponent, because it believes itself to be the most competitive supplier of services (service trade is, however, more difficult to measure than goods trade) and the US has a surplus in services trade (table 17.1), so further liberalization would help the US balance of payments. Among the services to be included in the GATT, the US and other developed countries have focused on skill-intensive or capital-intensive services (such as financial or management or information services) and do not mention more labor-intensive services such as construction (where NICs such as South Korea are highly competitive). The US position that the multilateral trade negotiations focus on trade in services, requiring no relocation of buyer or seller, has a similar bias against labor-intensive services in which developing countries may have a comparative advantage.

Disputes over which services to include, legitimate regulatory concerns, and the strength of vested interests all conspire to slow down progress in service trade liberalization. Within the EC, where barriers to factor mobility have been removed in principle, restricted rights of establishment, national regulations, and other NTBs have made the service industries very difficult to integrate, and they represent one of the most intractable obstacles to completing the unified internal market. GATT negotiations are also likely to make slow progress in this area, and the most that can be expected in the near future are "codes of behavior" which will be accepted by some GATT signatories and not by others; that is, a form of conditional MFN treatment will be ratified rather than bringing services into the GATT regime based on nondiscriminatory trade policies.

17.3 The Balance of Payments

The balance of payments is the name given to the international accounts recording a country's economic transactions with the rest of the world during a given time period. By definition, the international payments in which a country is involved must balance, because any sale of goods, services, or assets has its counterpart in the payment for that sale. In the pure trade models of the first three parts of this book, balance is automatic because exports are bartered for imports. Once money and assets are introduced it is possible to exchange goods for future claims, but the overall balance of payments must still balance, because any excess of imports over exports will be offset by the means of payment for the excess imports. Put another way, the balance of payments is constructed under the principles of double-entry bookkeeping (for example, an import is a debit which is matched by the credit item of the amount paid for the import) and, since every transaction is an equal-sized debit and credit, the two columns must be equal.

The balance of payments can be presented at various levels of aggregation and the entries can be divided into various categories. Table 17.1 gives 1987 data for several countries at a high aggregation level. The most usual broad distinction is between the current account and the capital account. The current account measures the country's net exports of goods and services. For all the countries listed, merchandise trade is more important than

Table 17.1 Balance of payments data, selected countries, 1987 (in US$ billion)

	China	Egypt	Japan	Mexico	UK	US	West Germany
77aad[a] Goods exports (+)	+35	3	225	21	130	250	278
77abd Goods imports (−)	−36	7	128	12	147	410	208
77add Service income (+)	+5	4	80	9	125	175	81
77aed Service payments (−)	−4	4	85	14	107	156	90
77afd + agd Unrequited transfers	0	+4	−4	+1	−6	−13	−16
77ad Current a/c balance	0	0	+87	+4	−4	−154	+45
77bad DFI	+2	+1	−18	+3	−15	−2	−7
77bbd Portfolio I	+1	0	−91	0	+27	+32	−3
77bcd Other long-term K	+3	0	−24	+1	0	−1	−4
77cd Basic balance	+6	+1	−47	+8	+8	−125	+32
77dd Short-term K	0	−1	+89	−3	−20	+50	−14
77ed + 78ad + 78cd	−2	+1	−3	+1	+9	+25	+9
78dd Performance balance	+5	0	+39	+6	−3	−50	+26

[a] The code letters are the lines in the source; 77ed + 78ad + 78cd is errors and omissions and valuation changes. The balances may not sum exactly because of rounding.

Source: IMF *International Financial Statistics*

service income and payments, but for the UK and the US the net credit on service items helps to pay for the deficit on goods trade. Service income, especially tourism and workers' remittances, is relatively important for Egypt, China, and Mexico, although in the case of Mexico it is more than offset by the high service payments (primarily interest on foreign debt). The last item in the current account, unrequited transfers, states how much of the above transactions involved no payment, and includes development aid in the form of gifts plus any other donations to foreigners (for example, for the US and West Germany private and public transfers to Israel). Adjustment for unrequited transfers is necessary to calculate the current account balance; that is, the amount which must be financed by transferring assets or which involves accumulation of assets.

The capital account contains all the remaining balance of payments items, which are characterized by involving some future claim on or liability to another country's residents. The balance of payments is in equilibrium if the desired accumulation or running down of international assets is exactly equal to the current account surplus or deficit. The difficulty here, of course, is to distinguish between which capital account items are desired for themselves and which are involuntary counterparts of the current account situation. The former are usually referred to as the autonomous items of the capital account.

Long-term capital flows are considered to be autonomous items because they reflect the underlying conditions described in section 17.1, such as differing relative endowments of capital and firm-specific advantages which can best be realized by direct foreign investment. Thus, the more developed countries in table 17.1 all have a net outflow of direct foreign investment, and the developing countries a net inflow. The situation with respect to portfolio and other long-term capital flows is more puzzling, with Japan as the leading lender and the US and the UK as major borrowers; this apparently reflects a higher savings propensity in Japan and higher marginal propensity to spend by American and British governments and consumers, which creates higher interest rates in the latter which draw in long-term capital from Japan (and to a lesser extent Germany). Another explanation of this pattern is that long-term assets which are readily tradable, such as US Treasury Bonds or British gilts, are as liquid as short-term assets, and can be considered as means of accepting essentially short-term IOUs, so that the distinction between this item and the next item, short-term capital flows, becomes unclear. For this reason, one commonly used measure of balance of payments disequilibrium, the basic balance, which consists of the current account plus long-term capital flows, may be a misleading guide.

The performance balance, given in the last line of table 17.1, is an alternative guide to balance of payments equilibrium. This measure includes short-term capital flows, other than transactions by central banks which involve reserves, plus errors and omissions, and valuation changes. The performance balance indicates that in 1987 the US and the UK were running down their stocks of reserve assets to finance deficits in their current account plus the autonomous items in their capital account (referred to as BOP deficits for brevity), while Japan, West Germany, Mexico, and China were accumulating reserves as a result of their BOP surpluses.

Two important limitations on using any single measure of BOP disequilibrium should, however, be noted. Firstly, it is intrinsically very difficult to distinguish autonomous from accommodating capital flows. Some private traders find themselves accumulating IOUs, perhaps ultimately in the form of bills (short-term assets) or liquid bonds (long-term assets), some of which they need as petty cash and some of which they might be happy to hold for the interest. Government accumulation and decumulation of assets is likewise difficult to classify, because some central bank transactions are commercial if it acts for state-owned companies or government departments, and even changes in reserve assets may be for exogenous prudential reasons rather than involuntary consequences of a BOP deficit.

In sum, the balance of payments is an accounting statement of the economic transactions between the residents of a country and the rest of the world. As such it contains the fundamental empirical information for the study of international economic relations. The principle behind the balance of payments is double-entry bookkeeping and, although in practice items may be amalgamated and the one-to-one correspondence of credits and debits obscured, the aggregate totals must balance. It is, however, useful for many purposes to draw lines in the balance of payments and derive above-the-line surpluses and deficits; for example, to measure the trade balance, the current account balance, or the overall balance. The last of these is the most difficult to define but is also the most useful, because it is the guide to the sustainability of the international economic relations which exist for their own sake. The next chapter focuses on what happens when BOP disequilibria exist, and on the role of trade policy as a corrective mechanism.

Further Reading

Dunning (1988) sets out the eclectic theory of DFI. Bhagwati (1987) discusses the distinctive features of trade in services and their place in the Uruguay Round.

18

Trade Policy when the Balance of Payments is in Disequilibrium

The analysis of trade policy in part III was based on the simplifying assumption that each country's trade was balanced. Although brief mention was made of the possibility of using trade barriers to reduce aggregate unemployment, this argument was dismissed on the grounds that "exporting unemployment" by running a trade surplus would invite retaliation by trading partners. The present chapter considers in greater detail the role of trade policy when trade is unbalanced: or, more precisely, since a trade deficit offset by an equal surplus elsewhere in the current account or in autonomous capital account items poses no problem, it considers trade policy in the presence of BOP disequilibria. We can already guess that trade policy will not be an ideal adjustment mechanism for removing BOP disequilibrium, but we must also consider whether it is any better or worse than alternative adjustment mechanisms given that something must happen.

At this point, money has to enter the picture. BOP disequilibrium implies the need for assets which can be held as IOUs. In addition, an accepted medium of exchange reduces transaction costs by eliminating the necessity for a double coincidence of wants, which is a prerequisite for barter. Within national boundaries there is typically a single currency which is legal tender and can be used as a medium of exchange or as a store of value, but international economic transactions are characterized by the existence of separate national monies. The relative prices of these monies are their exchange rates. The first section of this chapter discusses the determination of exchange rates, as a preliminary to analyzing alternative BOP adjustment mechanisms in section 18.2 and studying in more detail in section 18.3 trade policies as an adjustment mechanism.

18.1 The BOP and the Exchange Rate

The BOP is a statement of the economic transactions between a country's residents and the rest of the world. Each debit item represents a demand for foreign exchange and each credit item a supply of foreign exchange. Thus, imports ultimately have to be paid for in the supplier's currency and investment outflows require foreign currency to purchase the foreign assets, while visiting tourists or purchasers of a country's exports will need to buy the domestic currency. The interaction of this demand and supply determines the exchange rate, which is the price of foreign currency.

The foreign exchange market for the major currencies is efficient because it deals in a homogeneous product (a franc is a franc whether it is a crumpled or a clean bill, or an entry in a bank account), storage costs are low (although there may be a mark-up to buy banknotes rather than making transfers between bank accounts), information about prices travels fast, and market participants are interested solely in the best price for the currency they are buying or selling. Market efficiency implies, apart from small commission charges and minor variations depending on the type of transaction, the existence of a single exchange rate worldwide for any pair of major currencies.[1] Although much more could be said about the price variations and the institutions involved, in the present context we will only consider the determination of the spot exchange rate for immediate large-scale transactions.

18.1.1 The Traditional Approach

The proximate determinants of the exchange rate are items in the BOP. Since imports and exports are usually the largest items, they provide the traditional starting point. Figure 18.1 considers two countries, the UK and the US, whose only international transactions are commodity trade, and examines the demand for and supply of foreign exchange from the UK side (the analysis is symmetrical, so in a two-country setting it is irrelevant which way around it is done). The dollar price is on the vertical axes of panels (a) and (b) because we are interested in the price of foreign currency. Assume that exports are denominated in the supplier's currency, so that when the exchange rate changes the dollar price of US exports is unchanged but the dollar price of UK exports changes by the amount of the exchange rate change. Thus, when the pound falls in value from 2 to 1.5 dollars, imports become more expensive for UK consumers looking at their price in pounds,

[1]The word "major" is inserted because markets for minor currencies may be too thin to permit exact matching of buyers and sellers everywhere, so that transactions costs become larger and price variations possible (in practice, a Malaysian wishing to import from Nigeria will find the transaction priced in a vehicle currency, say US dollars, and will convert ringit into dollars, which the seller will then convert into naira). Many currencies are not freely convertible and are traded at varying prices in black markets or outside the country's borders. None of this applies to the major currencies in which the vast majority of international transactions are priced.

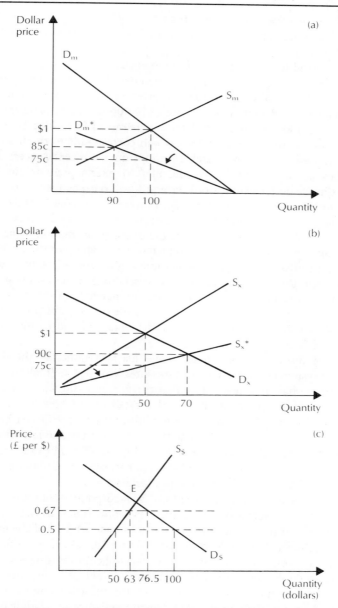

Figure 18.1 The traditional approach to exchange rate determination. The UK's demand for and supply of (a) imports and (b) exports at the exchange rate of 0.5 per $ are represented by D_m, S_m, D_x, and S_x. At the exchange rate of 0.67 per $ D_m and S_x pivot to D_m^* and S_x^*. The UK's demand for and supply of dollars is shown in (c).

but UK exports become more attractive to US buyers looking at their dollar price. These changes are represented by the shifts to $D_m\star$ and $S_x\star$ in figure 18.1.

The demand for and supply of foreign exchange at each exchange rate is given in figure 18.1(c). For example, when one dollar costs 0.5 pounds the UK wants $100 to buy imports and receives $50 for its exports, and when the exchange rate changes to 0.67 pounds per dollar the demand for dollars falls to $76.5 and the supply of dollars increases to $63.[2] The equilibrium exchange rate is the price of dollars which corresponds to the intersection point E. In figure 18.1 this is a stable equilibrium because the excess demand for dollars at, say, an exchange rate of 0.67 exerts pressure for further increases in the dollar's value until the equilibrium exchange rate is reached.

The foreign exchange market may, however, not have a stable equilibrium. The effect on the import side of a higher value of the dollar is to reduce both the equilibrium dollar price and the quantity of imports demanded in the UK market, thus reducing the demand for dollars. On the export side, however, the effect of a higher dollar value is ambiguous because the dollar price falls and the quantity exported increases, so that the supply of dollars may increase or decrease. In the latter case, an increase in the price of dollars may reduce supply by more than it reduces the demand for dollars, so that the excess demand becomes greater rather than less and equilibrium will never be reached.

Fears of disorderly foreign exchange markets underlay the desire to establish a system of fixed exchange rates after World War II, although more recently there has been less worry that the demand and supply curves are such that the type of disequilibrium described in the previous paragraph may occur. For a small country the equilibrium point, E, must be stable. Even for large countries, the elasticities of export supply and import demand are unlikely to be sufficiently small for E to be unstable. The exact condition for stability will be derived in the next section during the discussion of using the exchange rate as a BOP adjustment mechanism.

How can the other entries in the BOP be incorporated into this approach to exchange rate determination? In the 1950s and 1960s services trade and long-term capital flows were considered to be independent of the exchange rate, in which case they can be included in figure 18.1 as shifts in the demand and supply curves, which will alter the numerical equilibrium values but not the analysis. As capital markets have become larger and more open, it has become apparent that some of these flows are influenced by the exchange rate, but as long as they have stable demand and supply relationships they

---

[2]Note that the demand and supply curves in figure 18.1 are all drawn as straight lines for simplicity, but typically they will not be; and, specifically, diagram (c) is not the precise counterpart of the situation drawn in (a) and (b).

can be readily incorporated into the traditional approach to exchange rate determination. Short-term capital flows, on the other hand, may contain a speculative element, if buyers and sellers of currencies expect future exchange rates to differ from current values. If the expectations are in the correct direction then such capital flows will be stabilizing as they will be self-fulfilling and speed up the adjustment process, but if they are in the wrong direction then they will be destabilizing.

The government enters the picture in two ways. Firstly, it is a purchaser of foreign goods and services, and exporter of goods and services produced by public enterprises. These activities can be included in the preceding analysis of the current account, although they give the government some leverage in controlling the demand for and supply of foreign exchange in any period. Secondly, and more importantly, the government can build up or run down its holdings of reserve assets. Quantitatively, changes in reserves are a small BOP item, but they are important for exchange rate determination because they are not independent movements. Thus, in figure 18.1(c), if the British government decides to maintain an exchange rate of 0.5 pounds to the dollar, it can do this by reducing its reserves by $50. As long as the stock of reserves or the willingness to accumulate reserves is sufficient, the government can set and maintain any exchange rate by adjusting its reserve holdings.

Finally, capital flows are determined not only by the real forces described in the section 17.1 analysis of DFI and by speculation, but also by interest rates. Higher interest rates attract more savings. An important distinction between lending in domestic and in international capital markets, however, is that lending to a foreign borrower involves exchange rate risk for at least one side; for example, a German buying a US bond paying 10 percent interest will receive $10 per $100 invested, but his return per DM invested depends upon the difference between the exchange rate when he purchased the dollars and the exchange rate when he reconverts his funds into marks. Thus, the German investor's decision of whether to buy the US asset or to buy a German asset depends upon the interest rate differential and also on his view of what will happen to the exchange rate.

There is an important set of transactions where interest rate differentials affect the spot exchange rate regardless of future expectations, and that is the choice of where to hold forward cover. Suppose an Italian merchant needs dollars in 90 days' time: Should he buy the dollars now (and earn US money market interest rates for the 90 days) or should he keep his lire earning Italian interest rates and purchase the dollars when he needs them? In the latter case he can avoid any uncertainty about the cost of the dollars by purchasing them in the forward exchange market; that is, making a contract now to buy dollars with lire in 90 days' time at a specified exchange rate. The least-cost choice of where to hold forward cover depends only on the spot and forward exchange rates and the interest rate differential; it is independent of the merchant's expectations of the future, although he could speculate on the future exchange rate by not holding any forward cover at all. An example of covered interest arbitrage is as follows:

> Exchange rates: spot LIt1,000/$; forward (90 days) LIt1,025/$
> Annual interest rates: US 8 percent; Italy 20 percent
> (a) Buying dollars spot, each million lire will be worth $1,000 × 1.02 = $1,020 in 90 days
> (b) Buying dollars forward, each million lire will be worth 1,050,000/ 1,025 = $1,024 in 90 days

In the example given above it pays to hold lire now, but if the Italian interest rate fell to 18 percent or less it would be better to buy the dollars now. For given exchange rates, there is only one interest rate differential where the choice is evenly balanced, and with any other differential arbitragers can make a riskless profit by simultaneously buying a currency spot and selling it forward. Thus, in the above situation, arbitragers will boost the spot demand for lire and demand for lire-denominated assets, until the value of the lire increases and the Italian interest rate falls sufficiently to establish the appropriate balance between spot and forward exchange rates and interest differentials. Such arbitrage was relatively unimportant in the 1950s when capital flows were subject to national controls and international capital markets were poorly developed, but now the transactions costs are small and short-term capital moves in large quantities in response to the smallest interest differentials.

The traditional approach to exchange rate determination emphasizes real forces, in particular merchandise trade and long-term capital flows. The government can observe these forces and, if it wishes to maintain a certain exchange rate, change its reserve position to match the excess demand or excess supply of foreign currency at the desired rate. Capital flows can be incorporated into this approach, but because of the volatility of expectations and the role of interest rates they sit uneasily with the emphasis on slow-changing real forces and the omission of monetary considerations.

18.1.2   The Monetary Approach

An alternative approach to exchange rate determination was developed during the late 1960s as part of the monetarist critique of Keynesian macroeconomic theory. The monetary approach emphasizes the financial entries in the BOP. Since each real flow in the BOP has a financial counterpart, the traditional and monetary approaches to exchange rate determination could be viewed as mirror images, focusing on alternate columns in the double-entry bookkeeping behind the BOP, but by highlighting different sides of each transaction the two approaches yield different insights.

The basic building block to the monetary approach is the purchasing power parity (PPP) doctrine. This doctrine states that the exchange rate tends to the level which equalizes the purchasing power of the two national monies:

$$P = eP^\star, \tag{18.1}$$

where P is the domestic country's price level, $P^\star$ is the foreign country's price level, and e is the exchange rate (measured as the number of domestic currency units needed to buy one foreign currency unit). The micro-economic basis for purchasing power parity is the law of one price. If markets are competitive and transport costs are negligible, then the price of any good must be the same in all locations or else there will be opportunities for profitable arbitrage (that is, buying the good where it is cheap and selling it where it is dear).

There are some obvious drawbacks to assuming that purchasing power parity applies in the real world. Perhaps most fundamentally, the law of one price is an abstraction, just as factor-price equalization was in an earlier part of this book – both are logical implications if a series of assumptions all hold. In reality, there are transport and other transactions costs, as well as trade barriers and imperfectly competitive markets. Arbitrage cannot ensure that, say, car prices are identical in France and in Germany unless the price differential becomes sufficiently large to justify the effort, and car makers try to thwart such arbitrage and keep markets segmented (for example, by use of their dealer and after-sales networks) so that they can better use their market power. Moving from the microeconomic to the macroeconomic level, pur-chasing power parity will be distorted even if individual prices are the same, because consumption bundles differ from country to country so that the weights used in calculating the national price indices will differ; for example, the West German Statistisches Bundesamt publishes consumer currency parities using German and foreign weights, and with German weights $P/P^\star$ is lower because relatively popular items are cheaper in the home country and the purchasing power parity value of e is therefore smaller.

There is also a general bias in actual exchange rates' deviation from purchasing power parity. Poor countries tend to have lower price levels than rich countries, when they are both expressed in common currency units. Balassa (1964) explained this phenomenon in terms of the distinction between traded and nontraded goods. He noted that (i) labor inputs in non-traded activities are roughly the same in different countries, whereas labor productivity in the traded goods sector varies considerably, and (ii) the opportunity cost of labor is the wage rate in the traded goods sector which is determined by world prices and the marginal product of labor in that sector. Thus, in high-income countries, where labor productivity and the wage rate in the traded goods sector are high, the price of nontraded goods and services will be higher than in poorer countries. In a poor country $P_T = eP_T^*$ by the law of one price (assuming that international markets are competitive) but $P_{NT} < P_{NT}^*$, so that the overall price level used in expression (18.1) as a weighted average of the price of traded (P_T) and nontraded goods and services (P_{NT}) will not satisfy purchasing power parity; the actual exchange rate, e, will be greater than the PPP exchange rate, P/P^*, so that domestic prices will be less than foreign prices converted at the actual exchange rate ($P < P^*e$).

These considerations are important when making international income or cost-of-living comparisons. They also underlay a general scepticism toward the PPP doctrine during the 1950s and 1960s. A series of empirical studies, however, revived interest in PPP by showing that it worked well in explaining exchange rate movements during the 1920s, and for the few floating currencies (such as those of Canada, Mexico, Peru, and Thailand) in the 1950s, although PPP works less well when there are major restrictions on international transactions (as in the 1930s) or when governments maintain fixed exchange rates (as in the 1950s and 1960s – although then PPP was a guide to growing BOP disequilibria). The rehabilitation of PPP coincided with the rise of monetarism, and was combined with the monetarist view that the demand for real money balances is a stable function with a small number of determinants.

The simplest monetarist model of the exchange rate combines expression (18.1) with a money demand function and the condition for monetary equilibrium:

$$M_D/P = f(y,i,x), \qquad (18.2)$$
$$M_S = M_D, \qquad (18.3)$$

where y is real income, i is the real interest rate, x is the expected inflation, M_D is the money demand, and M_S is the money supply. Changes in money demand and money supply determine the price level and, since a similar process occurs in the rest of the world, the interaction of these changes at home and abroad determines the exchange rate. Thus, real variables can affect the exchange rate, but only via the demand for money. If the money demand function is stable, then the exchange rate is determined by the relative rates of money supply growth here and in the rest of the world.

This simple model can be modified to take account of nontraded activities by making the relative price of tradeables and nontradeables another exogenous variable. Such modifications can take account of the Balassa effect and other long-term deviations from PPP. The monetarist approach could explain why the mark's underlying strength increased during the 1960s (the fixed exchange rate regime meant that this was manifested in growing German BOP surpluses) when the German money supply grew more slowly than that of other large countries. Thus, the mark needed to be revalued in the 1970s, even though PPP alone could not predict the appropriate rate, because the relative price of tradeables to nontradeables seemed lower in Germany than elsewhere in western Europe or North America.

The simple monetary approach to exchange rate determination works well in hyperinflation episodes, when the inflating country sees its currency's value plummet in terms of the currencies of countries with low inflation. This approach was less satisfactory during the 1970s in explaining major exchange rates, which fluctuated much more than purchasing power parity would imply, and often in perverse directions in the short and medium term. This empirical deficiency encouraged the search for another approach to exchange rate determination, which would capture the volatility of unregulated exchange rates.

18.1.3   The Asset Market View

The asset market view of exchange rate determination starts from the observation that the exchange rate is the relative price of two currencies, and this price should be considered as an asset price. The prices of assets (such as stocks, bonds, and real estate) primarily reflect expectations about future conditions, such as the stream of returns coming from a share in a company or from renting land. In the short run, asset prices fluctuate with changes in expectations. Since expectations have a subjective element, the interpretation of the latest "news" may later be revised, so that if exchange rates are asset prices then they may be volatile.

The asset market approach can also explain the phenomenon of overshooting, where an exchange rate moves too far in one direction and has to move the "wrong" way later to correct the overshooting. Goods markets adjust more slowly than asset markets to a changed situation. An unanticipated fall in the money supply, for example, will lead to lower prices, but rigidities in the goods and labor markets mean that the price adjustment takes time. Meanwhile, the slow adjustment of money demand leaves an excess supply of money which requires higher interest rates to establish money market equilibrium. The higher interest rate attracts foreign capital and leads to a short-run appreciation of the domestic currency greater than that ultimately required by the change in prices due to the fall in the money supply. A classic example of overshooting was the appreciation in the value of the British pound in 1979–80 after Mrs Thatcher came to power.

These three approaches are complementary insofar as the traditional and monetary approaches to exchange rate determination focus on the long-run trends, and the variables identified as important are those which people look at in forming their expectations. In the short run, however, the asset market features are often dominant so that exchange rates may be volatile, especially if foreign exchange market participants are receiving unclear signals about future trends in prices (for example, from announcements about monetary policy) or imports or exports (for example, from business cycle indicators or fiscal policy announcements).

18.2   *Four Options for Removing BOP Disequilibria*

The previous section analyzed how exchange rates are determined. The proximate determinants of the exchange rate are the demand and supply components which appear in the BOP. Which are the key variables underlying the size of these components, and hence determining the exchange rate? The traditional approach emphasizes current account items plus the role of interest rates in monitoring covered interest parity. The monetary approach focuses on the money supply, and to a lesser extent on inflationary expectations and other determinants of the demand for money. The asset view emphasizes the nature of the exchange rate as an asset price and hence it is subject to volatility. All of these approaches to exchange rate determination can also be viewed as approaches to the BOP; for example, if the government is supporting a fixed exchange rate by changes in reserves then the theories of the previous section will help to explain the size of the BOP deficit or surplus.

Disequilibrium in a country's international transactions can be manifested either by the exchange rate being at an undesired value or by the BOP (measured, say, by the performance balance) being in surplus or deficit. What adjustment mechanisms can remove the disequilibrium? Another way of viewing this question is to ask how a country's external transactions will adjust to some change (such as an increase in imports or in military spending abroad) which disrupts BOP equilibrium and increases the demand for foreign exchange. There are four ways for this excess demand for foreign exchange to be removed:

1   Let the exchange rate adjust to the level which achieves BOP equilibrium under the new conditions.
2   Meet the excess demand by running down the country's foreign exchange reserves.
3   Ration the amount of foreign exchange available so that demand equals supply.
4   Adjust the domestic economy so that the aggregate demand and supply

curves underlying the BOP ensure equilibrium at the current exchange rate.

In practice all governments of the major trading nations use a combination of these four mechanisms, although the mix varies and is constrained at any time by the conventions of the current international monetary system. Analytically, however, it is convenient to treat the four options one at a time.

18.2.1 Exchange Rate Changes

The simplest adjustment mechanism for any change in demand or supply conditions affecting the BOP would be to let the exchange rate do the work; that is, to rely upon the price mechanism. The first question that arises is whether a stable equilibrium price of foreign currency exists; as we saw in the previous section, the possibility of a downward-sloping supply curve for foreign exchange means that stability is not guaranteed. The stability condition depends upon the elasticities underlying the demand and supply curves for foreign exchange. In the small-country case in which the elasticity of demand for exports and the elasticity of supply of imports are infinite, depreciation of the currency must improve the trade balance and the equilibrium will be stable. Conversely, if the demand for exports and the demand for imports are both perfectly inelastic, then equilibrium is unstable. Thus, the more elastic the demand for imports and exports, the more likely there is to be a stable equilibrium – in which case the price mechanism will function as an adjustment mechanism.

The most relevant case for "non-small" countries is that in which prices are fixed in the seller's currency, as in figure 18.1. The condition for stability is that the absolute values of the demand elasticities for exports and imports sum to more than one. This requirement, known as the Marshall–Lerner condition, is only strictly true if the supply curves are perfectly elastic, but it is a good guide in other situations. Does the Marshall–Lerner condition hold in practice? For almost all countries elasticities are sufficiently large for the condition to be satisfied in the long run. In the short run, however, elasticities are smaller and the initial reaction to an exchange rate change is likely to be in the wrong direction; specifically, after a currency depreciation (an increase in the price of foreign currency) the foreign currency value of exports which have already been priced in the domestic currency will fall so that the trade balance deteriorates. This distinction between the short-run and long-run consequences of a change in exchange rate is referred to as the J-curve effect, because the time path of the trade deficit following a currency depreciation looks like a letter "J."

Thus, if the Marshall–Lerner condition is satisfied, a market-determined exchange rate will achieve long-run external balance – if we only consider the current account. In this case, since trade imbalance is unimportant, all of the conclusions from the first parts of this book apply to a monetary economy; only relative prices matter for resource allocation, and money is just a veil. The existence of money reduces transactions costs; having to use national monies rather than a single global currency is a minor inconvenience for traders, but it does not affect the "real" analysis of trade theory.

Such a strong conclusion fits comfortably with the traditional view of exchange rate determination, which emphasizes the current account. The asset market view of exchange rate determination, however, implies volatile exchange rates and, even if there are pressures toward long-run equilibrium, the short-run volatility following reactions to "news" may seriously disrupt trade by giving confusing signals to traders and investors trying to act on the basis of future prices. Such problems are mitigated by the existence of forward exchange markets, but forward markets cannot cover all future time periods and even for the major currencies there are market gaps. The effects on the real economy of exchange rate volatility are a major reason why no government is willing to rely solely on the exchange rate as its BOP adjustment mechanism. This drawback is especially pronounced for small countries; even though the Marshall–Lerner condition holds, governments are unwilling to leave the exchange rate to be market-determined, because the small number of transactions would make large fluctuations likely.

18.2.2   Financing

A government faced with external imbalance and unwilling to allow the exchange rate alone to correct the imbalance can use its reserves or draw down reserve credit lines to limit the exchange rate movement needed to restore BOP equilibrium. This is known as financing a BOP deficit, and the basic mechanism was described in section 18.1.1; the change in reserves offsets the excess demand or supply in the foreign exchange market. The feasibility of financing as an adjustment mechanism is limited by the amount of reserves held by a deficit country or the amount that the government of a surplus country is willing to accumulate. A practical problem here is the definition of reserve assets, which are in principle anything accepted as a means of settling international debts but which can include holdings by quasi-governmental agencies in addition to the more obvious category of Central Bank assets; these problems, alluded to in discussing definitions of BOP disequilibrium, will be ignored in what follows.

Under the Bretton Woods system of fixed exchange rates, financing was the major short-run BOP adjustment mechanism of the 1950s and 1960s. As BOP disequilibria became more long-term (reflected in deviations of fixed exchange rates from PPP), however, speculators against overvalued currencies enjoyed a one-way bet; for example, in the mid-1960s speculators against the British pound would at worst find that the pound's value was unchanged, but if they happened to hold foreign assets in November 1967 they enjoyed a substantial gain when the pound's value fell from $2.8 to $2.4. Just as speculators profited from buying cheap and selling dear, the Central Banks who were committed to meet any excess demand for their currency by selling reserves ended up selling cheap and buying dear; for example, in early November 1967 the Bank of England bought pounds from eager suppliers at $2.8 apiece, and when it sought to rebuild its reserve-holdings at month's end the pounds were sold for $2.4 each, for a loss of 40 cents on each pound, or billions of dollars overall! By the early 1970s, financing had become a very expensive way of maintaining fixed exchange rates, as international capital markets were now sufficiently free that speculators could buy or sell currencies easily.

In the flexible exchange rate system which has existed since the early 1970s, speculation is not necessarily a one-way bet and Central Bank intervention in foreign exchange markets is not condemned to be loss-making. Governments use financing to reduce exchange rate volatility and to slow the pace of exchange rate adjustment. Whether or not such intervention is justified depends upon the relative costs of using resources to satisfy consumption or to increase future output, and of using them to accumulate reserve assets which can be used to reduce adjustment costs; the opportunity costs of holding reserves must be compared with the benefits.

Financing may be unnecessary if private capital flows are stabilizing. With perfect competition and perfect foresight, the real exchange rate will change in response to, say, reduced export demand, but the adjustment path will be determined by the time preference of individuals and cannot be improved upon by government intervention. However, this happy outcome will not be assured if there are capital market imperfections, if real wages are sticky, or if the government is better informed than the private sector about the state of the economy and its own policy intentions.

18.2.3   Direct Controls

Governments unwilling to rely on the price mechanism can adjust BOP disequilibria by direct intervention. They might ban certain international transactions or limit access to foreign exchange below the free market equilibrium quantity. The drawbacks of direct controls are relatively easy to analyze because the costs are similar to those from trade barriers.

Figure 18.2 illustrates a situation in which, at the exchange rate of 1.5 rupees to the dollar, there is an excess demand for foreign exchange. If the government decrees that all foreign exchange earnings must be turned over to the Central Bank, it must find some way of allocating the scarce foreign exchange. The most efficient method is to find the price at which demand

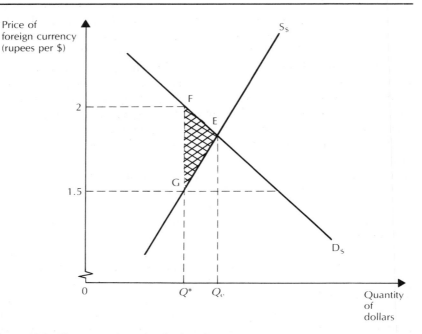

Figure 18.2 The operation of a dual exchange rate. $D_\$$ is the demand curve for dollars and $S_\$$ the supply curve. At an exchange rate of 1.5 rupees per dollar, the supply of dollars, Q^*, is less than the equilibrium value, Q_e. The market for the OQ^* available dollars can be cleared by selling them for two rupees each. By giving dollar-earners (exporters, and so on) less for each dollar earned and charging dollar users (importers, and so on) more, there is a resource allocation cost measured by the shaded area FEG.

would equal the available supply; in figure 18.2, this price is two rupees. Such a dual exchange rate system ensures that the available foreign exchange goes to the best use, if the market mechanism is working to ensure that price paid measures the social marginal benefit. Compared to the single exchange rate equilibrium, however, there is a national welfare loss, because residents would be willing to pay more for each of the Q^*Q_e units of foreign exchange than it costs the economy to earn them. The shaded area in figure 18.2 is analogous to the two welfare triangles in the partial equilibrium analysis of a tariff, and indeed a dual exchange rate has precisely the economic effects of a uniform tariff. The domestic redistribution consequences of the dual exchange rate are that the government benefits (by 0.5 rupees multiplied by OQ^*), exporters suffer and import-competing domestic producers benefit, while domestic consumers suffer.

More stringent or less simple foreign exchange restrictions will be even less efficient than a dual exchange rate, for reasons familiar from the analysis of nontariff barriers in chapter 11. Foreign exchange will not go to the best use, and resources will be diverted to rent-seeking rather than productive activities. Controls on currency transactions are more likely than restrictions on goods flows to lead to black markets, because money is homogeneous and difficult to trace; so enforcement costs are likely to mount if governments resort to tighter controls over foreign exchange transactions.

In sum, direct controls will involve net welfare losses if the demand and supply curves for foreign exchange represent the social benefits and social opportunity costs of foreign exchange. A case can be made in favor of temporary controls to smooth out temporary BOP disturbances or J-curve effects, if adequate reserves are unavailable. In the long term, however, the costs of using direct controls rise – including the consequences of growing black markets in inducing disrespect for the law and undermining business ethics.

18.2.4   Domestic Adjustment

The fourth adjustment mechanism is to change domestic variables which underlie the demand for and supply of foreign exchange. During the late 1940s and the 1950s the emphasis was on the relationship between aggregate domestic demand and the BOP, primarily via the marginal propensity to import. In the 1960s, with the rise of monetarism, there was renewed interest in the role of the price level, and today the main link between macroeconomic policy and the exchange rate is often seen in monetary terms.

BOP considerations can be introduced into a Keynesian model of the economy by including imports among the items determined by income and including exports as an autonomous item. Thus, in its simplest form, with no government activity, such a model can be expressed as:

$$Y = C + I_d + (X - M) = a + bY + I_d + X - mY,$$
$$Y = \frac{1}{(1 - b + m)} (a + I_d + X), \tag{18.4}$$

where Y is total output (GNP, which equals total expenditure by definition), C is consumption, I_d is domestic investment, X is exports, M is imports, a is the autonomous component of domestic consumption demand and of import demand, and b and m are the marginal propensities to consume and to import out of income. The multiplier for an open economy is smaller than it would be for a closed economy because imports are a leakage from the circular flow of income, which dampens the effect on aggregate demand of any change in autonomous variables. Thus, the open economy is subject to more shocks (from changes in the autonomous elements of X or M), but the magnitude of domestically induced cycles is less than in a closed economy.

Equilibrium in this simple Keynesian model occurs when the desired level of net domestic savings is equal to the trade surplus (using the identity $Y = C + S$ and expression (18.4) above):

$$S - I_d = X - M. \tag{18.5}$$

In figure 18.3 the initial equilibrium, Y^*, involves a trade deficit, which can be removed by depreciating the currency so that the X–M curve shifts to the right. But what if Y^* is the full employment level of output? Then the shift in output from domestic to export markets and the shift in demand from imports to domestic goods both generate excess domestic demand which will lead to inflation, offsetting the effects of currency depreciation until the X–M curve returns to its original position. Thus, in a full employment situation, exchange rate changes can remove a BOP deficit only if they are accompanied by changes in domestic variables; the latter adjustment mechanism is not only possible, but in this case (believed by most economic policy-makers

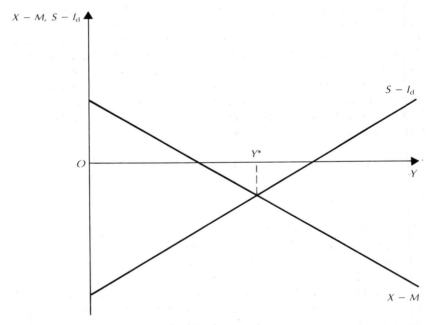

Figure 18.3 A Keynesian model of open economy equilibrium.

in high-income countries to be the normal case in the early 1960s) it is the only long-run alternative to direct controls. After introducing taxation and government spending into the model, it follows that the appropriate policy in the figure 18.3 full employment situation is to accompany the expenditure-switching policy of exchange rate depreciation by expenditure-reduction measures such as tax increases or government spending cuts.

Equilibrium in the simple Keynesian model ignores the monetary effects of trade imbalance. A BOP deficit involves a reduction in reserves, which reduces the domestic money supply, which in turn will lead to an increase in the interest rate which reduces C and I_d (and induces a capital inflow in a more complete model); that is, a BOP disequilibrium contains self-correcting mechanisms. The previous paragraph's analysis only applies if the government shortcircuits these mechanisms by offsetting the monetary effects of the BOP deficit by changing other components of the monetary base in a compensatory way; in other words, by adopting the appropriate policy toward its domestic claims, the Central Bank can ensure that any BOP imbalance has zero impact on the money supply. Breaking the link between the BOP and the money supply is known as sterilizing the monetary effects of BOP imbalance.

Sterilization is widely practised because governments wish to use monetary policy to achieve domestic macroeconomic goals, but there are two constraints on sterilization. Firstly, it is impossible to sterilize a long-run BOP surplus indefinitely, because the offsetting reductions in the domestic assets of the Central Bank will ultimately reduce those assets to zero and the reserves will equal the money supply (as in the pure gold standard system where reserves and money are identical). Secondly, to sterilize a BOP surplus the Central Bank must sell securities or increase commercial banks' reserve ratios in order to reduce domestic credit creation: in market economies the allocative mechanism is an increase in interest rates, which will lead to capital inflows and an increased BOP surplus. In the limit, with perfectly functioning international capital markets and no restrictions on capital mobility, it becomes impossible to sterilize the monetary effects of BOP disequilibrium even in the short run. Thus, although it was plausible to assume no monetary impact during the 1950s, this has become less plausible as international capital markets have become more efficient and as national controls on capital movement have been removed.

With no sterilization the two-way link between BOP and money supply ensures that BOP disequilibria are self-correcting. This was pointed out two centuries ago by David Hume and spelled out clearly in Ricardo's chapter on trade referred to in chapter 2. In the gold standard, the specie-flow mechanism is straightforward; a BOP surplus involves a gold inflow which increases the money supply, raising domestic prices and hence reducing exports and making imported goods more attractive, both of which erode the

BOP surplus. The same equilibriating mechanism is present in any situation where BOP disequilibrium changes the money supply. Therefore, in an important sense long-run BOP imbalance is a monetary phenomenon; that is, domestic credit is being extended too fast in a BOP-deficit country and too slowly in a BOP-surplus country.

The BOP imbalance as a monetary phenomenon can be seen even in the real economy model of figure 18.3. Without sterilization the trade deficit will involve a decrease in the domestic money supply leading to higher interest rates which will shift the $S-I_d$ curve to the left, so that currency depreciation can achieve full employment equilibrium. The general conclusion remains that, to remove a trade deficit in full employment domestic equilibrium, exchange rate depreciation must be accompanied by domestic deflation, either by fiscal or monetary contraction. Long-run disequilibrium must reflect an unwillingness to direct either form of macroeconomic policy to achieving external balance.

The existence of an automatic BOP adjustment mechanism (such as, the specie-flow mechanism or similar monetary process) does not imply that it should be left to function uninfluenced by government policy. If imports and exports respond slowly to price changes and if price reductions only occur with increased unemployment, then there may be a role for the government to use fiscal or monetary policy (or to use financing or temporary direct controls of the BOP) to smooth the adjustment process. The critical question for all national governments is which mix of monetary and fiscal policy can best achieve external balance, while allowing them flexibility in achieving domestic macroeconomic goals. Thus, a crucial reason for the end of the gold standard and again for the breakdown of the fixed exchange rate system in the early 1970s was the desire of governments to pursue independent monetary policies. The extent of policy independence was overestimated because in an interdependent world it is not possible to insulate the national economy from external shocks. The larger economies have some flexibility in pursuing independent macroeconomic policies, but only if they are prepared to accept the exchange rate consequences; France in 1981–2 was unwilling to accept the franc depreciation which followed the adoption of expansionary policies by the socialist government, but the UK in 1979–80 and the US in 1980–5 were willing to accept the exchange rate appreciation which followed tighter monetary policies.

Governments of smaller open economies, however, find it difficult to pursue independent monetary policies. If there is free capital mobility, then the domestic interest rate cannot diverge from the international rate without massive inflow or outflow of capital, so sterilization is impossible. Even with capital controls, if traded goods are a large share of GNP then exchange rate changes pass through very quickly into price and wage rate changes, thus eliminating the link between exchange rate changes and international competitiveness. Add to this the costs of thin markets for minor currencies (which have higher commission charges and greater volatility), then there are strong arguments for small open economies to accept the benefits of fixed exchange rates rather than pursue the illusion of monetary policy independence. Luxembourg has long tied its franc to the Belgian franc, and most developing countries peg their currencies to the US dollar, the French franc, or a composite such as the SDR.

Most members of the European Community fix their bilateral exchange rates within the European Monetary System, although the EMS currencies as a group float against other currencies such as the dollar, sterling, and the yen. Adjustment to BOP disequilibrium can be by exchange rate changes and there have been many agreed realignments since the EMS was founded in 1979, but such changes cause problems for trade, especially in agriculture where common support prices are enforced, and the EMS goal is to move toward irrevocably fixed exchange rates or, equivalently, a common currency. Adjustment within the EMS must therefore be primarily by adjustment of the domestic economy; that is, monetary and fiscal policy must maintain similar real interest rates and long-run economic changes are accommodated by factor movements. This is similar to the adjustment mechanism within the US, where Florida's trade deficit is offset by capital inflows and Alaska's windfall gain from oil discovery led to higher prices and labor immigration.

The choice of adjustment mechanism is thus one of taking the lesser of four evils – or if financing is considered as a strictly short-run measure, long-run adjustment involves three options. The next section will argue why trade policies, as one form of direct control, are likely to be a particularly inappropriate adjustment mechanism. The next chapter will consider the negative impact of exchange rate changes on trade flows. The major argument for relying on domestic adjustment as the long-run solution to BOP disequilibrium is that by foreswearing exchange rate changes the usefulness of money in international transactions is increased. The ideal situation for minimizing transactions costs would be to have a single world money, but governments are understandably jealous of their monetary autonomy and suspicious of giving this power to another government or to a supranational authority. The next chapter tries to assess one of the costs of retaining this autonomy.

18.3   Using Trade Policy to Reduce Current Account Deficits

There are two good ways to maintain long-run BOP equilibrium. One way is to maintain a fixed exchange rate and allow monetary mechanisms to achieve balance; that is, monetary policy independence is given up since monetary variables are endogenously determined by the external constraint. The other way is to have a floating exchange rate, although then fiscal policy is constrained by the requirement that domestic thrift $(S - I_d + T - G)$ is equal to the current account surplus $(X - M)$. Short-run adjustment costs or temporary disequilibria can be smoothed out by financing; that is, accumulating or running down the country's foreign exchange reserves. There is little room for direct controls as a first-best adjustment mechanism, and this applies equally to trade barriers, which have similar consequences to those shown in figure 18.2.

Trade barriers may be able to reduce a current account deficit, but they are a poor instrument because of the size of the resource misallocation costs. More fundamentally, they are an inappropriate tool because trade barriers are microeconomic tools and a current account deficit is a macroeconomic phenomenon. Thus, they are likely to involve more resource misallocation than even the foreign exchange controls analyzed in section 18.2.3. Even a uniform tariff favors some activities over others, because it favors import-substitute producers over exporters and because effective rates of protection will almost certainly vary so that some import-competing activities will receive more protection of value-added than others.

Furthermore, there is no presumption that trade barriers will in fact improve the current account. With flexible exchange rates, higher trade barriers will lead to appreciation of the currency unless there is a change in fiscal or monetary policy or in private-sector saving and investment behavior which adds to the net capital outflow (which will have its counterpart in a current account improvement). Several links between increased trade barriers and $T - G$ or $S - I_d$ are possible; for example, the increased tariff revenue may not be spent so that the budget deficit shrinks or the change in output mix after increased protection affects savings and investment patterns. These are possible mechanisms whereby trade barriers may reduce a current account deficit, but they are likely to be weak links and the impact on savings and investment could work equally well in the opposite direction.

A stronger case can be made for a positive effect of trade barriers on a current account deficit if there is a fixed exchange rate and excess domestic capacity; that is, unemployed labor and capital. In this case, alluded to in section 12.6, the reduced imports can be replaced by domestic goods, increasing output and also raising tax revenue and savings, which are both positively related to GNP. Assuming no retaliation, the improvement in the current account will continue as long as there is excess capacity. Once full employment is reached, higher trade barriers will lead to inflation rather than increased output, and the real exchange rate (the nominal exchange rate adjusted for inflation differentials) will appreciate as in the floating exchange rate scenario. Again, contractionary fiscal or monetary policy must accompany the imposition of the trade barriers if they are to affect the current account deficit.

In sum, there is a strong case for ignoring the link between trade policy and BOP disequilibrium. Trade policy can only improve a current account imbalance under certain circumstances and even then it is not the first-best adjustment mechanism. This was clearly realized during the 1930s when attempts to export unemployment by raising trade barriers led to retaliation and a drastic reduction in the volume of world trade, which harmed all countries by reducing the gains from trade and contributed to the severity of the depression. The issue was revived during the 1980s when calls were heard in the US for protection (or reduction of other countries' trade barriers) as a way of reducing the US current account deficit. Without a reduction in the budget deficit or an increase in domestic saving (or reduction in domestic investment), import restrictions would have been most unlikely to achieve the desired reduction in the current account deficit; the relevant analysis is that for a floating exchange rate and full employment, in which case higher import barriers will feed through into currency appreciation if there is no change in $G - T$ or $S - I_d$.

There are, however, several relationships between BOP disequilibrium or exchange rate movements and international trade and trade policy. Appreciation of the domestic currency harms producers of tradable goods; exports become less competitive in world markets and import-competing industries find it harder to compete with imports. Conversely, an undervalued currency helps the traded goods sector, and may be used as a tool of export promotion or of protection. This may be an element in explaining changes in protectionist pressure, which is likely to be stronger when the domestic currency is appreciating and weaker when it is depreciating in value. Aside from the level of the exchange rate, its volatility may affect international trade by creating uncertainty and thus deterring producers from diversifying out of domestic sales into exports. This is an important consideration in determining the relevant merits of the BOP adjustment mechanisms based on fixed and on floating exchange rates, which were analyzed in section 18.2. All of these issues will be addressed in the next chapter.

Further Reading

Dornbusch (1976) is the classic paper on overshooting. Mussa (1982) sets out a simple monetarist model of exchange rate determination. Frenkel (1981) documents the collapse of PPP during the 1970s. Corden (1960) provides the analytics of domestic economy adjustment to achieve external balance.

19

Exchange Rate Movements and International Trade

The previous chapter examined the relationship between trade policy and the BOP, focusing on the merits of trade policy as an instrument for removing BOP disequilibrium. This chapter reverses the question by looking at the effects of BOP disequilibrium on international trade flows. We will concentrate on the relationship between the exchange rate and trade.

Changes in the exchange rate obviously affect trade flows. Subject to the Marshall–Lerner condition, depreciation of the national currency will increase the value of exports and reduce the value of imports, and appreciation will reduce exports and increase imports. If a country reduces its tariffs or NTBs on imports, then a real depreciation of the currency must accompany the liberalization if the overall trade balance is to remain unchanged. To avoid increased unemployment after the trade liberalization, reduced employment in import-competing industries must be offset by employment gains in other industries; the currency depreciation will encourage expansion of production for export.

A striking example of the impact of currency appreciation on international trade was provided by the US during the first half of the 1980s. As the dollar increased in value relative to other currencies, American export and import-competing industries became less competitive. The precise effects depended upon the relevant elasticities and time lags, and on the degree to which foreign suppliers passed on exchange rate changes to US buyers or held dollar prices constant. Nevertheless, the aggregate impact was clear from the shift in the US trade balance from a small surplus in the late 1970s to a huge deficit by the mid-1980s. It was also apparent in the universal increase between 1980 and 1985 in the share of other countries' exports going to the US.

This episode generated fears in the US that the nation would become deindustrialized. Similar fears were expressed in the Netherlands, UK, and Australia when booming exports of natural gas, oil, and minerals led to exchange rate appreciation in the 1970s. Conversely, Japan and West Germany were widely believed to have benefited from "undervalued" exchange rates which stimulated their manufacturing sectors. There is a more general point here that applies to developing as well as to industrialized countries. When a country has a booming export sector there will be an impact on the rest of the economy; for example, when Nigeria and Indonesia experienced oil booms the lagging sector was agriculture. These issues will be analyzed in section 19.1.

Apart from the level of the exchange rate, fluctuations in the rate can also affect trade flows. In section 19.2 we will abstract from the direction of the movement and ask whether the volatility of exchange rates is important. Many commentators believe that the exchange rate volatility which has characterized the world economy since the early 1970s has had a negative impact on the level of international trade by increasing its riskiness.

19.1   Exchange Rate Protectionism

Exchange rate protectionism occurs when a country protects its traded goods sector (export and import-competing activities) relative to the nontraded goods sector by depreciating the exchange rate or preventing an exchange rate appreciation. Figure 19.1 shows a country's production possibility frontier between traded and nontraded goods. With the current account in balance the equilibrium is at point P, which is tangent to the highest attainable community indifference curve, and the domestic price ratio is the slope of K'K. If the government practises exchange rate protectionism by engineering a depreciation in the real exchange rate, then the domestic price line becomes flatter; that is, the domestic relative price of traded goods is increased.

Suppose that the government wishes to change the output mix in figure 19.1 to point Q, increasing the size of the traded goods sector. The domestic price line must be shifted to G'G, which can be done by devaluing the currency as long as the world price of traded goods and the domestic price of nontraded goods are fixed.[1] At the new domestic prices there is excess demand for nontraded goods and this can only be removed by reducing domestic demand; that is, a leftward shift in the G'G line. The new equilibrium will involve a current account surplus, because production of tradables at point Q is higher than consumption of tradables at point C. If the output mix Q is to be maintained, the monetary effects of the surplus must be sterilized: a policy of exchange rate protection can only last as long as sterilization can be sustained.

---

[1]Other assumptions would permit the same conclusion, but these seem the most reasonable. There must be some rigidity in the model in order for the nominal depreciation to lead to a real depreciation; with flexible prices, perfectly mobile factors, and so on, the economy would return to point P.

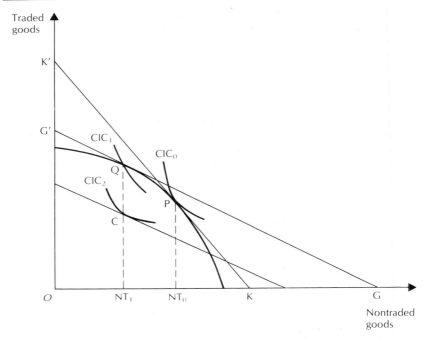

Figure 19.1 Exchange rate protection. The slope of K'K is the relative price of nontraded goods when the BOP is in equilibrium; point P is the output and consumption mix at that equilibrium. The slope of G'G is the domestic price ratio with an undervalued exchange rate; Q is the production point and C is the consumption point. The vertical distance Q − C is the trade surplus, which is here equivalent to the BOP surplus as we are ignoring the capital account. Output and consumption of nontraded goods fall from NT_0 to NT_1.

Thus, in the short run, exchange rate protectionism can be used to shield the traded goods sector from a decline in employment following an exogenous shock (for example, technical change in that sector). It might also be used to stimulate faster growth of the traded goods sector at the expense of the nontraded goods sector, if there are believed to be positive externalities associated with higher output of tradables. Even apart from the problem of sustainability, however, exchange rate protectionism is never the first-best policy. A subsidy for the production or consumption of traded goods financed by a tax on nontraded goods would be superior for reasons familiar from section 12.3. Even with the subsidy plus tax there is an inevitable welfare cost associated with shifting output from P to Q, because P is on the highest attainable community indifference curve. The consumption mix C, associated with the exchange rate protectionism policy, is on a lower indifference curve than Q. The additional welfare loss arises because the BOP surplus leads to the government holding an above-optimum level of reserve assets.

Exchange rate protectionism differs from the trade restrictions analyzed in part III because it shifts resources from the nontraded goods sector to the traded goods sector rather than shifting resources within the traded goods sector. It can be used to help part of the traded goods sector and will then have the advantage of not creating a distortion within that sector, but it will always have the added welfare cost associated with the BOP surplus. This choice of instruments has been relevant when countries have experienced rapid appreciation of their exchange rate due to a boom in primary exports and have wanted to avoid the ensuing decline in their manufacturing sector. The phenomenon was first observed when the Netherlands increased its natural gas exports in the 1970s, and is hence known colloquially as the Dutch Disease. Other cases are the Australian gold rush of the 1850s, and the impact of North Sea oil on the Norwegian and British economies in the 1970s. Even stronger Dutch Disease effects have been felt in some developing countries.

A boom in exports has both spending and resource movement effects. The boom increases income, and hence demand for nontraded goods and services, as long as the increased income is not invested abroad. At constant relative prices this leads to excess demand for nontraded items and excess supply of tradables. The latter creates a BOP surplus and hence exchange rate appreciation, which leads to a fall in sales by the lagging sector (nonbooming exports and import-competing industries) and a fall in the income of any factors specific to that sector (see the appendix to chapter 3). The resource movement effect consists of the shift of mobile factors out of the lagging sector and into the booming sector. The combined effect is to reduce the size of the lagging sector and the incomes of factors specific to that sector.

Faced with the Dutch Disease, exchange rate protectionism prevents the currency appreciation from taking place, and hence limits the deindustrialization process. The spending effect would be eliminated (it is offset by reduced absorption and a BOP surplus), and the resource movement effect is less than it would have been if the exchange rate had been allowed to appreciate. There is, of course, an inevitable welfare loss associated with slowing the deindustrialization, but this could be minimized by using a tax on the booming sector to subsidize the lagging sector. If the boom is viewed as temporary and the government wishes to avoid the adjustment costs and temporary income loss in the lagging sector which accompany the Dutch Disease, then the appropriate policy would be to use the windfall income gains to accumulate foreign assets which can be cashed in after the boom.

Neither a trade policy (a tariff on manufactured imports or a tax on the booming exports or a subsidy for manufactured exports) nor exchange rate protectionism is the first-best way to slow deindustrialization, but *a priori* it is not certain which of the two is least worst. The probability is, however, that exchange rate protectionism is the inferior policy because, although it avoids the distortion within the traded goods sector, it provides unwanted additional help to the booming sector as well as incurring the welfare cost associated with the BOP surplus. There may, however, be institutional reasons for resorting to exchange rate protectionism rather than trade policies when faced with a temporary Dutch Disease. Exchange rate protectionism is not in direct conflict with GATT obligations, and it may be easier to reverse the policy when the boom ends than it would be to remove legislated tariffs.

The above analysis of the Dutch Disease uses a specific factor three-sector model. When there is more than one mobile factor or when the lagging sector is decomposed into several subsectors, paradoxical results are possible with the lagging sector, or parts of it, expanding. Allowing international capital flows reinforces the output effects but reduces the boom's adverse impact on the income of capitalists in the lagging sector. International labor mobility often leads to immigration in response to the boom (the gold rush effect) which can reduce, but not eliminate, deindustrialization via the immigrants' spending. When the rents from the booming sector accrue primarily to the government and are put in a trust fund for future generations, this can also encourage a labor inflow in search of a share in the rents; this happened within Canada after the Alberta oil boom.

In sum, artificial undervaluation of the currency can increase the share of traded goods in total output and can help avoid Dutch Disease effects. Conversely, an overvalued exchange rate will promote the nontraded sector at the expense of the traded goods sector. Governments, and the general public, appear to be concerned about the output mix, although it is not obvious why manufacturing should be held in such universal high esteem – especially in an era of growing concern about the environmental impact of local productive activities. Even if there is agreement that one sector or subsector should be promoted, manipulating the exchange rate is not the best method (unless the sector to be promoted is the entire traded goods sector). The conclusion from chapter 12 still holds true; the best policy is the one which deals most directly with the perceived externality. In this case a subsidy to the activity is likely to be first-best. Exchange rate protectionism is likely to be even worse than trade policies, although in comparing two second-best policies such a conclusion can rarely be made with certainty.

19.2   Exchange Rate Volatility and Trade

Apart from the question of how exchange rate under- or overvaluation affects international trade, there is an analytically distinct question of whether exchange rate volatility is important. This has become an important question since the final collapse of the fixed exchange rate system in 1973, because rates of change in the major exchange rates of 1 percent a day or 5 percent a week or 25 percent a year have not been uncommon. Many critics of the current international monetary system have argued that such fluctuations have real economic costs insofar as they reduce the level of international trade and hence deprive the world of some of the possible gains from trade.

Here, as in the previous section, only changes in the real exchange rate matter. If purchasing power parity held everywhere at all times there would be no risk for traders from unanticipated changes in the nominal exchange rate. However, if PPP does not hold then exchange rate volatility can add to the uncertainty of producing for foreign markets or buying from foreign suppliers.

An individual trader can avoid uncertainty by invoicing in his own currency, but this option is obviously only available to the buyer or the seller, and not to both. The trader invoicing in a foreign currency can, however, also avoid exchange rate risk by buying the currency he or she will need to purchase the imports or by selling the proceeds from the exports in the forward exchange market. As long as well-developed forward exchange markets exist, there is only exchange rate risk if the trader chooses not to avoid it (that is, he or she chooses to be a speculator as well as a trader), and the cost of exchange rate volatility is reduced to the transactions costs of making a forward contract.

The negative impact of forward market imperfections and of related transactions costs on the level of international trade is an empirical question. It is a question which is difficult to answer directly because simple before and after comparisons of the fixed exchange period and the post-1973 international monetary system are dominated by concurrent changes (the oil crisis and global recession). In fact, a very small share of international trade transactions are protected from exchange rate risk by the traders taking forward cover. Nevertheless, the resulting uncertainty does not seem to have had any discernible impact on the volume of world trade (see Blackhurst and Tumlir, 1980).

19.3   Conclusions

At this point, it is worth repeating the microeconomic conclusion that trade is best served by a stable medium of exchange that minimizes transaction costs. Within the domestic economy this is achieved by imposing a monopoly on the supply of money, and by prudent management of the money supply. Within the international economy this situation does not exist because there are many national monies which are not perfect substitutes. In the absence of an international money, countries have to deal with BOP imbalances by one or more of the mechanisms described in the previous chapter. Exchange rate changes are likely to be part of the optimum policy mix.

If exchange rates are allowed to change in response to BOP disequilibria, this will have some real costs by requiring traders either to hedge against exchange rate risk or to become speculators. Section 19.2 concluded that such costs are small. Governments may also be tempted to regulate the exchange rate movements in order to affect trade flows – typically to help the manufacturing sector. Such a policy may be better than doing nothing; for example, if there are adjustment costs to allowing a traded goods sector decline temporarily only to be profitable once more when the exchange rate changes again – this is especially likely if overshooting occurs. It is, however, never the first-best policy; the exchange rate is a macroeconomic variable and its manipulation is a poor way to achieve microeconomic goals such as the desired output mix.

Further Reading

The analysis of exchange rate protection in section 19.1 is based on Corden (1981). Dornbusch (1974) provides an alternative treatment focusing on the relative price of traded and nontraded goods rather than on the output mix. The Dutch Disease is analyzed by Corden and Neary (1982) and Corden (1984). Forsyth and Kay (1980) deal with the impact of North Sea oil on the UK, Gelb (1988) with oil windfalls in developing countries, and Maddock and McLean (1984) with the Australian gold rush.

20

Conclusions

The most important concept in international trade theory is Ricardo's theory of comparative advantage. There are potential gains from trade as long as opportunity costs in any two countries differ for any pair of goods. This implies the strong policy conclusion that some trade is almost certainly better than none, in the sense that the total amount of all goods available to be consumed by the trading partners will be increased.

Actual trade policy debates are seldom over having some trade rather than none, but about marginal changes in individuals' freedom to trade. Here again a strong conclusion in favor of free trade can be reached if markets are perfectly competitive and prices reflect social costs and benefits. Trade barriers reduce both global welfare and the welfare of individual nations imposing the barriers.

The last conclusion no longer holds if a country has market power in world markets (that is, it is not a price-taker). A large country can suffer from immiserizing growth if the government allows pro-trade-biased growth to occur unregulated. More generally, the government of a country with market power can stop a deterioration or engineer an improvement in the nation's terms of trade by restricting imports or exports. Such a policy will, however, only work in the short run if alternative suppliers or markets or substitutes for the restricted product are encouraged (as in the Ghanaian cocoa or Japanese automobile examples, or after restrictions on trade in cotton textiles); the issue then is whether the short-run gains outweigh the long-run cost. Use of a trade barrier to improve the terms of trade (for example, the optimal tariff) may also fail if other countries retaliate by increasing their own trade barriers, leaving everybody worse off because of the foregone gains from trade.

When markets are characterized by imperfect competition, there are many theoretical possibilities for governments to use trade barriers to increase national welfare. Some of these arguments are similar to those in the previous paragraph because they aim to redistribute welfare, by protecting or promoting domestic firms' excess profits in world markets or by rent-snatching from foreign firms. The same considerations are relevant: Are there net benefits if profitable exports are promoted at the expense of domestic consumers paying higher prices, how will foreign firms and governments react, and so on? There is also a global-welfare-increasing argument that, in the absence of an international antitrust policy, national trade barriers may reduce the global costs of the abuse of monopoly power. In specific cases the argument may be valid, but there are likely to be better ways of regulating the monopolist's power than by using trade policies (such as enforcing a price ceiling).

In practice, the existence of imperfect competition is more likely to strengthen the case for removing trade barriers. Trade barriers always enhance firms' monopoly power in the domestic market, and allowing an unrestricted inflow of foreign goods is the best antitrust policy. Removing trade barriers will bring national benefits by reducing monopoly profits and forcing rationalization of domestic production, although the adjustment costs associated with trade liberalization are likely to be greater when economies of scale are present (and shifts in output may be discontinuous as whole industries shut down). On the whole, the imperfect competition revolution in international trade theory, although it established some novel arguments in favor of trade barriers which were seized upon by advocates of industrial policies and "strategic trade policies," strengthens the case for leaving markets open to competition from foreign suppliers (see box 20.1).

With competitive markets, intervention in international trade may be better than doing nothing if market prices do not reflect social costs and benefits. If the opportunity cost of producing the marginal unit is less than the market price (for example, because the wage rate overstates the social opportunity cost of labor) or if the social benefit from a unit consumed is less than a consumer is willing to pay, then an import tax will improve national welfare by increasing domestic output and reducing domestic sales. Import duties are also a source of government revenue. For all of these purposes, however, trade taxes are not the first-best policy. Other policies aimed directly at the source of the distortion, such as a subsidy if the value of output is understated by market prices or a sales tax to reduce consumption of a good, are superior because they avoid the side-effects of trade barriers.

The theory of distortions is the greatest postwar advance in international trade theory. It had long been accepted that trade barriers could be better than doing nothing if an industry deserved public support or a good was being consumed in undesirably large quantities, and advocates of free trade were identified as supporters of *laissez-faire* or no intervention in the economy. The theory of distortions breaks this link between free trade and *laissez-faire*. Policy-makers can pursue active policies to achieve domestic goals, but they should not use international trade policies for this purpose; trade policies could achieve the goals, but they are second-best (or worse) methods.

BOX 20.1 Edgeworth on Strategic Trade Policy?

The British economist Francis Edgeworth (1845–1926) wrote a biting criticism of the applicability of the infant industry argument to actual trade policy:

Thus the direct use of the theory is likely to be small. But it is to be feared that its abuse will be considerable. It affords to unscrupulous advocates of vulgar Protection a peculiarly specious pretext for introducing the thin end of the fiscal wedge. Mr Bickerdike may be compared to a scientist, who by a new analysis, has discovered that strychnine may be administered in small doses with prospect of advantage in one or two more cases than was previously known; the result of this discovery may be to render the drug more easily procurable by those whose intention, or at least whose practice, is not medicinal. . . . Let us admire the skill of the analyst, but label the subject of his investigation POISON.

A similar case can be made against policy-makers who hijack theories of "strategic trade policy," which can be derived under certain conditions of imperfect competition, and use them to justify wide-ranging trade barriers in any industry not characterized by perfect competition.

Source: *Edgeworth F.Y. 1925: Mr Bickerdike's theory of incipient taxes and customs duties. In* Papers Relating to Political Economy. *London: Macmillan, for the Royal Economic Society, vol. 2, 365–6. Quoted in the* Journal of Political Economy, *86(2), part 2, April 1978, back cover*

Two other major advances have been in the analysis of discriminatory trade policies and of alternative trade barriers. Trade diversion is the key concept with respect to discriminatory trade policies. Because discriminatory trade policies introduce a new distortion they involve second-best considerations, and preferential reductions in trade barriers may or may not be in the interests of the importing nation or of the world. Trade diversion itself is, however, welfare-reducing, so there is a presumption that a superior non-discriminatory policy exists. The problems are that discriminatory trading arrangements may have legitimate noneconomic motives (for example, the founding of the European Community) and that the participants may benefit at the expense of the rest of the world. The second problem implies that they are a legitimate area for international supervision, while the first problem means that they may be difficult to supervise in some cases.

The analysis of alternative instruments of trade policy has more clear-cut conclusions. Nontariff barriers to imports have the same effects as a tariff (because they also create a wedge between domestic and world prices) and under certain conditions may be equivalent. In general, however, nontariff barriers will not be equivalent to a tariff, and the additional consequences of NTBs are harmful. Thus, if a country wishes to use an import restriction, the best instrument is a simple tax on imports. In practice, governments have always used NTBs, and their relative importance is increasing. Among other reasons, NTBs are attractive because they are less transparent than tariffs and thus may not generate the same domestic and international criticism.

The GATT embodies the principles just described, and hence has a solid basis in trade theory. The basic principles of GATT are that trade restrictions should be nondiscriminatory and should be in the form of tariffs. The various rounds of trade negotiations which have taken place since GATT was signed in 1947 have aimed to reduce the level of tariffs and further regulate the use of NTBs. Because GATT has no true enforcement powers its ability to do good is limited, but it has played a major role in discouraging antisocial trade policies and preventing trade wars by laying down the circumstances in which retaliatory action is permissible and so discouraging policies which would trigger such reaction.

In sum, there is no perfect answer to the question of what is the best trade policy. But, as a general guide, free trade is a good rule of thumb. It is the policy which maximizes global welfare by allowing production to take place at the least-cost location. Trade restrictions can improve national welfare, but trying to exploit market power is confrontational and may not work, while using trade policies to achieve domestic goals is never the first-best policy. This last conclusion carries over to the use of trade policies to reduce aggregate unemployment or a BOP deficit; under certain conditions trade barriers could achieve these goals, but they are inappropriate tools because trade barriers are by nature microeconomic policies. There are interactions between macroeconomic variables and trade flows and vice versa, but the best approach to solving macroeconomic problems is to use macroeconomic policies.

If the arguments in favor of free trade policies are so strong, why are trade barriers so prevalent and trade policies so vigorously debated? Because any trade barrier has several consequences, there are always distributional effects; that is, in the absence of compensation there are gainers and losers from any trade policy change. When the conflict is in international markets, the outcome may be a mutually damaging trade war; this frequently happened before 1939, and is a major reason why nations signed the GATT and have on the whole abided by its terms. When the conflict is domestic, the outcome depends upon the country's institutional arrangements. Because import-competing producers are typically fewer than the consumers of their products, they are individually more affected by trade barriers, and will put more effort into lobbying politicians or officials to obtain protection than consumers will put into opposing protection. The success of such lobbying will vary from country to country, but it is seldom futile. These directly unproductive, or DUP, activities add to the costs of having trade barriers (rather than a trade policy based on the rule of free trade), and are a further reason why a strong commitment to open trade policies is in the national as well as the global interest.

Further Reading

Krugman (1987) and Bhagwati (1989) reflect on the broader policy implications of recent developments in trade theory.

References

Arrow, Kenneth 1951: *Social Choice and Individual Values*. New Haven: Yale University Press.

Balassa, Béla 1964: The purchasing power-parity doctrine: a reappraisal. *Journal of Political Economy*, 72, 584–96.

Balassa, Béla 1966: Tariff reductions and trade in manufactures among industrial countries. *American Economic Review*, 56, 466–73.

Baldwin, Richard E. and Krugman, Paul R. 1988: Market access and international competition: a simulation study of 16K random access memories. In Rob E. Feenstra (ed.), *Empirical Methods for International Trade*. Cambridge, Mass.: MIT Press, 171–97.

Baldwin, Robert 1971: Determinants of the commodity structure of US trade. *American Economic Review*, 61, 126–46.

Baldwin, Robert 1982: *The Inefficacy of Trade Policy*. Princeton, N. J.: International Finance Section, Dept. of Economics, Princeton University.

Baldwin, Robert 1985: *The Political Economy of US Import Policy*. Cambridge, Mass.: MIT Press.

Baldwin, Robert and Murray, Tracy 1977: MFN tariff reductions and developing country trade benefits under the GSP. *Economic Journal*, 87, 30–46.

Baldwin, Robert E., Mutti, John H., and Richardson, David J. 1980: Welfare effects on the US of a significant multilateral reduction. *Journal of International Economics*, 10, 405–23.

Basevi, Giorgio 1968: The restrictive effect of the US tariff and its welfare value. *American Economic Review*, 58, 840–52.

Bhagwati, Jagdish 1958: Immiserizing growth: a geometrical note. *Review of Economic Studies*, 25-6, 201–5.

Bhagwati, Jagdish 1974: *Illegal Transactions in International Trade*. Amsterdam: North Holland.

Bhagwati, Jagdish 1982: Directly unproductive, profit-seeking (DUP) activities. *Journal of Political Economy*, 90, 988–1,002.

Bhagwati, Jagdish 1987: Trade in services and the multilateral trade negotiations. *World Bank Economic Review*, 1, 549–69.

Bhagwati, Jagdish 1988: *Protectionism*. Cambridge, Mass.: MIT Press.

Bhagwati, Jagdish 1989: Is free trade passé after all? *Weltwirtschaftliches Archiv*, 125, 17–44.

Bhagwati, Jagdish N. and Hansen, Bent 1973: A theoretical analysis of smuggling. *Quarterly Journal of Economics*, 87, 172–87.

Bharadwaj, R. 1962a: *Structural Basis of India's Foreign Trade*. University of Bombay.

Bharadwaj, R. 1962b: Factor proportions and the structure of Indo-US trade. *Indian Economic Journal*, 10, 105–6.

Blackhurst, Richard and Tumlir, Jan 1980: *Trade Relations under Flexible Exchange Rates*. GATT Studies in International Trade, No. 8. Geneva: GATT.

Boadway, Robin and Treddenick, John 1978: A general equilibrium computation of the effects of the Canadian tariff structure. *The Canadian Journal of Economics*, 11, 424–46.

Brander, James 1981: Intra-industry trade in identical commodities. *Journal of International Economics*, 11, 1–14.

Cheh, John H. 1974: United States concessions in the Kennedy Round and short-run labor adjustment costs. *Journal of International Economics*, 4, 323–40.

Cline, William R. et al. (eds) 1978: *Trade Negotiations in the Tokyo Round: A Quantitative Assessment*. Washington, D. C.: Brookings Institution.

Constantopoulos, M. 1974: Labour protection in Western Europe. *European Economic Review*, 5, 313–18.

Cooper, Charles A. and Massell, Benton F. 1965: A new look at customs unions theory. *Economic Journal*, 75, 742–7.

Corden, W. Max 1957: The calculation of the cost of protection. *Economic Record*, 33, 29–51.

Corden, W. Max 1960: The geometric representation of policies to attain internal and external balance. *Review of Economic Studies*, 28, 1–22.

Corden, W. Max 1966: The structure of a tariff system and the effective protective rate. *Journal of Political Economy*, 74, 221–37.

Corden, W. Max 1971: *The Theory of Protection*. Oxford: Clarendon Press.

Corden, W. Max 1974: *Trade Policy and Economic Welfare*. Oxford: Clarendon Press.

Corden, W. Max 1981: Exchange rate protection. In Richard N. Cooper et al. (eds), *The International Monetary System under Flexible Exchange Rates*. Cambridge, Mass.: Ballinger.

Corden, W. Max 1984: Booming sector and Dutch Disease economics; survey and consolidation. *Oxford Economic Papers*, 35, 359–80.

Corden, W. Max and Neary, J. Peter 1982: Booming sector and deindustrialization in a small open economy. *Economic Journal*, 92, 825–48.

Crandall, Robert W. 1984: Import quotas and the automobile industry: the costs of protectionism. *Brookings Review*, 2, 8–16.

Deardorff, Alan V. 1984: Testing trade theories and predicting trade flows. In Ronald W. Jones and Peter B. Kenen (eds), *Handbook of International Economics*. Amsterdam: North Holland, 467–517.

Deardorff, Alan V. and Stern, Robert M. 1979: *The Economic Analysis of the Effects of the Tokyo Round of Multilateral Trade Negotiation on the US and Other Major Industrialised Countries*. Washington, D. C.: US Government Printing Office.

Deardorff, Alan V. and Stolper, Wolfgang F. 1990: Effects of smuggling under African conditions: a factual, institutional and analytic discussion. *Weltwirtschaftliches Archiv*, 126, 116–41.

Dixon, Peter B. et al. 1977: *ORANI, A General Equilibrium Model of the Australian Economy*. First Progress Report of the Impact Project, vol. 2. Canberra: Australian Government Publishing Service.

Dornbusch, Rudiger 1974: Tariffs and non-traded goods. *Journal of International Economics*, 4, 177–85.

Dornbusch, Rudiger 1976: Expectations and exchange rate dynamics. *Journal of Political Economy*, 84, 1,161–76.

Dornbusch, Rudiger, Fischer, Stanley, and Samuelson, Paul A. 1977: Comparative advantage, trade and payment in a Ricardian model with a continuum of goods. *American Economic Review*, 67, 823–39.

Downs, A. 1957: *An Economic Theory of Democracy*. New York: Harper & Row.

Dunning, John H. 1988: *Explaining International Production*. London: Unwin Hyman.

Eastman, Harry C. and Stykolt, Stefan 1967: *The Tariff and Competition in Canada*. Toronto: Macmillan.

Finger, J. Michael, Hall, H. K., and Nelson, D. R. 1982: The political economy of administered protection. *American Economic Review*, 72, 452–66.

Flamm, Kenneth 1985: Internationalization in the semiconductor industry. In Joseph Greenwald and Kenneth Flamm, *The Global Factory*. Washington, D. C.: Brookings Institution, esp. pp. 48–54 and 68–79.

Forsyth, P. J. and Kay, J. A. 1980: The economic implications of North Sea oil revenues. *Fiscal Studies*, 1, 1–28.

Frenkel, Jacob 1981: The collapse of purchasing power parities during the 1970s. *European Economic Review*, 18.

Gelb, Alan 1988: *Oil Windfalls; Blessing or Curse?* New York: Oxford University Press for the World Bank.

Greenaway, David 1984: A statistical analysis of fiscal dependence on trade taxes and economic development. *Public Finance*, 39, 70–89.

Greenaway, David and Milner, Chris 1986: *The Economics of Intra-industry Trade*. Oxford: Basil Blackwell.

Grubel, Herbert and Lloyd, Peter 1975: *Intra-industry Trade*. London: Macmillan.

Hamilton, Carl 1986: An assessment of voluntary restraints on Hong Kong exports to Europe and the USA. *Economica*, 54, 339–50.

Hansen, Bent and Nashashibi, Karim 1975: *Egypt*. New York: National Bureau of Economic Research, Columbia University Press.

Helleiner, Gerald K. 1977: Transnational enterprises and the new political economy of US trade policy. *Oxford Economic Papers*, 29, 102–16.

Helpman, Elahan and Krugman, Paul R. 1985: *Market Structure and Foreign Trade*. Cambridge, Mass.: MIT Press.

Helpman, Elhanan and Krugman, Paul R. 1989: *Trade Policy and Market Structure*. Cambridge, Mass.: MIT Press.

Hillman, Arye 1989: *The Political Economy of Protection*. Harwood: Chur, Switzerland.

Hirsch, Seev 1967: *Location of Industry and International Competitiveness*. Oxford: Clarendon Press.

Hocking, Robin 1980: Trade in motor cars between the major European producers. *Economic Journal*, 90, 504–19.

Houthakker, Hendrik 1957: An international comparison of household expenditure patterns. *Econometrica*, 25, 532–51.

Hufbauer, Gary C. 1966: *Synthetic Materials and the Theory of International Trade*. London: Duckworth.

Hufbauer, Gary C., Berliner, Diane T., and Elliott, Kimberly A. 1986: *Trade Protection in the United States: Thirty-one Case Studies*. Washington, D. C.: Institute for International Economics.

Johnson, Harry G. 1954: Optimum tariffs and retaliation. *Review of Economic Studies*, 21–2, 142–53.

Johnson, Harry G. 1955: Economic expansion and international trade. *Manchester School of Economic and Social Studies*, 23, 95–112.

Johnson, Harry G. 1960: The cost of protection and the scientific tariff. *Journal of Political Economy*, 68, 327–45.

Johnson, Harry G. 1965: An economics theory of protectionism, tariff bargaining and the formation of customs unions. *Journal of Political Economy*, 73, 256–83.

Johnson, Harry G. 1970: The efficiency and welfare implications of the international corporation. In I. A. McDougall and R. H. Snape (eds), *Studies in International Economics*. Amsterdam: North Holland.

Jones, Joseph M. 1934: *Tariff Retaliation: Repercussions of the Hawley–Smoot Bill*. Philadelphia: University of Pennsylvania Press.

Jones, Kent 1984: The political economy of voluntary export restraint agreements. *Kyklos*, 37, 82–101.

Jones, Ronald W. 1965: The structure of simple general equilibrium models. *Journal of Political Economy*, 73, 557–72.

Jones, Ronald W. 1971: A three-factor model in theory, trade and history. In Jagdish Bhagwati, Ronald W. Jones, Robert A. Mundell, and Jaroslav Vanek (eds), *Trade. Balance of Payments and Growth: Essays in Honor of Charles P. Kindleberger*. Amsterdam: North Holland, 3–21.

Jones, Ronald W. 1987: Heckscher–Ohlin trade theory. In Eatwell, John, Milgate, Murray, and Newman, Peter (eds), *The New Palgrave Dictionary of Economics*, vol. 2, 621–7.

Kalt, Joseph P. 1988: The political economy of protectionism: tariffs and retaliation in the timber industry. In Robert E. Baldwin (ed.), *Trade Policy Issues and Empirical Analysis*. Chicago: University of Chicago Press, 339–64.

Karsenty, Guy and Laird, Sam 1987: The generalized system of preferences: a quantitative assessment of the direct trade effects and policy options. *Weltwirtschaftliches Archiv*, 123, 262–96.

Katrak, Homi 1977: Multi-national monopolies and commercial policy. *Oxford Economic Papers*, 29, 283–91.

Keesing, Donald B. 1966: Labor skills and comparative advantages. *American Economic Review*, 56, 249–58.

Kemp, Murray 1964: *The Pure Theory of International Trade*. Englewood Cliffs, N. J.: Prentice-Hall, 110–31.

Kemp, Murray and Wan, Henry 1976: An elementary proposition concerning the formation of customs unions. *Journal of International Economics*, 6, 95–7.

Kenen, Peter 1965: Nature, capital and trade. *Journal of Political Economy*, 73, 437–60.

Kindleberger, Charles P. 1951: Group behavior and international trade. *Journal of Political Economy*, 59, 30–47.

Kravis, Irving B. 1970: Trade as a handmaiden of growth; similarities between the nineteenth and twentieth centuries. *Economic Journal*, 80, 850–72.

Krueger, Anne O. 1968: Factor endowments and per capita income differences among countries. *Economic Journal*, 78, 641–59.

Krueger, Anne 1974: The political economy of the rent-seeking society. *American Economic Review*, 64, 291–303.

Krugman, Paul 1979: Increasing returns, monopolistic competition and international trade. *Journal of International Economics*, 9, 469–79.

Krugman, Paul 1980: Scale economies, product differentiation and the pattern of trade. *American Economic Review* 70, 950–9.

Krugman, Paul 1987: Is free trade passé? *Journal of Economic Perspectives*, 1, 131–44.

Laird, Sam and Yeats, Alexander 1988: A note on the aggregation bias in current procedures for the measurement of trade barriers. *Bulletin of Economic Research*, 40, 133–43.

Lary, Hal 1968: *Imports of Manufactures from Less-developed Countries*. New York: National Bureau of Economic Research.

Lavergne, Real P. 1983: *The Political Economy of US Tariffs: An Empirical Analysis*. Toronto: Academic Press.

Leamer, Edward E. 1980: The Leontief Paradox reconsidered. *Journal of Political Economy*, 88, 495–503.

Leamer, Edward E. 1984: *Sources of International Comparative Advantage: Theory and Evidence*. Cambridge, Mass.: MIT Press.

Leontief, Wassily 1953: Domestic production and foreign trade; the American position re-examined. *Proceedings of the American Philosophical Society*, 37, 332–49.

Lewis, W. Arthur 1980: The slowing down of the engine of growth. *American Economic Review*, 70, 555–64.

Linder, Staffan 1961: *An Essay on Trade and Transformation*. Stockholm: Almqvist and Wiksell.

Lipsey, Richard G. and Lancaster, Kelvin 1956–7: The general theory of 'second best.' *Review of Economic Studies*, 24, 11–32.

Little, Ian, Scitovsky, Tibor, and Scott, Maurice 1970: *Industry and Trade in Some Developing Countries*. London: Oxford University Press.

McCalla, Alex F. and Josling, Timothy E. 1985: *Agricultural Policies and World Markets*. New York: Macmillan.

MacDougall, G. D. A. 1951: British and American exports: a study suggested by the theory of comparative costs. *Economic Journal*, 61, 697–724.

Maddock, R. and McLean, Ian 1984: Supply shocks; the case of Australian gold. *Journal of Economic History*, 44, 1,047–68.

Magee, Stephen P. 1972: The welfare effects of restrictions in US trade. *Brookings Papers on Economic Activity*, 3, 645–707.

Magee, Stephen P. 1980: Three simple tests of the Stolper–Samuelson theorem. In P. Oppenheimer (ed.), *Issues in International Economics*. London: Routledge & Kegan Paul, 138–53.

Magee, Stephen P., Brock, William A., and Young, Leslie 1989: *Black Hole Tariffs and Endogenous Policy Theory*. Cambridge: Cambridge University Press.

Mayer, Wolfgang 1984: The infant-export industry argument. *Canadian Journal of Economics*, 17, 249–69.

Meade, James E. 1951: *The Theory of International Economic Policy;* vol. 1, *The Balance of Payments*. London: Oxford University Press.

Meade, James E. 1952: *A Geometry of International Trade*. London: Allen and Unwin.

Meade, James E. 1955: *The Theory of International Economic Policy;* vol. 2, *Trade and Welfare*. London: Oxford University Press.

Messerlin, Patrick A. 1981: The political economy of protection: the bureaucratic case. *Weltwirtschaftliches Archiv*, 117.

Minhas, B. S. 1962: The homohypallagic production function, factor intensity reversals, and the Heckscher–Ohlin theorem. *Journal of Political Economy*, 60, 138–56.

Mundell, Robert A. 1957: International trade and factor mobility. *American Economic Review*, 47, 321–35.

Mundell, Robert A. 1964: Tariff preferences and the terms of trade. *Manchester School of Economic and Social Studies*, 32, 1–13.

Murray, Tracy 1977: *Trade Preferences for Developing Countries*. London: Macmillan.

Mussa, Michael 1974: Tariffs and the distribution of income: the importance of factor specificity, substitutability and intensity in the short and long run. *Journal of Political Economy*, 82, 1,191–203.

Mussa, Michael 1982; A model of exchange rate dynamics. *Journal of Political Economy*, 90, 74–104.

Ohlin, Bertil 1933: *Interregional and International Trade*. Cambridge, Mass.: Harvard University Press.

Olson, M. 1965: *The Logic of Collective Action: Public Goods and the Theory of Groups*. Cambridge, Mass.: Harvard Unversity Press.

Petith, Howard C. 1977: European integration and the terms of trade. *Economic Journal*, 87, 262–72.

Pincus, Jonathan 1975: Pressure groups and the pattern of tariffs. *Journal of Political Economy*, 83, 757–78.

Pomfret, Richard 1986: On the division of labour and international trade: or, Adam Smith's explanation of intra-industry trade. *Journal of Economic Studies* 13, 1986, 55–62.

Pomfret, Richard 1988: *Unequal Trade: The Economics of Discriminatory International Trade Policies*. Oxford: Basil Blackwell.

Pomfret, Richard 1989: Voluntary export restraints in the presence of monopoly power. *Kyklos*, 42, 61–72.

Posner, M. V. 1961: International trade and technical change. *Oxford Economic Papers*, 13, 323–41.

Preeg, Ernest H. 1970: *Traders and Diplomats*. Washington, D. C.: Brookings Institution.

Reich, Robert R. 1990: Who Is Us? *Harvard Business Review*, 68, January/February, 53–64.

Ricardo, David 1817: *On the Principles of Political Economy and Taxation.* London: John Murray.

Richardson, J. David 1988: *Empirical Research on Trade Liberalisation with Imperfect Competition: A Survey.* OECD Department of Economics and Statistics, Working Paper No. 58 (November).

Riedel, James 1977: Tariff concessions in the Kennedy Round and the structure of protection in West Germany. *Journal of International Economics*, 7, 133–43.

Riedel, James 1984: Trade as an engine of growth in developing countries, revisited. *Economic Journal*, 94, 56–73.

Robson, Peter 1984: *The Economics of International Integration.* London: Allen and Unwin.

Rosenstein-Rodan, Paul N. 1943: Problems of industrialization in eastern and south-eastern Europe. *Economic Journal*, 53, 202–11.

Rybczynski, T. M. 1955: Factor endowment and relative commodity prices. *Economica*, 22, 336–41.

Sampson, Gary P. and Snape, Richard H. 1980: The effects of the EEC's variable import levies. *Journal of Political Economy*, 88, 1,026–40.

Samuelson, Paul A. 1939: The gains from international trade. *Canadian Journal of Economics and Political Science*, 5, 195–205.

Samuelson, Paul A. 1948: International trade and the equalisation of factor prices. *Economic Journal*, 58, 163–84.

Samuelson, Paul A. 1949: International factor price equalisation once again. *Economic Journal*, 59, 181–97.

Samuelson, Paul A. 1962: The gains from international trade once again. *Economic Journal*, 72, 820–9.

Samuelson, Paul A. 1971: Ohlin was right. *Swedish Journal of Economics*, 73, 365–84.

Schattschneider, E. E. 1935: *Politics, Pressures and the Tariff: A Study of Free Private Enterprise in Pressure Politics, as Shown in the 1929-1930 Revision of the Tariff.* New York: Prentice-Hall.

Simkin, C. G. F. 1970: Indonesia's unrecorded trade. *Bulletin of Indonesian Economic Studies*, March (reprinted in Bhagwati, 1974, pp. 157–71).

Spraos, John 1980: The statistical debate on the net barter terms of trade between primary commodities and manufacturer. *Economic Journal*, 90, 107–28.

Stern, Robert M. 1975: Testing trade theories. In Peter B. Kenen (ed.), *International Trade and Finance: Frontiers for Research.* Cambridge: Cambridge University Press, 3–49.

Stolper, Wolfgang and Roskamp, K. 1961: Input–output table for East Germany with applications to foreign trade. *Bulletin of the Oxford University Institute of Statistics*, 23, 379–92.

Stolper, Wolfgang and Samuelson, Paul A. 1941: Protection and real wages. *Review of Economic Studies*, 9, 58–73.

Svedberg, Peter 1979: Optimal tariff policy on imports from multinationals. *Economic Record*, 55, 64–7.

Tatemoto, M. and Ichimura, S. 1959: Factor proportions and the foreign trade: the case of Japan. *Review of Economics and Statistics*, 41, 442–6.

Tumlir, Jan 1985: *Protectionism: Trade Policy in Democratic Societies*. Washington, D. C.: American Enterprise Institute.

Vanek, Jaroslav 1959: The natural resource content of foreign trade, 1870–1955, and the relative abundance of natural resources in the United States. *Review of Economics and Statistics*, 41, 146–53.

Vernon, Raymond 1966: International investment and international trade in the product cycle. *Quarterly Journal of Economics*, 80, 190–207.

Vernon, Raymond 1979: The product cycle hypothesis in a new international environment. *Oxford Bulletin of Economics and Statistics*, 41, 255–67.

Viner, Jacob 1950: *The Customs Union Issue*. New York: Carnegie Endowment for International Peace.

Wahl, D. F. 1961: Capital and labour requirements for Canada's foreign trade. *Canadian Journal of Economics and Political Science*, 27, 349–58.

Weiss, Frank D., Heitger, Bernhard, Jüttemeier, Karl Heinz, Kirkpatrick, Grant, and Klepper, Gernot 1988: *Trade Policy in West Germany*. Tübingen: J. C. B. Mohr.

Whalley, John 1985: *Trade Liberalization among Major World Trading Areas*. Cambridge, Mass.: MIT Press.

Index